Kansas City's
Fairmount Park

~

Carnival ~ Electric 1 & 2 ~ Fairyland
Forest ~ Swope ~ Troost ~ Winnwood
& Washington Parks

By John M. Olinskey

With Debra Topi & Leigh Ann Little

DEDICATION

This story is dedicated to my big brother, Staff Sergeant Raymond Joseph Olinksey, 1,023,810[th] USMC, 1950-1954, 155s.

Everyone needs a charity, either to give or receive. Ours is the Sugar Creek CCRC (Civilian Civic Relief Committee). $1 will be donated per story.

INTRODUCTION
i.e., Why This Book

I remember Fairmount Lake. It was 1949, and I was three. It was the Fourth of July celebration at the Sugar Creek Ball Diamond. The lake at night was the prettiest thing I'd seen, except for my mother. There was a fireworks display after sundown, making what was left of the lake seem to be on fire. There were also street lights, at the place a road cut through, where, unknown to me, trolley tracks once unloaded thousands of city people. Soon after, I heard the adults excited about the lake's dam mysteriously giving way, bringing a lot of water via the Sugar Creek, downhill, into the Missouri River. A few years later my mom and dad would talk about the "good old days," meaning the 1920s, not the 1930s. Mostly they talked about the auto my dad had won at Fairmount Park. Mom told me her favorite ride was the Mountain Speedway, a mile-long roller coaster. As a little girl, it was her last ride before going home. She and her best friend talked about as little girls always dancing and having fun. Later, while hanging out at the main Kansas City library, reading old newspapers, I found in an 1896 Kansas City Journal an Indian on a horse at Fairmount Park. I was hooked. Twenty-five years later, I'm done.

Foreword
By Judge Alex Petrovic

Nestled in the hills of Northeast Jackson County, Sugar Creek was probably the only town in the shadows of Kansas City and Independence who cared about Sugar Creek.

Supported early on by the tax dollars of the Standard Oil Company, Sugar Creek grew in stature by some talented athletes and made a name for itself by virtue of some notable merchants and area entertainers known for amusement park entertainment. People like the Carlisle family's enterprises that succeeded in business and enjoyable entertainment, bringing companies from Kansas City and its environs to host parties and social events for their employees.

People like former Kansas City Police Chief and FBI Director Clarence Kelly made their early days living by peddling Creek water to patrons of Fairmount Park. Since Standard Oil Co. was the principle employer, refining products supported area families in good style. Sugar Creek Elementary Schools and later Northeast and William Chrisman Schools educated its residents; local talented athletes of baseball skills were often offered scholarships, and big league contracts to others. Local pride in its Slavic ethnic background, urged male suitors to mate with their area counterparts.

The Portland Cement Co. hired many locals to produce a nationally known brand of building products. The Missouri river on the south ran along Sugar Creek city to support river traffic form the east and west of town. Recreation opportunities were available to the area.

Historians like John Olinskey documented the contribution and the importance of this community from a rich history of accomplishment by Sugar Creek, to the growth of area progress.

Politics was a by-product of our notoriety. Public office hopefuls campaigned for local and state office in Sugar Creek. Harry Truman, famous names like Robert Kennedy, Stan Musial, Haskell Holman, Bill Randal, Stewart Symington, Ed Long, Warren Hearns, and Edward Dalton spoke here to the largest crowd of Missouri Democrats, second only to the Springfield rally. This community was solely all Democratic. Sugar Creek was never seriously challenged by a competing party.

Having lived here since my discharge from the Marines, I would be remiss if I didn't acknowledge the most far-thinking man I ever met. Pete Saxton was the only proud Republican around. Every major improvement had Pete's goal behind it. New roads, Harrison Park, the ball park, swimming pool, Onka Building, schools, and much more. Saxton should have some kind of recognition for his accomplishments. Pete Saxton had the ideas, plans, and the urge to make Sugar Creek a place of low taxes and a good place to educate our children.

If anyone would have been a better mayor than Pete, they didn't exist. Name a building, school, road, or park after him.

Judge Alex Petrovic
Guadal Canal – WWII,USMC
Missouri House of Representatives, District 11 1962-1966
Eastern Judge, Jackson County, Missouri, 1966-1970

Chapter 1: 1887 – 1892

Did you know that Mount Washington Cemetery was once an amusement park called Washington Park?

Also, that one of the first airports in Kansas City is now called R. J. Roper Stadium in Sugar Creek and it was then called Fairmount Park, located between 24 Highway and Kentucky Ave? That what is now Northern Boulevard was the bed for a railroad that ran through Fairmount Park to Kansas City? Or that Red Skelton, star of the stage, screen, radio and TV performed there in the 1930's? He married a Fairmount girl, moved to Hollywood and "He Dood It," as he would say.

In the 1880s Kansas City was a boom town and was referred to in the newsprint of the day as the "New Chicago". The population was 55,785 in 1880 and more than doubled by 1885 to 124,474. On June 29, 1886, the newspapers announced that the Dummy Line was being revived. The Winner Investment Co. had just purchased property near the Bethsaida Springs, and the Kansas City-Independence Park Railway Co. line was to be completed by winter time. The next year, Rock Creek was dammed and a large 20 acre lake was filled, which was to be Swan Lake at Washington Park. Rock Creek ran through Independence to the Missouri River. Four hundred acres were set aside for the park.

Early on, family picnics were in fashion. As the park became more popular and the area developed, fortunes were made. A park at the end of a rail line was a common practice in other parts of the nation, and because of an influx of capital from eastern cities such as Boston, Kansas City was on the cutting edge of the new technology.

In the Washington Park area, developers began selling land around the proposed park raising prices and value. At the time, Independence was known as the Royal Suburb, and land speculations were rife. The headlines in the KC Journal (June 20, 1888) read:

"MOUNT WASHINGTON!: 5 miles east of Kansas City, 18 minutes from Grand Avenue, upon a high elevation with views of the surrounding county and the Missouri River of miles, sloping to the south, and covered with sugar maples. The Missouri-Pacific Railroad, with12 suburban trains daily, just to the south. The Kansas City-Independence Park Railroad (an electric road) is graded almost to the addition."

W. V. Lippincott, Jr. 129 W 6th St., Kansas City MO

In June of 1888, a reporter for the Kansas City Times reported that in his opinion, "Washington Park was the most picturesque spot between the Allegheny Mountains and the Rockies." Washington Park was huge, 382 acres, one mile east to west, one and a half miles north to south, covered with blue grass, rocks as big as houses, and beautiful wild flowers and ferns. Horse drawn open summer cars were boarded on 12th St. and 15th St. and slowly headed east. They crossed a then crystal clear Big Blue River at 15th Street, detraining at the bottom of the big bluff.

Because of the Park's large size, both ends had entrances. After a long walk up the bluff, the west, i.e., the first entrance was at Stark Avenue. Another entrance was by Rock Creek, and one in the middle. The north entrance was where the bus stop is now. Many of the patrons would enter the park at one end and, after a day of fun, return to the city from the other.

The high ground on Blue Ridge was then called Bald Nob. A 107 foot lookout tower was built and a museum at its base featured old coins, books, and other historical curiosities. Several rustic foot bridges crisscrossed Rock Creek, linking nature with the man made attractions. The springs were linked by a bridge to the double L-shaped pavilion, which included a large restaurant. A band stand was already in use, attracting many quality musicians.

The flat ground from where now there is a Dairy Queen, north to Al Waits Service Station, was the ball field, the hill to the east were the bleachers and above this was the camping ground. The 20 acre lake featured an island for picnickers. Two steam-powered boats were already in dry dock and workmen were optimistically painting oars and John-boats, in preparation for the liquid fun. No dancing or ball playing on Sunday and, of course, gambling and strong drink was never allowed. Admission to the park was free and uniformed watchmen always patrolled the grounds.

However, even with all the hoopla, Washington Park never did catch on. It did set the stage for Fairmount Park, when, in August, 1891, the ninth annual reunion of the ex-Confederate Veterans of Missouri, was held in Washington Park. Across the state, there were 1500 members and more than a third attended. Jackson County alone had more than 1800 former rebels. Among the notables were Generals Jo Shelby, Joe Blackburn and Elijah Gates. They led the divisions in parade from 6th & Broadway to 15th & Grand, where the soldiers boarded trains for Washington Park. Besides the thousands of soldiers of both armies, there were three senators and various state, county and city VIPs. Next came the fire department, the retail clerks, the 3rd Regiment and Battery B. For 2 days the park was transformed into a military camp. North of the 15th Street tracks there were 5 command tents and 250 smaller ones. Tables to feed 2,000 people at a time were spread out under the trees.   An old vet put it this way:

> "Jackson County was the hot bed of strife during the war. The animosities here were the strongest just after the war. Now our children have been raised and educated with the children of Union Soldiers. They have formed lasting friendships and our sons and daughters have married the children of the men we fought. Here we want to meet them and bury our animosities."

As many as 40,000 people passed through the park in those two days. The veterans paid a dollar for each badge to identify them and their unit. The money went to the veterans home, just purchased in Higginsville; $18,500 for 362 acres. Many of the men were destitute; causes being wounds received while serving the Confederacy or were disowned by family. These men did not have to pay for their badge or anything else at Washington Park.

On May 23, 1891 an open-door meeting led by Arthur Stilwell was held in Independence where details of the new Air Line (an electric trolley line that ran from 2nd and Wyandotte to Fairmount Park) were discussed. A large crowd was present. 70 acres was purchased from J. D. Cusenbary, including the spring. An earthen dam was scooped out of the ground and what resulted was an 18 acre lake. Arthur called it "The Air Line" because, he said later, it was financed by hot air, not money.

In 1892 Cusenbary Springs (later known as Fairmount Park) opened to the masses. By the 4th of July the park had a pavilion, band stand, gymnasium, shooting gallery, merry-go-round and a beautiful lake with a fleet of boats. On the 4th of July 8,000 people celebrated Independence Day in what was to be the first of 40 there. The newly formed artillery band made music all day while Battery B fired the cannon.

After the 4th of July in 1892, every Sunday afternoon and evening was concert time at both Washington and Fairmount Parks. In early August, gymnasts such as the Vorwaerts and other Turner groups, ventured to the park. At 2 pm sharp a program of athletic exercises began which lasted all afternoon. It started by a grand drill of 200, next an iron wand exercise by a class of 50, after which a class of 40 from each society gave an exhibition on 3 vaulting horses. Then there was a grand display of ladder pyramids, followed by an exhibition on both the horizontal and parallel bars.

On the lake, a canoe spear combat created much merriment and the whole performance concluded with tug-of-war contests between the societies. The balance of the day was spent dancing to music of the band, which played until the last train left, taking the Turner Societies home to some Ben-Gay.

A three cornered debate was held on Labor Day weekend, September 5, at Fairmount, between three well-known politicians in a time of much labor unrest. One's name was Cyclone Davis, a name well deserved. To make a long afternoon short, everyone got drunk and gave the politicians hell.

On September 17, the Kansas City Star featured a small ad on the amusement page informing the public that from now on Cusenbary Springs would be known as Fairmount Park. The cafe was newly opened and the electricity had been turned on. An electric fountain had been built in the lake. Fairmount Park featured the finest boats and the best band in town. The last weekend of the season featured Alphonse King, "who could walk on water".

So ended the first year of Fairmount Park.

Chapter 2: 1893

It was a depression year. In Kansas City the bottom dropped out of the real estate market. But you couldn't tell that at Fairmount Park on Opening Day, Sunday, May 14. The weather was beautiful, high in the mid 80s and mostly sunny.

A lot of the improvements had been made during the off season and no more alcohol would be allowed in the park this year (once was enough!).

The Kansas City Boat Club had moved from Washington Park to Fairmount Park, which was a good sign for Fairmount Park, but not for Washington Park. A boat house was build 2 blocks north of 24 Highway and 50 feet east of Northern Blvd. They spent $2000 on it. The 2nd floor had a gymnasium and a club room. The lake featured a 1/2 mile boat race course marked by buoys and many regattas (races) were planned for the season. Just west of what is now the tennis courts in Sugar Creek was a lovely flower garden with rock walls and hundreds of flowers, mainly roses, creepers, and vines.

A new bath house had been erected at a cost of $1,500, featuring a subterranean tunnel leading to the beach. Across the lake, park management had big plans for an athletic field (now known as R. J. Roper Stadium).

A bicycle track, baseball field, and tennis courts were planned. The dance pavilion was newly opened and the First Artillery Band was playing at the band stand.

The water from the springs was very popular and was advertised thus:

> Cusenbary Spring Water. Now ready to introduce this long celebrated spring water for your family. No other water compares with it for purity. Address for lowest terms and plan for delivery. J. H. Pickering, General Superintendent, 2nd & Wyandotte. Telephone 2393

The area around and leading to the spring was known as the Cascade Glen, which was the lovers resort and led down to the springs. Rustic seats and benches were made out of the trees that were cleared while making the park. A gazebo had been built around the springs; an arc light set the area aglow.

The following Friday afternoon after opening day, the Kansas City Commercial Club boarded three newly purchased summer cars (open trolley cars) on the Air Line, an electric trolley line that ran from 2nd & Wyandotte to Fairmount Park. They left promptly at 2:30 pm and, after a couple of stops, arrived at Fairmount Park in the middle of a hail storm. Walnut sized hail rained down on the group, delaying their tour. When the rain ceased, the party walked over the ground, giving special interest to the mineral spring. Below the springs a large mineral pool had been added and was very popular. The weeks that followed were filled with balloon ascensions and parachute leaps.

In June, a reporter from the Kansas City Journal took a trip out to Fairmount Park and was much impressed. His trip was made mid week, mid June. He boarded a car at 2nd & Wyandotte early in the afternoon for the 20 minute trip along the high ground overlooking the Missouri River valley, "As the train pulls into this beautiful spot and stops under the broad pavilion overlooking the lake." His first stop was the boat house where hundreds of boats are cared for by very competent men. A narrow wooded path led from the boat house to the Kansas City Boat Club Building, which, like a lot of other things, was described as the "best in the West." The Ladies Boat Club had a reception room and was in the process of being fitted out. It was located on the second floor and from the balcony it gave a wonderful view of the lake and the surrounding countryside.

The bathing beach was nearing completion after much hard work. At that time all the big-time bathing facilities were back east and it was obvious that someone had paid a lot of money duplicating a popular eastern resort. The bath house was a large 2 story building, located where now the intersections of Northern and Hink Drive meet.

A well known swimming teacher and his wife had been put in charge of the bathing and swimming, giving free lessons to anyone who needed help. Suits were furnished for a price and there were hundreds to choose from. The ladies dressing room was located on the 2nd floor and gave an exclusive view of the lake. Stairs led down to the bathing beach via a vine-covered tunnel; a white sand floor changed into a small sand beach. Ladies were given the privilege of having the morning to themselves. Many bathing clubs were formed and every afternoon the beach was filled with society's elite. Bathing suits owned by the bathers were cared for at Fairmount Park for free.

After a good swim the cafe was open for business. Its location is now the first house on the north side of Northern and Lexington Avenue, just west of the tennis courts. It was a large white building with a round rock patio facing the lake and a mostly screened in English style dining room with a fireplace. The cuisine was French and was some of the best eating in town. In the evening the place to be seated was on the cafe patio which faced east toward the lake. A new electric fountain (where the tennis courts are today) was in place and in the evening it was turned on creating an enchanting scene of multicolored lights in a shell of mist. It must have seemed quite spectacular to people, some who were seeing this new technology for the first time.

North of the cafe was the Crystal Maze. There were only three in the world; one in Paris, one in New York, and now Fairmount Park. Crystal Maze was a building in which hundreds of mirrors were placed in every conceivable position, reflecting hundreds of times the image of the visitor. The Crystal Maze was built at a cost of $5,000, a tidy sum in 1893.

The springs were manned by 4 young men with cups to accommodate the hundreds of people that lined up to take a drink of the famous Cusenbary Spring water, reported to be shipped all over the known world at that time. The Cascade Glen was magnificent. The sides were hedged with brambles and curtained with twining vines and honeysuckle. An outdoor gymnasium, complete with everything, was free to all and was very popular with both boys and girls.

In the evening as the day merged into night, the electric lighting was quite popular with the society set, who would sometimes take a late trip to the park to catch the transformation of the park into "one big bower of loveliness".

On Sunday, June 18, Joseph Leuvenmark, champion diver of the world, set the first of many world records that would be set at the park. He dove 90 feet from the tower at the north end of the lake.

The following Thursday was the Grocers Picnic. Now, they knew how to have a good time! Many arrived early in the morning and before the day was over 10,000 people were in attendance. The whole park was leased for the day and opened to the public. The best parts of the picnic besides the food were the great prizes and a lot of winners. There were five bicycle races on the athletic field (R.J. Roper Stadium), three one mile and 2 half mile races, with prizes like a new boys 24 inch bike, food certificates, five dollar gold pieces, a gold watch, and racing shoes. There were 27 activities called "other events", which included boat and foot races, sack and fat man's races, a boxing match, cake walks, and a tug-of-war. There was a greased pig and duck catching contest.

In the evening a fireworks display that was to be launched from a boat in the lake caught fire and the spectators were treated to a spectacle that can only be imagined. The pyrotechnician escaped with his life by jumping into the lake as the show commenced to blow up, burn, and sink, much to the merriment of the crowd.

The 4th of July in 1893 came on a Tuesday and wasn't the seemingly dull event that it is now, like sparklers and lady fingers. There were some spectacular fireworks. Young boys threw small bombs and the big boys carried pistols to shoot in the air to celebrate the nation's birthday. It wasn't a one-day affair, either. It usually began the weekend before and lasted until the 4th. This year the place to go was Fairmount Park. The crowd was believed to have been 25,000 to 30,000 people. The Air Line was "feathered out," a term meaning the cars were not only full, but they had people hanging off the sides. Many people at the 2nd & Wyandotte Street depot gave up after a few hours in frustration and never made it to the park. The big attraction of the day was the Crystal Maze. Somehow it was possible for a person to sit in a small room and be seen without being found, because a very pretty girl was seen eating ice cream, but was never found. The park that day had 50 ice cream stands and 6 soda stands going and was very busy.

A baseball game took place on the new athletic field. A high dive by Professor Leuvenmark and a fireworks display capped off the evening.

Towards the end of the season, much fun with bicycles came to the park. One attraction was a one-legged man by the name of Kilpatrick, whose claim to fame was that he had ridden his "wheel" down the steps of the White House in Washington, D.C. Not the east steps that were only 40 feet long, but the west steps that were 100 feet long and at an angle of 45 degrees. Each step had an 8 inch drop and there were 82 of them. Now he traveled the country duplicating the feat.

At Fairmount Park the steps built for him were 110 feet long and 50 feet high. There were no side rails and they were only 5 feet wide (sounds very dangerous!). He started out a little rough but settled the bike down halfway to the bottom. His wheel finished the bottom half as if moving over glass, his one foot on the pedal. When reaching the bottom he continued to travel across the field for several hundred feet; this done twice a day thru the weekend.

Following the Wild West show on Sunday, August 26, there was a small disaster. Upon the mass exit, a wooden bridge collapsed, sending 100 people into the ravine. Most were only slightly injured, some serious. Everyone got muddy. The support had been washed away and a section, 15 feet long, fell into the muck. Many of the victims were women in white dresses, and children. Some of the forty injured went home, a few went to the hospital. Physicians from Kansas City were rushed to the park in a special trolley car. After the excitement had played out, things at the park returned to normal.

A bicycle tournament was held there the 1st of September and featured champion cyclist Arthur A. Zimmerman.

Chapter 3: 1894

The third season of Fairmount Park began on Sunday, May 6, 1894. The mirrors in the Crystal Maze had been rearranged "making it more puzzling than ever." The cafe was also open this year under the management of Mrs. George McClean, a well known caterer. The Third Regiment Band was again at the park and gave concerts every day and twice on Sunday. Fifty acres of picnic and timber land were added to the park. The boats this year were under the command of the Thompson brothers and the bathing beach was opened and was advertised as being the "best in the west," and probably was.

The seventh season of Washington Park was the first one with a lot of money spent on improvements. Until then, it was like a 400 acre zoo with a lake, but in 1894 things changed. The cars going to Fairmount Park went by Washington Park and Fairmount Park drew more patrons. A bathing beach and bath house were built, costing $10,000, and a restaurant was also added. A wild beast show appeared in June. Sir Charles Wombell of London brought his performing leopards, and Miss Mili Nana and her Hypnotic Lions thrilled the people as she entered the cage blindfolded. A parachute leap was also on the agenda, where a lady, in full evening attire, jumped 5,000 feet from a helium balloon. Washington Park also emulated Fairmount Park in that the water from the spring in Washington Park was sold as Bethsaida Spring Water. It was delivered in a 400 gallon horse-drawn wagon and sold door to door. "For a free sample call 2536." In addition, the park also featured Shetland ponies, boats, swings, a bowling alley and a shooting gallery. It was 15 cents round trip on the Dummy Line.

The latest style in ladies' beach wear was very important. Mohair was the popular material of the season, replacing flannel, which could drag a small lady in a big suit under. A rainbow of colors was now more popular, replacing the traditional blue of previous summers. Only the face and the arms, just below the elbows, were exposed to the sun, long stockings covered the legs and of course they were color coordinated. Ruffles were in, and the cap just had to have a bow in front. Sandals were also a good idea.

Fairmount Park surged ahead. In early June and going into July, "the greatest balloon exhibition ever witnessed" was booked. Two hot air balloons carried a large cannon to an altitude of 5,000 feet and blasted an aeronaut into mid-air, where he descended to the lake with the help of a specially designed parachute. Chicko, the Brazilian flying man who acted like a monkey, worked the trapeze gig, while Professor Kearney P. Speedy, tied in a gunny sack, jumped off or was pushed into a tank 70 feet below, with only 6 inches of water to stop him.

The parks, at that time, were the lungs of the city. People came to breathe the fresh air and a cop never awoke a sleeping patron. They were a melting pot, where the rich and poor came and mingled. Boys flirted with girls and girls could flirt with boys. Some came to eat the park food and many brought their lunches in a picnic basket. Bachelors would wander about the park looking for a friendly face in hopes of getting some home cooking. The most common sight would have been the family group: mom and dad, with a youngster or two (later to become our great-grandparents).

There was also the crime element. Juvenile delinquents strolled in groups, smoking cigarettes, with their collars turned up and wearing yachting caps, making grandstand remarks for the pretty girls to hear. There was park statuary, too. People stretched out on the grass or on a park bench away from the crowds. The young lady with a book who came to the park early in the afternoon and read until dark hoping to meet Prince Charming. The old man who sits all day thinking about the time he shot a prairie chicken where the lake is now located. Young boys, in dog drawn carts noisily crisscrossing the park, and couples in love strolled everywhere, hand in hand.

The 4th of July was better than any celebration in town. Fairmount Park was really neat and many new attractions greeted the thousands that attended. The Toboggan Slide had just opened to the public and a trapshooting park opened just north of the springs; all day, 7 days a week, with guns, shells, and targets all furnished. The people with the cannon were there again. Speedy jumped into the lake from a height of 100 feet, a world's record, and a young lady dove 85 feet into the lake. The Obertie Brothers were a new act and worked with a burning ladder. At 9:00 P.M. a tremendous fireworks display, costing $1,000, took off and the evening ended with a bang!

Washington Park also had unique attractions. A troupe of seven juggling; Japanese were there and the lions and leopards were still there. In the afternoon, two members of the gun club had a match, using 50 live birds, with 25 targets a piece (Society for the Protection of Animals, where were you?)

At 4:00 P.M. on Sunday, July 14th, "As You Like It," Shakespeare's popular comedy, was presented at Fairmount Park's new open air theater, by the Kemper Stock Company. A new bridge had been built across the ravine, located where Northern Blvd. is now (at Hink Drive), leading north to the newly acquired 50 acres, expanding the park to Kentucky Avenue and Appleton.

In the shade of the oak trees, the "Theater in the Woods" made its debut, with room for 5,000 spectators. Although interrupted by rain on the first day, the play was a huge success.

After arriving at the depot, passengers would detrain and step onto a wooden platform that was open to the air and roofed over. It was a two city block walk to the bridge over the ravine, the lake being on the right, the cafe and the Crystal Maze on the left. The pretty white cement bridge over the ravine led north and on the left was the recently opened shooting range. The path headed down to where the tickets were accepted; $1.50 got you a chair on the front couple of rows, $1 was a bench right behind them, 50 and 75 cents was general admission, standing room only. Over the entrance was printed, "The entire world's a stage". Two tents were set up for the cast as dressing rooms and the stage was grass, with the trees as the scenery.

There were 75 players in the Kemper group. Some were local actors, but many had performed at the Chicago World's Fair in '93. The costumes were from Hermann's Emporium in New York City and cost over $2,000. The Third Regiment Band performed instrumental music, while an octet from the Apollo Vocal Club added a bit of charm to the performance. Underbrush was cleared away and what was left was used by the actors to make their entrances. The play, written in 1599, was described as a "rustic comedy." The original script was set in the woods, so the forest probably saved some money on back drops. Several cloudbursts interrupted the performance, but the show must go on, and it did. Hundreds of umbrellas popped open and "your umbrella, please," was repeated many times as they obscured the view. The play ran one week and was very popular, but there were no more outdoor productions that year at Fairmount Park. Washington Park, true to form, put on a Gilbert & Sullivan production in its own outdoor theater.

In August, the action at Fairmount Park shifted to the new athletic field (now R. J. Roper Stadium) northeast of the lake. On Saturday the 4th, the Kansas City Athletic Club met for their monthly meet. The number of contestants was small, but the events were exciting. Among the events were the 100 yard dash, 12 lb. shot-put, pole vault, hammer throw, 440 yard dash, and 120 yard hurdle. Bicycle races were also held; one to ten miles on a 1/4 mile track.

A second rail depot was opened at 2nd and Walnut to help handle the masses. Special trains were to run daily, for Dr. W. F. Carver was coming to town. Champion shot of the world, decorated by emperors, kings and presidents, he would perform daily with a rifle, from horseback and on foot. His high-diving horse amazed the crowds, jumping from a height of 30 feet into the lake. She swam like a duck and ate sugar out of ladies' hands. Beginning on the 26th, a $20,000 Wild West show was presented by Dr. Carver; 200 cowboys and Sioux Indians filled the new field. New bleachers were built and the athletic field has been in service for over 100 years.

"Methods of attack and warfare as practiced by the Indians, the circle of death, the attack on stage coaches, burning of the settlers' cabins, rescue by Dr. Carver and his cowboys, sports on the plains roping and riding wild broncos and steers, trick and fancy riding by the greatest horseman on earth, the cowboy camp and village..."

The show was held every afternoon at 3 and every evening at 8:00, with a magnificent grandstand seating thousands of people. Box seats were $1.00, three reserve rows were 75 cents, grandstand 50 cents, and 25 cents for general admission.

The Fairmount and Washington Parks competitive wars began in earnest in '94, fueled by money from the Holmes family, Washington Park's new owners. Kansas City's Labor Day Parade, which was a huge attraction, conveniently ended at 2nd and Wyandotte at 10:00 A.M., where rail cars were boarded for Fairmount Park and thousands spent the day. Dr. Carver's show was still there and everything was free... from boating to bowling and swimming, for the laboring man and his family.

Next year, 1895, would begin the first of two golden eras for Fairmount Park.

Chapter 4: 1895
The First Golden Era Begins

1895 was a year of business upturn and the new attractions at Fairmount Park just kept on coming. The park opened on Sunday, May 12th this year and the Third Regiment Band was again on board. Concerts were given every day and twice on Sunday. On Saturdays, children were treated to a free concert at the Pavilion and on Thursday afternoons there were concerts at the cafe.

Washington Park's main attraction this year was "Takazawa's Troupe of Japanese," billed the best acrobats in the world. Fairmount Park featured Paul Alexander Johnstone, the great mind reader. At 3:30 PM, on Sunday May 19th, Mr. Johnstone ran a train blindfolded, from the downtown depot at 2nd and Walnut to Fairmount, a distance of 7 miles. Another of his many feats was finding a needle on the bottom of the lake (Sure!).

At 8:15 P.M. Saturday night, June 1st, the new Fairmount Auditorium opened. It was located just west of what is now Northern Blvd. and Hink Drive. Gilbert & Sullivan's "Mikado" was presented and the players, just for this performance, were transported by train from New York City. Many international actors were among the 42 in the cast, 35 in the chorus, and their 10 piece orchestra, along with many pretty girls. $6000 was spent on a building that today would cost a hundred times more, with seating for over 1,000 and a wood interior that was beautiful.

"The Mikado," with British humor, Japanese costumes and American actors, most from the "Big Apple," was written halfway through Gilbert & Sullivan's partnership in 1881. It was considered their masterpiece, a satirical comic opera that managed to slam both Victorian England and the Japanese Empire. At the appointed hour, the Honorable E. H. Allen, former president of the Kansas City Board of Trade, delivered a speech and at 8:15 the play began. A theatrical tradition of the time was to bring a baby on stage, so in the first act, George Paxton, who played the title role of Mikado, brought out of the audience Theodore, 6 month old son of Herman Brumbach, a well known attorney of local note.

In the second act a most unusual and wonderful thing happened. The entire rear of the stage area was thrown open, exposing the natural scenery of the park, decorated with Japanese arches, pagodas, and hundreds of Chinese lanterns. The opera played for one week and was critically acclaimed. Ticket prices were 25, 30, and 50 cents.

A new and improved Electric Fountain had been built, at great expense, in the lake. The Cascade Glen now had a small lake with a jet of water that shot 40 feet in the air and on sunny days created a rainbow. Another first was the Electric Theatre, which opened on Sunday, June 2nd and was similar to the one at the World's Fair. It was located by the bowling alley which was where Northern Blvd. runs one block north of 24 Highway now. It featured "A Day in an Alpine Village" which included sunrise, sunset, storm clouds, and other events of the day. The price of admittance was 10 cents and it had to be one of the first commercial ventures of its kind in the world.

A greenhouse had been built east of the lake. It had its own water tower and was responsible for the miles of sweet pea vine, thousands of roses of different colors, geraniums, pansies, and other varieties which decorated the park. Where the shelter house now stands in left field of R. J. Roper Stadium there was an ice house. In the winter, when the lake froze, men working with saws cut and stored tons of ice for use in the summer.

If the new things didn't appeal to you there were always the established attractions like boating, bathing, outdoor gymnasium, fishing, bears, a dance pavilion, the Crystal Maze, bowling, swings, shooting, a photograph gallery, and a merry-go-round.

On June 9th, Professor F. A. Squires, aeronaut, released 25 small parachutes from 2,000 feet, each containing a prize, such as a pair of gents fancy garters from Wolf Brothers, umbrellas and a ton of coal from Central Coal and Coke Company, free delivery.

The big attraction for June was the good Rev. Sam Jones who, on the 23rd, brought Southern style evangelism to the park. For several days in late June and 25 cents you could hear the great orator speak on "sawciety," the world as it was and the world as it should be, according to him.

The warm summer sun had finally warmed the water in the lake and 500 new bathing suits had been purchased, but remember, Washington Park was just up the road and had such acts as the Flying Jordans and the Four Nelson Sisters.

The nation's birthday in the 1890s was much more patriotic that today and much louder. Bulldogs (fireworks), pistols with blanks and a small bore cannon could constantly be heard from early morn till late at night. Orators praised grandfathers who fought and died at places like Valley Forge. The 4th of July was on a Thursday that year and the weatherman promised a sunny warm day, so of course it rained most of the day.

The people at Washington Park did not let the weather interfere with the celebration. A hot, humid morning was interrupted by a strong cool front that passed through about noon, dropping the temperature 10 degrees, bringing thunder, lightning, and rain. Mother nature let go with a big bang and hundreds of smaller ones were followed by rebel yells and other verbal responses. After less than half left the park, many stored their clothes at the bath house, put on swimming suits and took boats out on the lake, armed with cannons, men rowing while the ladies fired. Soon the lake was obscured by smoke from the mock fire fights.

Mayor Webster Davis of Kansas City was the keynote speaker, followed by D. E. Stoner of the City Council, who recited the Declaration of Independence. Professor Zimmerchied's band played patriotic tunes such as "Dixie" and "The Star Spangled Banner", which could hardly be heard over the yelling and explosions.

Meanwhile, back at Fairmount Park, not as many people left, probably because there were no political speeches and not as much rain. Most of the attractions were open to the public, and the ones that did charge didn't charge much.

New wide, white sidewalks crisscrossed the park. Ladies in wet, white dresses and men in duck trousers (made of duck cloth, a fabric somewhere between canvas and cotton) were seen everywhere. A game of La Crosse on Shetland ponies was played at the athletic field and music from the opera "Erminie" came from the new auditorium. Crowds followed the Third Regiment Band as it marched around the park. A world class equilibrate, Carl Charles, tied a rope between two trees, 40 feet above the ground, and walked across with only the help of a balancing bar. The traditional fireworks display took place at 8:30 P.M. and went off without a hitch. People stayed until the last train headed back to the big city.

The remainder of the summer at Fairmount Park was outstanding. At the auditorium, prices had doubled and the Kemper Stock Company turned a one week engagement into two, because so many people had to be turned away at the door. Shakespeare's comedy, " A Mid Summer Night's Dream," played from Monday, July 8th to Sunday, July 21st. It was followed by the same actors in another gem by Mr. S., "As You Like It." August at the auditorium was filled with Vaudeville, which was just now entering its second decade. Music, jokes, skits, and juggling were some of its trademarks. Admission was 25 cents and featured acts such as The Bison Quartet, W. S. Gilbert, European aerial hook artist, The Hale Sisters, who were a local song and dance favorite, and The Dark City Circus.

Outside, Professor Squires and his wife and the rest of the family, including his two dogs, leaped from a balloon with parachutes. Later, astride a donkey, he jumped from 3,551 feet. The "mother of all picnics" was held on August 15th by the Irish American Society, while the Walton Mandolin Club played on the cafe veranda. The third annual bicycle races were held on the athletic field the 30th and 31st. Every night ended with a fireworks display of one kind or another. One favorite display was Niagara Falls, where the lake appeared to be on fire.

The big news at Washington Park for the late summer of '95 was the boat that had been built in the middle of the lake and used as a stage for plays such as Gilbert & Sullivan's "Pinafore," performed by a traveling company of actors from New York. Not a unique idea, but at least they didn't' steal it from Fairmount Park.

September was to show just how much of a social melting pot Fairmount Park was. Labor day of '95 came on a Monday, the 2nd, and the parade led to Fairmount Park. Among the speakers in the new auditorium was Mayor Davis, of Kansas City, and Jerry Simpson from the Medicine Lodge. Many sporting events were held both on the lake and at the athletic field; foot races, boating and a game of tug-of-war, capped off by a game of 9's (baseball) between the plumbers and bricklayers. The 5 inning game was won by the bricklayers 7-3. 10,000 people journeyed to Fairmount Park that day and just about maxed out the system. Trains were packed from 11:00 A.M. until dark. Management liked to brag that there were 100 attractions at the park. The 101st would be a doozy.

On July 21st, the Missouri, Kansas and Texas Trust Company announced that a Horse Show would be held at Fairmount Park September 3rd, 4th, 5th, and 6th. It was the brainchild of Tom Bass, a former slave, who would someday be a world-famous horse trainer. A purse of $2,500 was to be offered and A. E. Stillwell was named trustee. The purpose of the show was to bring together horsemen from all over the southwestern United States. Fairmount Park was chosen for two reasons: (1) the amphitheater (Roper Stadium) with seating for 3,500 and its 1/4 mile race track and (2) horses could be unloaded right from the train inside the park. By September 3rd, the purse had been increased to $3,300 in prizes and $400 in gold medals. At 2:30 P.M., the trumpet sounded, calling the entries to take their place, beginning the first annual fancy Horse Show. There would be several more at Fairmount Park in the coming years, but it would eventually move to Downtown, Kansas City and evolve in 1900 into the American Royal of today.

Major C. H. Buford called out the classes and was superintendent of the grounds. There were 54 classes and 383 entries with 400 different horses. Only the fancy horses need apply, such as carriage horses, coach roadsters, saddle animals, hunters, and Shetland ponies. The spectator stands read like a Kansas City street guide, such people in attendance such as Gillham, Sterling, Armour, Holmes, Scarritt, and Wilson (you get the picture?). Arc lights were strung around the track and searchlights reached for the sky. The four days of competition ended with only one casualty, a broken arm from a fall. On the 6th an auction was held and many good horses were sold. The quality of livestock was not yet as good as the east coast's, but there was always next year.

Chapter 5: 1896

Last year it was the new auditorium, this year it's the new hotel, "The Fairmount," built on the high ground overlooking the lake. Opening day was May 8th, a warm spring day with the air temperature at 86 degrees and the water temperature at 70. The Third Regiment Band, conducted by H. O. Wheeler, began its 4th season by giving two concerts on Sunday, May 10th, and things were again on a positive note. Except for some lying politicians and a few truant kids, there was, as yet, no crime at Fairmount Park.

The Fairmount Hotel was built to accommodate the many people from the big city who wanted to spend a few quiet days in the country. There were 52 rooms in the hotel and nine cabins just south of it. Many people found rest and relaxation in the U-shaped two story building, with two screened in front porches, used for sitting and watching the world go by. A cafe seating 50 people was open, managed by Mrs. George McLean, who as also in charge of the park cafe. The Sunday dinner was 75 cents, which doesn't sound so cheap when the average wage for a 60-hour work week was just $12.

Washington Park, which opened May 23rd, had not changed a whole lot in the last two seasons. The trains now ran every couple of minutes. Boating, fishing, the bathing beach, the cafe, and the Shetland ponies for kids were again the main attractions. The Washington Park Military Band was very popular, but other that that it had just about seen its day.

Beginning May 30th and lasting two weeks, the first annual Chautauqua was booked at Fairmount Park. New York State, where the first one was held in 1874 and from there spread all over the nation. It was kind of like a correspondence, mainly for adults, with a Bible-thumping theme. Among the many speakers was Methodist Episcopalian John Vincent, who founded the movement, and William Jennings Bryant, a young oracle, who was to be the Democratic presidential nominee for that year. The "great commoner" debated a man from Massachusetts named Horr; the subject being the silver issue. Special train rates for people within 150 miles of Fairmount were in effect. A tent city sprang up along the sloping ground just north of where Ralston Avenue runs into Lexington Avenue. Over 100 tents were rented from the park management and pitched. Most of the campers cooked under the trees and it took on a picnic atmosphere. The highlight had to be on Saturday afternoon, June 6th when a pretty young lady by the name of Clevenger fainted while waiting to recite. Almost 3,000 people received a diploma at the end of the tortuous affair, which ended on June 13th.

On Saturday, June 20th, the National Circuit bicycle races were held at Fairmount Park's amphitheater (Roper Stadium). There were two classes, professional and amateur. It was easy to spot the pro's in the crowd: they were the ones with the bruises and bandages. The event was sponsored by the Kansas City Bicycle Dealers Association. $600 in gold coin for the professionals and $235 in silver and jewelry for the novice, were offered. Twenty-five professional wheel men from New York City to San Francisco were drawn to town. The 1/4 mile track was a combination of cinders and dirt and was described as "one of the swiftest in the country." Over 2,000 people attended the events and while no new records were broken neither were any bones. It rained early Saturday morning so there were a few spills. Sixty-two locals wheeled around the oval track competing for prizes like silver service sets, diamonds, gold watches, opera glasses, etc.

The weekend before the 4th of July, the 4th annual picnic for the Kansas City Railroad Passengers Men was held. They arrived from all over the Midwest, on Saturday, June 27th. On this day the picnic area of the park was located where now Willow and Ralston dead end into Lexington. Rustic tables were covered with food and were already set up. After lunch, a couple of hours of speeches, introductions, and much toasting were in order. At 5:30 those that could still walk took a dip in the lake and teased the other bathers. When 7:00 rolled around, the trains were again boarded and the railroad men began, for some, a long journey back from where they came.

Following the fireworks, fun, and festivities of the fifth 4th of July at Fairmount, the fabulous frolic returned to its former functions. The heat of July sent many patrons to the lake to cool off. Boating and a well-stocked lake guaranteed, at least, a bite on the end of your fishing line. The Auditorium was in its second year. Two groups of actors, one local and one nomadic, merged into the new "Fairmount Park Stock Company." Together they were signed to stay the season. Because of its popularity, "The Merry Wives of Windsor" was held over for two days and was followed by "The Lion's Mail," a play about some poor guy getting his head cut off in France. "Twelfth Night" finished out the month.

A club house for the local bicycle enthusiasts was built at the athletic field and on Sunday, August 2nd, anyone on a bicycle was admitted to the park free. Many people from all over the greater Kansas City area wheeled out to Fairmount Park. A new macadam (a fitted, stone road) had been built, running from the end of Independence Avenue to the park, for them to try out. Competition to separate the bicyclist from his money was intense. A good bike cost at least $100 or more, while a buggy, back then, cost less. On the same Sunday afternoon, the Kansas City Cyclist Club rode to Parkville and the Pathfinders Bicycle Club left their clubhouse at 2:15 P.M. for a ride to Washington Park for a dip in the lake. The

Independence Athletic Association announced that their new bicycle club would hold a 10-mile run out to the Salem Track on the 28th of August. This event was open to residents of Independence only. A wheel man of local fame, Joe Hocker, made the big time. With a little training he earned the opportunity to race with the pros. He was invited to join the national circuit, as he was very impressive that June at Fairmount Park.

At the park theater, four new moving pictures, called Vitascopes, were added to the bill, with titles like "Corbett vs. Courtney" boxing match rounds, Cissy Fitzgerald, in her famous wink and kicks, sea waves off Dover, England, and a fire rescue scene. The auditorium featured live Vaudeville weekend afternoons, acts like Casino Comedy Four or the Grierson Sisters, both from New York. Seven evenings a week the Fairmount Stock Co. put on plays like "The Talk of the town." Prices were 25 cents and 50 cents.

In mid August, the park was visited by five adult elephants and after their Saturday matinee, Professor Lockhart, their trainer, marched them to the lake for a bath. Some skeet shooters spooked the pack-o-dermis by blasting some clay pigeons. If they were to panic, they would stomp the hell out of the park, not to mention the patrons. "Tails-O, tails-O!" ordered the trainer and they stomped a doughnut in the grass. The day was mostly rainy and cool, but when the sun shined through the clouds, they took to the water, standing on their heads, sparring and splashing about. "Elephants have just as much sense as a man," said Professor Lockhart.

Getting to the park for the second Fancy Horse Show, was much improved over last year's dusty trip. Thanks to the new fitted stone road from Independence Avenue, many people no longer had to take the train. The buggies and bicycles could make the trek without getting stuck in the mud.

"What a beautiful park," remarked Dr. Charles S. Turnbill, a judge for the show who hailed from Philadelphia, upon entering Fairmount Park. On Saturday afternoon, September 5th at 2:30 pm, the 2nd Annual Fancy Horse Show got underway. The elephants led the parade into the amphitheater, followed by the many entries, 559, twice as many as last year, and 180 more than the New York or London horse shows. Riding the famous "Miss Rex" was the soon-to-be-world famous horse trainer, Tom Bass. He was awarded the $1,000 Stilwell Stake.

Chapter 6: 1897
"The Prettiest Park in the U S of A"

Soon after the end of last year's Horse Show, a magazine, "Horse Show Monthly" eulogized the show. The horses and Fairmount Park were touted for public interest. "The Fairmount Riding and Coaching Club" was organized. Its goal was to bring equestrianism to the natives. To accommodate, the athletic field was again the object of much construction. The bluff to the east (Sterling Ave to Sterling Terrace and Lake St.) was linked by a wide, rustic wooden bridge, where the riding school and stables were built. An oval track for driving and riding horses was surrounded by a larger bicycle track that went under the bridge, giving the amphitheater dual roles. Horse school lessons included tandem, coach, and carriage driving. Hurdling, polo, and other riding sports were practiced. For amusement, egg and spoon races, umbrella and cigar races and an obstacle driving range were added. For a small fee a horse could be quartered at the stables or "house" horses were rented to the public by the hour.

The 6th glorious season began on Sunday, May 9th. The new 25 piece Fairmount String Orchestra, under the direction of Mr. H. O. Wheeler of last year's third regimen band, held concerts every Sunday at 3:30 P.M. Both the park and the hotel's cafes were now under the management of Mrs. Emma Mills, with her specialties of fruits, ices, delicacies, and fine meats. The month ended with the park's first felony. A 17 year old boy was shot by a lady who lived at the athletic field with her child and husband. The lung wound was not fatal, but it wasn't for the lack of trying.

Early June was the second annual Chautauqua invade from the 1st to the 12th. A lot of the newness was gone, but for those in attendance it was still spiritually rewarding. As soon as the summer school pulled out things got back to normal, i.e., much fun. At the theater, Vitascope was replaced by the next generation of movie technology, Magniscope, which was soon replaced by a more familiar name, Cinematography. It was still a 10 cent admission charge.

To usher in the third season of the auditorium, two free concerts were given by the Pickaninny Band on June 13th at 3:30 and again at 8:00 P.M., on a warm Sunday. Twenty-five Black musicians and the Slayton Jubilee Singers sang plantation music. The next day Vaudeville returned. It, too, had evolved. Short skits had replaced longer plays, due in part to the influence of the moving picture. At a time when a laboring person might make $20 a week, top drawer actors sometimes could make $300 to $500 a week. This brought many from the big shows back east to Fairmount Park. "Any Seat in the House 25 Cents."

Gold coin was the carrot and the stick was the railroads, who also owned a piece of the parks. Everything was in readiness for the National Bicycle Races, held on Saturday of the following weekend at the amphitheater. Cracks (professional bike riders) from across the country were entered. Last week they were in St. Louis and next week they will be in Omaha, Nebraska. A rivalry between the amateurs of St. Louis and Kansas City developed; the locals getting waxed. Two Independence men, D. D. Dunkin and B. F. Wallace, entered the amateur one mile race, but didn't win. A novelty of the races this year was a quadricycle, a four person bike that did a pretty good mile.

America's 121st birthday came on a Sunday, creating a 3 day weekend. Not everybody went to the parks. Some could not afford it and on many a train ride the dads were absent from the family outing. Many had to stay home with their friends and drink beer. Those that could afford it took trains destined for a small town like St. Joseph, while others would cruise Independence Avenue from Woodland to Gladstone in their buggies, dressed in their best. Most large, vacant lots became ball parks. Many cemeteries served as picnic groves and if you wanted to wager a bet there were the horse races at Exposition Park. Many in the city liked to ride their wheel (bicycle) out to Independence. New stone roads had been laid to both Salem and Blue Springs. The suburban road system was beginning its infancy. The country clubs offered golf and tennis.

Fairmount Park and its many attractions was that place to be. Six years of smart investment had turned a forest into a silver mine. Kansas City was being nickeled and dollared, but they loved it. From disembarking the trains until time to go home, vendors hawked such things as popcorn, peanuts, soda water and cheap candy. Parents could trust the park to protect their children if they wanted to go to the theater. The park was like a 70 acre baby sitter. A small zoo was located where Northern and Ohio meet. Bears, a deer petting pen and Shetland ponies for riding kept the kids busy. On the lake "The Admiral," a canvas covered powered boat plowed around the 18 acre lake.

Two big Vaudeville shows were the feature attractions at the auditorium; trapeze artists, singers, clowns, sketches, and moving pictures. Day and night fireworks lit up the outdoors. The Third Regiment Band played from morning until the last person had left the park.

Washington Park's popularity this season was really off from previous years. Many still preferred its quiet beauty, with its acres of flowers and huge oak trees (some 5 feet in diameter) to Troost Park's monkeys or Fairmount Park's crowds. Bands, large and small, played concerts and many big names were invited to perform. The lake was a big draw and the boating, fishing, and bathing beach were first class. Rain interrupted many a visit to the park, but the only cover was the leaves on the trees, as there were not many buildings.

After the 4th of July at Fairmount, a blue ribbon bicycle race was held for the Convention Hall Fund. Kansas City's best riders entered. On a rainy Saturday afternoon, several track records were broken and one state record tied. Admission was 25 cents and there were many spills and plenty of seats due to the inclement weather.

August 1st the Salvation Army invited all poor mothers in the Kansas City area to attend Camp Stilwell. A tent city was erected and educational and medical facilities were made available. The park was also at their beck and call.

An attempt to interest Kansas City's youth in boating flopped. On Friday afternoon, August 27th, a regatta by the newly formed Kansas City Naval Cadets failed to draw much of a crowd. Plans for a lighted night parade on the lake were cancelled.

The 3rd annual Horse Show began on Saturday, September 4th. A lot of changes were made since last year's show. Special rates by the railroads boosted attendance. Anyone within several hundred miles of Kansas City (like Texarkana) could purchase a ticket for $4.50. This was a doubling of the circumference over last year's show. One thing that this show would have that the first two didn't was class. First, the number of entries, 500 or so, was about the same as last year, but there were more horses from out of town. Many had been in shows in Chicago or Philadelphia. Along with the horse was the horseman or horsewoman, they all had money, most had class.

Last year there were two shows a day, in 1897 there was one show a day, seven days a week from 2:00 P.M. till almost dusk. This year the contestants entered the arena from the stables at Sterling Avenue and Lake Street, then called "Horsey Hill", using the new bridge. For drainage, six inches of cinders was laid on the dirt arena floor. The cinders then were covered by six inches of tan bark. Dimensions of the arena floor were 350 feet north to south, 250 feet east to west. The weather was also different. Last year it had rained almost every day, this year it was very hot with temperatures into the 90s.

Ninety percent of the people rode the Air Line to the park, but some rode out in their buggies, arriving with dust from the macadam road. Taking a bicycle to a horse show would be like taking a Yamaha to a Harley run. The amphitheater soon filled with 7,000 spectators and "Horsey Hill" was also filled with the overflow of people who watched for free.

The United States Calvary from Fort Riley, Kansas was sent by the War Department to entertain and educate the civilian population. They camped north of the bear pit; their perimeter is now the Northern, Kentucky, Appleton, and Ohio Street square. This was only the second time a military unit had put on a show, the first being in Madison Square Garden. This was a Nineties version of an air show.

Commanding 48 horsemen, 32 cannon men, over 100 horses and mules and 2 cannons was Captain T. T. Knox, with 24 years of service and veteran of two Indian Wars. He would send a full report back to Washington, who was interested in the civilian response to these shows.

Everyday at 8:00 P.M., Labor Day through Friday, the horse soldiers would perform, getting more reckless by the day. Riding like Cossacks they put on one hell of a show. Several were hurt doing tricks like back flips. They certainly earned their $20 a month average pay. Several Calvary horses were entered in the horse show. They were large animals, some weighing a half ton, all jumpers. Next summer they would be in Cuba without their horses, commanded by Leonard Wood and Teddy Roosevelt. They were going to be the Rough Riders.

The First Calvary was the hit of the show. The hero was Ed Stutte. His two horses, Gambler and King Salisbury, and buggy got away from him while showing them to the judges. For six laps they ran wild; the crowd cheered. Finally the horses tired and came to a stop in front of the grandstand. When congratulated for his horsemanship he said, "What else could I do?"

Mules were also in the show. A fox hunt and trumpet blowing contest and much more were held.

During the Horse Show on the afternoon of Saturday, September 11, at precisely 3:30, a loud cannon went off and a huge banner unfolded, announcing that the last spike had been driven in the Kansas City, Pittsburg & Gulf Railroad, another venture conceived by Fairmount Park founder Arthur Stilwell. From Kansas City to the Gulf town it was now connected with by rail, Port Arthur, Texas, people celebrated in the streets. The celebrating would be short-lived, however, as a hurricane fell upon Port Arthur early the next morning which killed fourteen people, including four who had sought shelter in Stilwell's KCP&G roundhouse.

In spite of all this, Horse Show #3 was a huge success, with 40,000 people attending the show this year. Fairmount Park was becoming very well known.

Chapter 7: 1898
WAR

In April of 1898, the United States of America declared war on Spain over Cuba. The war lasted 112 days. 2,400 young men from the Greater Kansas City area who were members of the 3rd and 5th Regiments had been mobilized to a place called Camp Mead. Along with the men went the band which had played at Fairmount Park for years.

A new open air band stand had been built for the Third Regiment's band. It was very impressive. The stage was 60' long and shaped like an egg cut in half. The acoustics were so perfect that the softest notes could be heard at the Dance Pavilion. Its location was 500 feet east of the auditorium, just north of the intersection of Lexington and Hedges Streets. It was closed in back and the front was in the shape of an arch facing south. It worked like a giant speaker. The cost was over $1,000 and had bench seating for 2,000 people.

By May 15th, the new Fairmount Park Military Band had been organized. Under the baton of J. P. Zimmerschied, 30 musicians would occupy the new band stand.

Not just world events worked against Fairmount Park this year. The weather was bad. A wet, cool spring delayed the bathing beach from opening until late May. The 30th annual Memorial Day weekend, however, began sunny and warm, though not yet warm enough for swimming, so boating and fishing became the most popular water sports. Because of the war, the fleet of boats had been repainted various colors. All but one had been named after American heroes or boats, the Admiral Dewey (named after the hero of Manilla Bay) being most popular. A yellow and red boat named Admiral Cevera (someone's idea of a joke?) was peppered with rocks by small boys all day. The banks of the lake were lined with fisherman and kids, beckoning several large crappie from the comfort of their home in the lake.

Close to the merry-go-round, where now Ohio Street meets Northern was the deer corral. Twelve May births increased the herd to 41. Grass cut by park maintenance mixed with corn was their diet. The animals were not only a big draw for the children, they were also for profit. Next year several would be sold as venison. One of the local dogs that tried to take off with some baby deer steak got his head shot off by park security.

This year's 4th of July celebration brought forth fireworks and a patriotic explosion. Even Washington Park came alive. It was still open, but doing a little feebly. Fireworks were dropped from a balloon twice a day. A goose was also thrown from the balloon at 5,000 feet, with a reward of $10 for the finder. Only 3,000 people were in attendance.

If it was baseball that you wanted, Exposition Park featured a double hitter between the first place Kansas City Blues and Omaha, the first game at 10:00 A.M. and the second game at 3:00.

One thousand dollars in fireworks, Lenge's Military Band and many more attractions drew 20,000 to Troost Park. Troost's location was its greatest asset, being only a few minutes south from downtown, with the city rapidly growing in that direction.

Fairmount Park featured a "grand patriotic celebration" in honor of Dewey's great victory at Manila Bay and the fall of Santiago. One thousand five hundred dollars is the amount management claimed to have spent on fireworks. The latest in pyrotechnics was the Bombshell Batteries: several mortars firing projectiles into the night, exploding several times in the air, throwing out Roman Candles which exploded again in red, white, and blue, lighting up the sky. Napoleon Repeating Bombshells showed as many as six different designs. The Japanese type exploded into moons, dragons, chrysanthemum, and mushroom clouds. Some of the fireworks exploded into pieces showing pictures of Dewey, Sampson, Miles, & President McKinley. The heroes of the war were used magically. The auditorium was filled to capacity. "The Chimes of Normandy" was given by the Bennett and Olmi opera company.

Two city records were set; 100,000 transfers were issued, meaning that over half of the population of the city had used the trolley that day. Because of the dry weather 24 fires were attended to, breaking the record set on July 4, 1892 of 11. All were caused by fireworks, most of them from boys throwing small bombs on wood roofs that had not seen rain for several weeks.

After the Fourth, the Salvation Army ran into money problems. Last year's Open Air camp for the poor mothers of Kansas City was a great success with 140 mothers being helped. Because of the war this year there was an even greater need. Many soldiers had left, leaving mothers and children in financial jeopardy. This year, instead of everyone coming to camp ("Brigadier Harry Stillwell") all at once, 25 women and their children would attend per week, followed by another 25 the following week.

One of the attractions they would have seen, reflecting the militaristic mood, was the Knaben-Kapelle, or Royal Hungarian Boys Military Band of Budapest. Billed as the "Kaiser's Own", 33 young musicians, ages 8 to 13, played music such as Sousa's marches, Strauss's waltzes, Wagner's massiveness, etc., stirring and moving music from people who knew how to march. Their discipline was amazing. Very early in the morning they would fall out for roll call and march to breakfast. They were quartered at the Fairmount Hotel, sleeping 4 to a room. The only fun they were allowed to have was the 30 minute dip they got to take in the lake every other day. Talk about contrasts; 1,000 youths from the Kansas City area spent a day at the park courtesy of the good people at the Kansas City Star. Their job was to cheer the boys up and maybe to get one to defect...

In September our soldiers were finally on their way home. Finding them a place to stay while they were mustering out was a problem for the military. Both Burge Park and Fairmount Park offered to accommodate. Burge proposed to give the entire 80 acre park, blue grass sod, drill ground, city water, free transportation on the Northeast Electric Line and 1,000 pounds of ice a day for free. Fairmount's proposal was much the same, although farther from the city. Fairmount won. A good cafe, bathing in the lake and Cusenbary Spring water swayed the powers that be.

The parade downtown went off with out too much trouble. School was let out, children waved American flags with 45 stars and pretty girls with red, white, and blue sashes on their shoulders lined the streets. A lot of hurry up and wait and a shortage of sandwiches failed to dampen the festivities.

Camp Jackson, at Fairmount Park, was another matter. It rained a lot. A soldier could go home if (1) he lived locally and (2) he wasn't in the brig. Many were and some were fined their whole $16 a month salary. Food wasn't always the best or plentiful. Some local farmers came up missing chickens, and some chicken thieves lost their chickens to other chicken thieves before they could cook and eat them. Sick call was very popular. A shortage of beds meant that some had to sleep on the ground, rolled up in their ponchos.

One poor guy was killed by a train en route from a good time in the city. Major Will T. Stark angered his troops when he forced them to parade by his home in Independence, a round trip of 8 miles in the rain and mud, just to impress a couple of women. On the 16th of September, almost everyone received a 30 day furlough. One Company was left behind to guard government property. That wasn't too bad, for they could go to the Horse Show.

Horse Show #4 was a social hit and a financial miss. A total of $23,000 was lost by park management, the equivalent of 23 new bandstands. That was one hell of a lot of money back then, let alone now.

There were several reasons for the loss, (1) Rain ruined 4 of the 7 shows, holding the attendance down, (2) The show which was held on Labor Day in the past was delayed in hopes that the troops could attend, (3) the annual carnival downtown started right after the Horse Show, cramping the availability of both hotel rooms and the local amusement dollar, and (4) a lot more money was spent on entertainment this year and the prize money was also increased.

This year's show started with a ton of enthusiasm. A ball was held by the Algonquin Club the first evening of the first show at the Dance Pavilion. A canvas awning was stretched from the pavilion to the hotel to keep the people out of the elements. Black and Old Gold were the official colors for this year's horse show, the bleachers had a new coat of white paint. Everything was at the ready.

Among the many features this year was the 3rd Regiment Band, but just in case they would not be able to make it even at this late date, a backup band was booked. The "Ladies Boston Military Band" was a great treat.

Polo pony races were also held for the first time. Firemen from as far away as Omaha competed to see who could hook up their horses to their equipment and race to the finish line first. The usual horsey stuff filled out the show.

Chapter 8: 1899
VAUDEVILLE

Last season's 4th annual Horse Show was the last, blowing 23K hurt. The local entrepreneurs now had the new Convention Hall downtown to invest in. Horses were losing their value and bicycles were also seeing depreciation. Sales would soon plunge. A new word was creeping into the vocabulary, au-tow-mo-bil, with the accent on the second syllable.

Park Management also changed. Mrs. E. C. Loomis was now in charge of the Fairmount Hotel, while the park now had two managers, Mr. Lehman and Mr. Rosenthal. The season was under the thumb of the Orpheum Amusement Company.

Fairmount Park's eighth season was unlike any other. For the first time there were no new expensive projects. Things also got started late. Professor W. O. Wheeler was again put in charge of the new Fairmount Park military band. The 3rd Regiment Band, which had been so popular in the years past, would not return. On Sunday, May 21st, concerts were given at 3:00 P.M. and then again at 8:00 P.M. in the band stand. Weekday concerts were put on hold.

The grand opening of the new "Fairmount Park and Orpheum" was Sunday, June 4th. This season's emphasis was on Vaudeville. Nine big acts were the draw. In the theater there was a complete high-class bill, like Melville and Stetson, Reno and Richards, Lorenz and Allen and the Four Nelson Sisters. At the lake a gent by the name of Charles Marsh dove from a height of 49 feet into a lake with his bicycle. Lenge's Orpheum Band was in the stand. The park's mottos this year were "Cost You Nothing," "Everything For Free," and "Something Going On All The Time."

On an enchantingly beautiful Sunday afternoon, the Old Settlers Association held a basket picnic. Some of the local history makers were in attendance. Talks were given by military men like Major Warner. General Blair sent a letter regarding the battle of Westport. Fighting Joe Hooker arrived by train. There were politicians like Congressman Cowherd. The cloth was represented by Father Dalton. Some who could not attend, many due to their health, sent histories for others to read. Mrs. Sarah Lykins Russell, one of the oldest settlers to this area, read a paper on the early history of Kansas City. Oldsters from both Kansas City, Kansas and Independence were invited to partake.

Toward the end of June, the champion lady swimmer of the world, Cora Beckwith, a British subject, visited the park. One hell of a swimmer, she had swam the English Channel when she was just 15 years old. A few years later she floated for 12 hours a day for 40 days! She was already credited with saving 49 lives, so she demonstrated what to do to save a drowning person. She also showed off the famous Beckwith Backward Sweep. Another European feature was the Faust family of some fame. The former Horse Show grounds were again being used for baseball. Teams like the Kansas City Billiard Makers played Bruce Lumber Company.

Fairmount's 4th of July celebration reflected the worldliness of the new America, a world power. Burmese Football is similar to soccer, except the ball is made out of wicker; whoever touches it or lets it hit the ground loses. Good players, like Moung Toom and Moung Chit could pass it back and forth for hours without a foul. Juggling was their forte. Bubble thin glass balls that broke at the slightest wrong move were used, glistening in the sun like crystal, never touching their hands. In the band stand was Lenge's Military Band. A musical battle of Manila, complete with cannon, rockets, rifle fire and flashing lights, gave two performances a day. The Manhattan Four comedy team headed the Vaudeville bill in the theater. The usual fireworks display on the lake was again the biggest in town and "It Cost You Nothing!"

In the popularity contest this 4th of July, Fairmount Park came in first, Troost Park second, and Washington Park was almost deserted. Only 300 people spent the day there, in what was to be the park's last 4th.

The remainder of the season was given to Vaudeville, for that was what the Orpheum Amusement Company was all about. Martin Beck owned 10 Vaudeville theaters and a piece of 25 more from Chicago to San Francisco.

There were two types of Vaudeville; big time and small time. Big time Vaudeville paid well, from $50 to $3,000 a week. That was before expenses, but it still wasn't too bad. There were two or three shows a day. Small time Vaudeville was the pits. It paid lousy and sometimes played 6 to 10 shows a day. Fairmount was somewhere in the middle.

Vaudeville was described as an enemy to responsibility and worries. Admission was 25 cents for a balcony seat and 10 cents for general admission. A bill consisted of six or seven 20 minute acts twice a day; matinee at 2:00, evening at 8:30. Shows throughout the circuit were all about the same. The opening act was always a silent act like a bunch of dogs or a juggler; something to get the late arrivals to their seats. A comedy team might be next, followed by a skit. Before intermission, a dance or musical group would give you a reason to come back. After intermission was a comedy single, followed by another musical number.

Last would be something like a troupe of European trapeze artists in bright red costumes, something to tell your friends about.

At that time, Vaudevillians were made, not born. A few grew up in middle class, but many were orphans. Learning a trade was better than begging. Many started by either dancing or juggling. Working your way up the ladder was tough, as there were only a few headliners at any one time.

Many very talented people appeared at Fairmount Park's Vaudeville shows this season, like Henry Lee, impersonator of famous people of his time (he not only did the mannerisms and voice, he would also dress in their likeness), Francesca Redding, one of the first dramatic actresses of legitimate theater to play Vaudeville, and the Howard Brothers and their Flying Banjos, two of the greatest in their profession.

Erich Weiss, Hungarian born magician and escape artist, who took the name Harry Houdini, was not yet famous. Harry and his wife Bess had struggled for years, till by chance he met Martin Beck of Chicago, owner of the Orpheum Co. He was hired in at $60 a week. Kansas City was his second stop, where he escaped from the Central Police Station in August. At Fairmount Park he had the local cops apply handcuffs from which he soon escaped. Next year he went to Europe and came back in 1905 worth $1,500 a week. Vaudeville was not yet in its golden age but was already playing a huge part in American culture.

The season came to an early end this year. Fridays had been amateur night since the 4th of July, and proved to be very popular. So, as the month of August and Houdini's act slipped into memory, Fairmount Park had Amateur Week. Lenge's Band provided accompaniment for the outdoor extravaganza held in the band stand. Admission was free. Prizes and maybe a job were offered for those with talent and lots of moxie. So ended another successful season.

Chapter 9: 1900

On Saturday, May 17th, the Kansas City Driving Club opened its gate to the public. It moved over to the area vacated by the Horse Show, which had evolved into the American Royal. $35,000 was spent on a rustic club house with a white picket fence, half-mile track, and is now Mayor R. J. Roper Stadium.

At 2:30 in the afternoon 117 contestants, 50 married couples, 17 single women, 4 married women, 44 misters and two doctors competed for a blue ribbon. Also new to the park was an outdoor theater built on the high ground with bench seating for 600 and plenty of standing room under the big trees.

But Old Fairmount Park was doomed. Electric Park opened in June next to the Heim Brewery and began as a huge keg party. It was located in the East Bottoms (now Guinotte and Chestnut).

Local commercial production of beer began in the 1850s. In 1886, Fred, Joe, and Mike Heim bought the Kumpf brewery. After acquiring a few more and thinking that the masses would want to visit the East Bottoms, $96,000 was spent on the Heim Electric Line. Finished in 1899, it wasn't very popular so they built an amusement park with a dance pavilion, bandstand, rides, fountains, and a German village beer garden. Electric lights were strung throughout the park allowing patrons to stroll late into the evening, and sip ale.

The battle of the parks had begun. While admission to Fairmount Park was free, transportation wasn't. Electric trollies cost a dime at a time when a pair of calf shoes were $1.48 or a round-trip to Chicago via the Chicago & Alton Railway was $14.50.

Over the Fourth of July holiday, the Democrats held their National Convention in Kansas City. William Jennings Bryant and Adlai E. Stevenson were nominated to run against William McKinley and Teddy Roosevelt. Bryant would lose and McKinley soon would be shot.

KC's population had grown to 215,000 with about 75,000 more in the suburbs. Somehow everyone had a room, 100,000 visitors found a place to stay. All three parks, Troost, Fairmount, and now Electric, competed for their $ & ¢. Fairmount spent $10,000 on fireworks, and Troost almost as much. In addition to fireworks, Electric had Vaudeville. A slack-wire walker was featured. A description of the festivities from the Kansas City Journal follows:

In the German Village, five singers will render songs typical of the Fatherland. In the theater, Melville & Stetson, the well-know comedian, will be featured. Buns & Nina did acts like paper-tearing, monologues, juggling, singing and dancing. Miss Nina will do a new spectacular dance at the close of the program. Van Brothers have a novel musical act and they have been billed as the foremost exponents of music and comedy. Kelly and Violet are well known in this city. Miss Violet is one of the handsomest women on the stage. Marie Rose, a lyric soprano, has been engaged for the week. She is one of the best singers in Vaudeville. Lou Hawkins has a monologue that is a wonder, and he writes his own songs.

And on it went until 1901, which would be the last year of the first Old Fairmount Park.

Chapter 10: 1901 - 1903

The grand opening for the tenth and final summer of fun at old Fairmount Park wasn't until June 2, 1901. It got off to a rocky start when six top vaudeville acts were scheduled for the amphitheater which was not completed. Since it wasn't done, the acts were transferred to the bandstand. The lack of shade and seating made the gig a bummer, and by the end of the first show most everyone had left.

For the first time in park history, summer cottages had some vacancies, and the Kansas City Driving Club had moved to a new location, 35K went south, as in a better part of town, to Cleaver Boulevard, not far from the Plaza.

The new amphitheater was shaped like an eggshell, located on the high ground in the center of the park, facing the lake, between Ralston and Hedges south of Lexington.

A quote from a reporter from the Journal told in a footnote to the opening day activities, "The crowds at the park were not as large for an opening day and the park is not so pretty as in past seasons owing to a seemingly lack of attention. The Vaudeville was the only special attraction."

Vaudeville seemed to be going well, two shows a day seven days a week and attendance was excellent, as was the talent, like "Techows's Cats", fifteen in number, that took their cues in German and performed like a bunch of dogs, the kids loved it. Also on the bill was the Four Flying Banvards, an aerial act made up of two adult males and two young girls; Amiel, the contortionist; Leonzo the famous juggler: working with things like hammers, knives, and rolling pins, he could juggle anything; the musical Kleists singing, dancing, and the black arts, whatever that was. Last on stage were Raymond & Clark acrobatic comedians, backed up by Lenge's Concert Orchestra.

On June 23 the last vaudeville production for quite a while played out. About ten o'clock that night John A. West closed the show by playing a variety of musical instruments and he was good. Back at Washington Cemetery, fishing was no longer allowed at Swan Lake. For the Fourth of July, Electric Park had a big fireworks display. Troost Park had a movie, "A Trip to the Pan American Exposition", Fairmount went all out, the world famous Bellstedt Band, conducted by Herman Bellstedt. The New Orleans Picayune called it the best band in the United States, and they would know. With 45 musicians and 8 soloists, the band was advertised as "one of the crack bands of the East". Crack, meaning something far different than it does today.

The band gave a concert in the amphitheater twice a day. Originally booked for only a week, they stayed on for most of the month. About this time a man by the name of George Shultz of KC, formerly of Independence, claimed to have, after 40 years of effort, invented a flying machine and wanted to fly it at Fairmount Park on August 10, the 80th anniversary of the admittance of Missouri into the Union.

Starting on July 12, the Salvation Army opened a camp amongst the trees just north and west of the lake. Every week from July to September, 100 different women and children from the city's poor neighborhoods were transported free to the park. Here a tent city was built which included sleeping quarters for all, a huge kitchen with 500 pounds of ice daily to keep things fresh, a twelve-bed hospital tent was set up along with a library. Although not mandatory, everyone was encouraged to take a dip in the lake first thing every morning. In the afternoon and evening, the kids were marched to the amphitheater, military style, to hear whoever happened to be there. There was plenty of adult supervision to keep the little brats from pulling up flowers and running amok. The end of July brought a new and novel attraction to the park, "The Mystic Fleet," described as a "grand pyrotechnic and aquatic spectacle". In reality it was a bunch of boats on the lake illuminated by fireworks. In the afternoon, Lenge's Military Band put on a concert along with Mile Verne and the Nebraska Wesleyan Male Quartet.

In the fall of 1874 some locals got drunk, hopped in a wagon, and tried to spread cheer throughout the city. Next year they did it again, it was the end of harvest and that was something to celebrate. Slowly growing, similar to the St. Patrick's Day celebration, started in 1973 when Mike Murphy, 710 AM, and some friends walked from one watering hole to another on St. Patty's day.

In 1877, some locals went to the Mardi Gras in New Orleans. After seeing the floats and balls, they came back to make a little bit of New Orleans in KC. They formed the Kansas City Karnival Krewe, the good old KKK. Nothing racial, it was just all Caucasian. It was a big deal from 1887 to 1924 when they merged with the Shriners. In April of 1901 the end of the festivities were predicted by the Journal. But it was not to be. They would have their party. But beginning on July 21, the KKK and the POP, or Priests of Pallas, endeavored to auction off the land around Fairmount Park. The occasion was the first great MINITOKA festival, standing for Missouri, Iowa, Nebraska, Indian Territory, Texas, Oklahoma, Kansas, and Arkansas. The plan was to sell 500,000 chances, or half a million dollars cash in silver certificates. Five hundred lots, with 50 of those lots having houses, were to be auctioned off in October during carnival week at Fairmount. Valued between $750 - $6000 each, a house valued at $2,000 looked like a Hollywood mansion and a $6,000 house looked like a castle. Suckers were asked to pay $1 per chance, which also gave the chump four passes to the fairgrounds. For $5, they got 20 admissions to the park and a ticket for two to the ball at Convention Hall. Backing this project were some of KC's finest capitalists.

Getting wind of the fall festivities, Mr. Shultz, local aeronaut, proposed flying out of the fairgrounds. He claimed to be 100 years ahead of everyone else, claiming he could fly to St. Louis in 2 hours or Chicago in 4, carrying 3 to 5 people. He didn't do it. For most of August, THE BANDA ROSA filled the park with patrons, probably the greatest military band ever, second only to the U. S. Marine Corps Band. 50 red-coated soloists, the most celebrated in all Italy, broke attendance records, 13,000 to 15,000 attended some of the weekend concerts. During the weekday, as many as 3,500 came from the city to catch the matinee. In the evening, hundreds parked themselves on Fairmount Knoll, where now there is a hole in the ground due to political incompetence, south to 24 Highway.

On August 24, the Karnival Krewe met to plan this year's parade. Nothing was mentioned about using Fairmount Park as part of Karnivale this October, nor was anything said about the great MINITOKA festivities, and especially nothing was said about any money that was given them for the 50 houses that were never built, the 500 lots, or a return of the money.

Meanwhile, back at the park, the KC Ladies Boat Club and the Missouri Canoe Club held their annual races. The following Thursday, September 5, all the grocery stores in both KCs and St. Joe shut down for the Seventh Annual Grocer's Picnic, all of which were at Fairmount Park. From noon till seven, sandwiches, pies, cakes, bananas, peaches, pickles, and cups of coffee were served free. After the feast baseball, races, etc, etc filled the afternoon and was the last organized activities at old Fairmount Park.

There were a lot of losers due to the decision to close the park. One of the biggest was the Kansas City Athletic Club, founded by our friend Arthur E. Stilwell, in 1894. The club was very exclusive, with a membership of 200, they were the cream of KC's young male yuppies. The club kept a clubhouse during the summer. Some of the members would spend the night there and after a dip in the lake, off to work downtown. But no more. In 1902, Troost and Electric were the only parks open to the public. Electric built two new rides, the Loop the Loop, where people go down a track and go upside down, and a Ferris wheel.

An article in a 1903 paper informed people that Troost and Fairmount would be closed permanently, but like so many things you read in the paper, it was not true. How could they know that the richest man who ever lived would be coming to this pristine little valley, well, at least his money? Like four million dollars of it. Mr. John David Rockefeller, America's greatest Capitalist.

Chapter 11: 1904
Sugar Creek, the Town

The first white men to trample on the land now called Sugar Creek were the people of the Louis and Clark expedition to the West Coast via the Missouri River, on June 23 to June 25 in 1804.

In 1834 the Mormons, facing persecution, fled Independence and camped along the bluffs just west of the present day VFW before they could escape across the river.

In 1849 an ox-drawn railroad was built between Wayne City, a riverboat landing about a mile down river from the creek, to the Independence Square, financed by some Independence entrepreneurs led by William Gilpen. The enterprise was the first commercial railroad west of the Mississippi. Starting in Wayne City the tracks ran west to the creek in between the bluffs. It then turned south along the creek (now Sterling) for a short distance to Elizabeth street. Turning east from there it wound its way up Forest to Sugar Creek Boulevard, and where U. S. 24 Highway and Crysler intersect is the only remaining physical reminder of the old railroad. Behind the business building now at 2421 U. S. 24 Highway is an earthen railroad trestle. From there it snaked its way to where the Independence Post Office is today, but there was a turn-around and stable then. The oxen were loaded on board so that the train could coast back down hill to the river. When a sandbar and a plague in 1855 killed the project, freight and passengers moved a few miles up river to a town originally called Possum Trot (now Kansas City, Missouri). The Civil War Order #11 screwed things up, Major Gilpin was one of many to be run out, and later became Governor of Colorado.

A county map drawn in 1877 showed the owners of Sugar Creek to be James Mallinson, 80 acres, J. D. Cusenbary, 160, J. Kronehart, 80, William Chrisman, 90, I. W. Duncan, 220. J. Foster owned 59 and had a house exactly where someday there would be an oil refinery.

In early 1889 oil was discovered in southeastern Kansas and Northeastern Oklahoma. In 1897 Standard built a refinery in Neodesha, Kansas. Meanwhile electricity was replacing nasty-smelling, black smoking, dangerous kerosene. In 1885 there were 250,000 light bulbs in use by Americans; by 1902, 18,000,000. Soon only the country folk would be burning kerosene. Something had to be done.

The oil fields back East were playing out. South of Paola, Kansas, Oklahoma, and Texas were like a mini Saudi Arabia. The oil was coming out of the ground faster than the Neodasha refinery could refine. In 1896 production was 500 barrels a day. By 1903 production had risen to 2,500 barrels a day while the oil being brought out of the ground was as much as 13,000 barrels a day. Pits were being dug in roads and ponds were made out of oil.

Standard was in the thick of it. Two miles north of Neodasha, Mr. Rockefeller, Inc., bought 320 acres and spent 1.5 million on a tank farm with 40 tanks holding from 37,500 to 60,000 barrels each. He soon had $3 million worth of oil stored by Spring, 1904. To bring the oil to the farm, pipe was laid by 400 skilled and semi-skilled laborers. Standard would lay pipe to any rig producing 50 barrels a day or more. That cost another million. When, in 1900, Prairie Oil and Gas Co. was incorporated, it was the point of the spear for Standard. If you bought stock in Prairie you were okay but there were some stocks that were worthless, like the Gold Standard Oil Company of Arizona. But there were some people who made money. George Banks, a farmer living near Independence, Kansas, was making $100 a day from just three wells.

At that time, America was an oil exporting country and 80% of the oil and gas was used East of the Mississippi river. On January 24, 1904, it was announced by Standard that a pipeline was going to be built from the Kansas Oil Fields to the refinery at Whiting, Indiana. The 700 mile 6-inch pipe would cost $4 million and take 2,000 men 7 months to complete.

In February of 1904 a stranger to Kansas City called Mr. Allen came to the Sugar Creek valley and within 2 weeks bought 70 acres at $200 per, he said, for a dairy farm. Mr. William Mallinson sold 30 acres, George Collins 20, and Hugh McElroy 20, all of the land east of the public highway which is now Sterling Avenue, but for years would be called Fairmount Avenue.

On Tuesday, March 1, the headline on the front page of the Kansas City Journal announced the Birth of Sugar Creek. It read:

"SITE CHOSEN"

It wasn't announced to be a site for an oil refinery, but for a railroad repair shop. Since this area stayed above water in last year's flood, it was the perfect place for something dangerous. By April the ground was being cleared and locals began asking questions, like one asked of Mr. J. D. Cusenbary, longtime resident, whose land Fairmount Park was built on. "What's going on?" by a reporter from the Journal. "My home is in the vicinity of the land which Mr. Allen recently purchased, ostensibly for dairy purposes, and I am in touch with affairs in my neighborhood. While I do not know for certain that the Missouri Pacific is the real purchaser behind Mr. Allen yet I have reason to believe that such is the case." But he went on to say that for the last several days people from the railroad, along with several strangers, had been walking among the hills and paying detailed attention to the landscape.

In 1903 the Missouri Pacific Railroad bought 40 acres from Judge Edward Gates of Independence. It was flat and didn't flood. Word soon got around to what was really going on.

Meanwhile, back in oil country, the good people of Kansas were getting teed off. The price of oil Standard was paying recently dropped 20 cents a barrel to $1.19. Producers complained that they were paying for the new refinery. On top of that, the $1 per foot first rumored for right-of-way turned out to be 20 cents per rod (16 1/2 feet). The whole price Standard paid for pipeline right of way was only $11,000. But the farmers were hired to build the pipeline. They worked in three waves, first came digging a 1 foot to 5 foot deep trench (depending on the terrain). Second came the crew laying the 210 miles of 8 inch pipe, last were the people to cover the thing and stomp it down. Soon Standard put a cap on the amount of oil that they would buy, from 1000 barrels per district per day to 600. It was to eliminate any competition. In 1902 an oil man with 27 years in the field back East named C. D. Webster, came to Humbolt, Kansas and opened an independent oil refinery to compete with the Standard Oil refinery in Nevada. For a while things went fine, many stores in Humbolt and the surrounding towns bought his kerosene at 20 cents a gallon. In May of 1904 well dressed representatives of The Octopus, i.e. goons, came to the area with a proposition the store owners couldn't refuse. Buy from Standard or they will open a store in every town and sell it for 5 cents a gallon. Soon Mr. Webster's independent oil refinery was the pumping station for oil heading for Sugar Creek.

It didn't take long for the local investors to see opportunity. Filed on March 22, the Sugar Creek Townsite Company Inc. What they did was pool their money, $10 thousand, borrowed $20 thousand, and purchased all of the land around the proposed venture.

Ten men bought shares at $50, 200 shares were issued. T. T. Crittenden, Jr. of Kansas City led the way with a purchase of 70 shares, while E. F. McElroy, a local, kicked in $500 for 10.

Article IV of the incorporation documents stated that the corporation would go on for 50 years, which didn't happen. The town outgrew their land.

From the Jackson Examiner, April 8, 1904, page 3:

A New Town Already Started at the Oil Refinery Site now a Railroad Stop.

A new town is springing at the mouth of Sugar Creek where the workmen are laying the foundations for the big Standard Oil refinery. Electric roads and county roads are headed for this point and there will be a population of several thousand here within a short time. The Kansas City Times of Thursday says, "The Santa Fe railroad has a depot at Sugar Creek, the site of the refinery to be erected by the Standard Oil Company. It is only an old freight car but the officials say that it fulfills its purpose more adequately than the Union passenger depot used by the railroads in Kansas City. A sign 'Sugar Creek' adorns the box car and trains stop there regularly. The station will appear on the next issue of the Santa Fe time cards."

"The Santa Fe has nearly completed the 4,000 foot switch it is building at the refinery site. Considerable material has been unloaded at the site and two warehouses have been built and are now loaded with the material which will be used in the construction of the refinery. Active work has begun and within six weeks 400 men will be at work putting up permanent building."

In reality, there were many more than that.

By June 1, 600 to 700 men were employed and working ten hour days, six days a week. First were hundreds of common laborers, paid 17 1/2 cents per hour, led by W. A. Eaton, at 37 cents per hour, T. J. Griffith, and W. E. (Whitey) Moore, earning 27 1/2 cents per. There were 36 carpenters, 40 cents, and 19 carpenter helpers, 17 1/2 cents, four water boys, fourteen people in the office, and two messenger boys, all 17 1/2 cents. Ten watchmen worked around the clock, seven days a week, some working over 100 hours a week at 25 cents per hour. The boiler shop had 235 employees, paying from 40 cents to employee # 1169, Charles Mallinson, who was paid 14 1/4 cents an hour for seven hours on June 30, earning 83 cents before quitting. Some didn't last that long, it was very hot, dirty work. The masons, all 29 of them, were the best paid, earning 62 1/2 cents an hour, for an eight hour day. Helpers got 21 7/8 cents. The two men in the blacksmith shop and three men in the machine shop earned from 35 to 20 cents. The pipe shop had 180 earning 30 cents to 17 1/2, bringing the amount of money being dumped into the local economy at around $30,000 a month. Cold beer was 5 cents, and there were no taxes.

On June 23, Michael and Sophia Onka, Mike being a former soldier in the Austro-Hungarian army, bought two lots for $300 at 6% interest on Evans Street, which was named after J. E. Evans, the boss of bosses at the refinery. They opened a grocery store and boarding house, accompanying up to 90 men, and many watering holes and bordellos, along with barber shops and cafes, soon lined the dirt street. There would be no murders or cops; everything else was fair game. On July 6, a quote in the Journal spoke of possible doom for the new boom town. "Independence is casting its eyes towards the Sugar Creek refinery. The refinery town cannot incorporate because no town can incorporate within two miles of another." The reason, taxes.

August began the selling of stocks to the public from a number of oil related corporations. Kansas Petroleum Company, on August 2, ran a full page ad in the Journal with a photo of "THE GREAT STANDARD OIL REFINERY NOW UNDER CONSTRUCTION AT SUGAR CREEK." Stocks were offered at 5 cents per share. On August 28, another ad promised that this was the last chance to buy at 5 cents because on the first of September the stocks would be sold at 10 cents per share. It was never heard from again. At that time Standard Oil stock was hundreds of dollars per share.

On September 26, the pipeline from Humbolt to Sugar Creek was finished, and on October 24 at 5:00 in the morning, the building of the refinery was complete, with the first product being kerosene.

Many of the men who worked on the refinery were from the Whiting, Indiana refinery, like Whitey Moore, who stayed here and raised a family that turned out to be good plumbers and pool players. On January 5th, under the headline, "HELP SUGAR CREEK" since the $4 million refinery was growing even more money was to be put into expansion. Already $1 million more had been spent. Sugar Creek, then being called "The Oil City". Train service known as the Sugar Creek and Maywood Railway Company's tracks were lined with tank cars being filled for the trip back east, the tracks creating a lake in Fairmount named after Colonel Crisp.

190,000 barrel storage tanks were built. Six million gallons of water was being used in October. By January, 1905, water usage was up to 12 million gallons, by summer 20 million was projected. Already the plant boasted a gas plant, fire department, and water works. Electricity would come later.

Rumor had it that the refinery in Whiting was to be shut down as would rumors a few years later about Sugar Creek. But it would survive for 75 years. Meanwhile, the once-tranquil valley, quietly eroding over the eons, grew expeditiously into one hell of a great place to grow up, producing a bunch of heroes. Best of all, Fairmount Park is going to reopen, and be open for 30 more years. The best was yet to come.

Chapter 12: 1905
New Fairmount Park

1905 was an up and very down year for Sugar Creek, while it was the beginning of thirty years of more fun for Fairmount Park. For Sugar Creek, the year started off on a positive note. On January 15 Judge Albert Allen married Andrew Markham to Mary Cabay. It was the first marriage in Sugar Creek. Later a new church was built in the area of Putnam and High Streets. On Monday, December 18 the Examiner sent one of their elitists to Sugar Creek. He made it official, the Bohunks were gone, the definition of a Bohunk being a skilled or unskilled foreign loser, mainly from Eastern Europe. From 10 busy saloons and many houses of pleasure, the boom town was reduced to two or three not so busy watering holes. Half of the wooden commercial buildings on Fairmount Avenue were already deserted, while the refinery continued to expand.

There was also talk of building a cement plant downstream from the refinery. Cements plants needed power, petroleum and rock, which was of unusual quality and quantity.

On Thursday, May 18, construction of another oil refinery for the area was announced in the newspaper. $1,000 an acre was reportedly paid for 90 acres. The venture capitalists were *The Producers Refining and Fuel Company*, an independent and enemy of Standard. Located east of the Blue River to Rock Creek, north of Mt. Washington cemetery to the river. Intended to compete with Standard oil of Sugar Creek. Will they never learn.

Meanwhile, Fairmount Park was having a second Grand Opening. Thousands spent opening day on Sunday, May 28, at the new Fairmount Park. Fifty new boats, 1000 brand new bathing suits and many new attractions greeted the city folks, like a Ferris wheel and merry-go-round. Admission was free and for a nickel you could ride to the park from anywhere in the city, thirty three more cars were added as the day progressed. The lake hadn't been fished in three summers and was pristine, the lawns were immaculate. Cusenbary Springs free water was now operated by an electric pump. Charles D. Carlisle owned the lake.

The main feature was a one-legged man who coasts down a 100 foot incline in an automobile twice a day. Zimmerschields Band of 25 played two concerts a day at 3 and 8 p.m. Vaudeville was back featuring a comedy act called *The German Fifth* by Rapier and Knopp. Singers, hoofers, magicians, pugilists and devices called the Funagraph and Terriscope.

On June 8 the Fairmount Lake claimed its first victim. An 18-year old Independence youth named Lloyd Highman drowned within the ropes in 10 feet of water.

The Fourth of July was especially popular as park records were broken. The Standard Oil refinery had a huge impact on the tax base of the county, increasing it by $1,172,065.56. Standard paid $1,200 in taxes for 1904 but this year would pay several times as much. Is it any wonder that there is a Dairy Queen where there was supposed to be a competitor to The Octopus?

Chapter 13: 1906 ~ 1907
Portland Cement, Etc.

The big news for these two years was the acquisition and beginning operation of the new cement plant, while the Sugar Creek area bloomed, Fairmount Park boomed.

On May 27, 1906, a full-page ad in the Kansas City Journal touted the *New Kansas City Portland Cement Plant* as a great investment. They didn't give a price for their stock or a phone number, just an address: K C Portland Cement, 708 Heist Bldg, K. C. M. O. along with the names and professions of the major entrepreneurs, a drawing of the plant and a description of future operations were included. Quality cement was in great demand to the point where America was importing 20,000,000 barrels a year and much of it was needed west of the Mississippi River. Samples of the 280 million year old limestone were sent to some of the best chemists in the land, including Cornell University, all reports came back declaring it of "unusually high quality". 73 acres were purchased for the enterprise. Buildings on the site included a stock house, cinder mill, engine room, kilns, dryers, machine shop and office, all made out of cement or brick. Most of the finished product will be shipped out by rail. Three 2,000 horsepower engines will drive the mill, which will produce 1,400 barrels a day, fuel supplied by a pipeline from Standard next door.

Early in 1907 an Iowa firm bought 120 acres by Courtneyville to build an even bigger cement plant, one producing 2,500 barrels a day. But the deal fell through.

In late October of 07, the Examiner sent a reporter to the site of the latest jewel of the industrial area now springing up just outside of Independence's grasp. C. H. English, the boss of Cement City had appeared in front of County Court asking that the terrible, wild hemp-lined road to the plant be improved. After a bone-jarring ride by the court to the plant along said road, it was deemed to expensive.

The 2,000 horsepower engines, here in reality, turned out to be two 600 horsepower and one 175 horsepower, but still impressive to a newspaper person. 300 people, many being of Mexican descent, worked at the plant, some living in a four story hotel atop the bluffs known as Lover's Leap. Among his description of the area was to mention that the old river landing called Wayne City was now a fisherman's shack.

Meanwhile, in April of 1906, the Bowman- Hicks Lumber Company of Sugar Creek was selling out. "Everything must go Quickly" including a 34 x 80' shed and 20,000 feet of lumber. The building boom was over.

In July Sugar Creek got its first and only hotel, "The Standard". Standing two stories, some of the 20,000' of lumber went to good use. Located northeast of the intersection of Sterling and Elizabeth where now a fence company exists, the creek at that time being farther south. Besides being a hotel with large, airy rooms, the people going to Fairmount Park were encouraged to walk the half-mile through the dusty little town to get a country-style dinner for 50c, open from 1pm to 8pm and no phone.

In February 1907 transportation between Independence and Sugar Creek became easier, for 10c each way a person could get on a trolley near the Independence Square and get off in Sugar Creek, or vice versa.

While things were going good for Standard of Sugar Creek, the same can not be said for Standard. The attorney general was on the war path in Cleveland. In an article entitled, "Closing in on Standard" he subpoenaed as witnesses the honchos of the Lake Shore Railroad, hoping they would furnish more damning testimony against Standard. The federal government was building a case that in 1911-13 would threaten the very survival of the company town.

The oil boom that swept Kansas and was responsible for the Sugar Creek Refinery was over. The price of a barrel of oil had fallen to 65c and the gushers were a thing of the past. The pipe that once helped bring in the oil was sold for scrap. Thousands of barrels of oil were stored about the area by many small companies. Prairie, i.e., Standard, had 23,000,000 barrels stashed in their tank farms. It was a lot back then, now it's about a days' worth.

New Fairmount Park's second season began on May 27 with the "Daredevils of the Clouds", the main free draw. Two huge balloons lifted a large cannon high into the sky, on a signal from the ground, the cannon was fired and a man and a woman with parachutes landed in the lake.

One of the new attractions this year was a ride called the "Figure Eight", rising 60 feet above the park and giving a great view of the area, did exactly what its name implied. You paid ten cents for an adult and five cents if you looked younger, after which you did a figure eight in a plush, leather cushioned car.

Admission to the park again was free but once inside you were penny, nickled, and dimed. Picnic baskets could be checked all day for 5 cents. Plates, glasses and silverware could be rented and ready-made custom picnic baskets could be delivered anywhere in the park for a price.

The Fourth of July was a blast. 40,000 people packed the park on the preceding Sunday, with the Fourth being on a Wednesday. The main attraction on the Fourth was the destruction of Naples by Mt. Vesuvius. $4,000 was spent on a carload of pyrotechnics including 30 pounds of dynamite. Laid out at the south end of the lake, a scale model of Naples made with combustible material was destroyed and could be heard for miles. The feature was so well received that the next Saturday night it was repeated across the lake (east) from the bathing beach. Soon after the Fourth, professional divers and swimmers, both men and women, were hired as instructors. Next year two new parks would open in Greater Kansas City.

Chapter 14: 1907
The Parks of Kansas City

1907 is the beginning of a golden age for KC's commercial parks and a lot of competition for Fairmount. Two new parks opened this year, Carnival Park and the new Electric Park. Forest was popular, but Troost was struggling.

The new Electric Park at 46th and the Paseo had everything, band concerts, vaudeville, Electric Fountain, ballroom, natatorium (an indoor swimming pool), German village, alligator farm, chutes, Dips Coaster, Norton slide, penny parlors, novelty stand, Japanese rolling ball, scenic railway, pool room, a Hale's Tour of the World, Electric Studio, boat tours, old mill, a Temple of Mirth, Flying Lady, Double Whirl, Circle Swing, soda fountain and ice cream shops, knife rack, doll rack, shooting gallery, air gun gallery, giant teeter, boating, outdoor swimming, carousel, clubhouse cafe, Casino 5c theater, fortune telling and palmistry, covered promenade and horseless buggy garage.

New Electric's grand opening was Sunday, May 19. Admission to the park was ten cents. The Ellery band played at 2 and 8 pm., seven days a week, "Rain or Shine". The vaudeville in the German Village was free, but the beer wasn't yet allowed. There was a legal hassle about the transfer of the liquor license from the old park location to the new park.

The prohibitionists were trying to curb the devil rum. A law had been passed in KC that until the population of the city reached 400,000 no more liquor licenses would be granted, and then only 1 for every 1,000 population of increase. But on May 16, a liquor license for Fairmount was proposed by park management. In front of the county court many people, mostly women with babies, protested and gave to the court a petition with 905 signatures. The signatures weren't valid because the women could not vote. The license for a saloon was granted. Fairmount for the first time in a long time was wet.

Opening day at Electric Park was electric. 100,000 light bulbs, one every few inches, lit up the sky. One thing Fairmount Park had going for it was its trees; Electric had few. Directions to the Electric Park were as follows:

"Take Rockhill and Troost cars direct to park. Passengers brought to main entrance of the Promenade. Vine Street car entrance at 45th and Woodland Ave. Carriage, automobile, and pedestrian entrance at 46th and Lydia."

The new park was packed and declared a success by the public.

Meanwhile, Carnival Park had its grand opening at 7:00 pm on Saturday, May 25th. It was located at 14th and Minnesota Avenue in Kansas City, Kansas. To get to the park from KCMO the new Intercity Viaduct served as the artery. Attractions featured a scenic railway, Chute the Chutes, dancing and roller skating. Vaudeville four times a day and a dog and pony show. Only 15 minutes from downtown Kansas City, Missouri.

Forest Park opened in 1903 while Fairmount was in a coma. Located in the Northeast park of KC, south of Independence Avenue and Hardesty, where the old Quartermaster building still stands. Built by Col. Hopkins for $195,000 on farm and orchard land owned by the Michael, Ancel & Mattie Collins family for decades. Distorted mirrors greeted the guests where they entered, a $15,000 English Carousel, Vaudeville, swimming, etc. It was the only park, maybe in the whole world, that had a dress code. But neither Carnival nor Forest lasted long. Carnival closed in 1911 and Forest in 1912, due mainly to 1) Electric and Fairmount Parks' popularity and 2) in 1909 the city doubled in size to 50 or so square miles and land was growing in value.

New attractions like the Saloon delayed the opening a few days so Fairmount was the last park to open. Balloon races between two and sometimes three professional aeronauts was the opening free draw. Car fare to the park was still five cents each way.

On Sunday, June 9, at 1400 hrs. "B" Battery MO National Guard put on an exhibition just north of the park to Kentucky, which was now used as the picnic area. The old picnic area was now the hill which was now a zoo and other attractions. The artillery exhibition, led by Captain George R. Collins, featured 7 75mm field pieces that were manned by 45 men. Both days they marched to the park in the morning and set up camp, then made a lot of noise.

The success of last year's Fourth of July extravaganza encouraged park management to try and top it. A crew of 10 men was brought to construct this year's volcano from New Orleans, where that sort of thing happens all the time.

A reporter from the Journal took a trip out to Fairmount Park on the Fourth. The cars were running as quickly as they could be loaded, about one minute apart, starting in the morning and running that way until late at night, first crowded one way, then crowded the other. His first stop was at the zoo. Two hundred different animals, including a male lion named Moses. His claim to fame was that he attacked his trainer, Dolly Castle, last winter in Wichita where she thus spent 17 weeks in the hospital ... why would she give him a second chance? One of the main interests besides the cute little bunny rabbits was a groundhog that had been captured on the park ground. There were also pony, dog and monkey shows going on constantly.

Next he touted the refreshments, all made at the park. The ice cream was fresh and cost $1.25 a gallon and was delivered anywhere in the park for free. The same cream used for the ice cream is used to make butter for the popcorn, bought locally and daily from nearby farmers. A Japanese tea room encouraged ladies' card clubs, parties, receptions, etc., free. All supervised by Mr. N. E. Newman, phone 713.

The rides came next, the longest lines were for the Circle Swing. Next came the figure-eight roller coaster, then the merry-go-round. Next he visited the Mystic Caves where the main attraction of the new attractions was called, "Chinatown Charlie". In April of last year, the city of San Francisco had a devastating earthquake and fire. Exposed in a part of the city known as Chinatown, sections of buildings were exposed to the outside world. Found were opium dens, so Fairmount built a replica of Chinamen taking part in the highly addictive poison. There were many other attractions in the Mystic Cave like Lovers' Lane, and a big surprise at the end, 10 cents. Also on "The Hill" was Doreen the Snake Charmer, also ten cents. He also checked out the Fairmount Hotel, claiming the dinner was superb.

One thing he didn't mention, but the Jackson Examiner did, was a homicide. The Poindexter brothers from Kansas City broke the neck of a 22-year old Teamster, also from KC, James Wilson. The two were arrested by Capt. Rice of park security and taken to the Independence Jail for safekeeping. It was said that this was the end of a long feud. The disposition of the case is unknown.

After the Fourth the Kansas City Chautauqua would dominate the park for twenty days. Several VIPs like senators and congressmen from the state of Kansas spoke and gave slideshows of things like the progress of the Panama Canal. Many Christian Indians from various tribes were in attendance. The rest of the season was given to picnics, the Kansas City druggists picked the hottest day of the year (August 7) to have their day of frolic. The heat caused the baseball game to be cancelled, so many went swimming. The grocers had theirs the next day. Both went off without any heat-related casualties.

Later in the month the 8th annual reunion of the Army of the Philippines, including General Arthur McArthur, father of you-know-who, General Irving Hale, Col. W. F. Metcalf, Maj. L. B. Laughton, and Congressman E. C. Ellis. Next the "Modern Brotherhood of America" passed through. Both brought not just people to the park but to Kansas City. Fairmount was good for the growing city.

They were not going good for Standard Oil of the World. In May, a federal investigation headed by Herbert Knox Smith gave to President Teddy Roosevelt a report spelling out the alleged atrocities conducted by Standard in 1904, same year as the birth of the Sugar Creek facility. The report titled "How It Controls" states:

"It is apparent that the dominating position of the Standard Oil Company in the oil industry has largely been secured by the abuse of transportation facilities 1) By flagrant discriminations obtained from railroads 2)By a refusal to operate its pipeline system so as to extend to independent intrinstics the benefits to which they were both morally and legally entitled, at the same time the Standard has prevented such independent interests from constructing their own."

Standard's refineries produced 86% of the country's total output of illuminating oil (kerosene) and transported through its pipeline 90% of all crude oil in the oil fields and 93% in the new fields in the Midwest, Kansas, Texas, and the Indian Territories (Oklahoma).

In June the state of Kansas was also hot because Prairie Oil i.e. Standard, was not paying its fair share of taxes. In response in July, the Boss of Bosses and at that time, not yet as rich as he was going to be, spoke out calling Standard "A blessing". In Chicago, Rockefeller stated:

"Since the enactment of the Interstate Commerce Law in 1887 the Standard Oil Company has carefully observed its provision and in no case has willfully violated the law. I welcome the passage of the law and the principle of equality which was embodied in it. The old system of special rates or rebates was obnoxious and was never a source of profits for the company." etc, etc.

The Bull continued for about a half an hour.

Also in Chicago about this time, a judge was studying the 1,462 count indictments of Standard Oil. Each carried a fine from $1000 to $20,000. The maximum could be as much as $29,240,000. The subject of this probe was Standard of Indiana which on paper was only worth $1,000,000 while Standard of New Jersey was valued at $100,000,000. For Uncle Sam it was like squeezing money from a turnip.

Chapter 15: 1908

1908 is the year that my family started to arrive via a steamship from Europe, lucky to escape the future horrors of WWI. My grandma, Anna Novak, 1892-1967, told of arriving here with a friend at the R.R. depot, being met by a man that could not speak their language, driving through a pathetic looking, dusty town and finally meeting friends known from across the ocean. Surely word got back to certain areas of "The Old Country" that friends were here, also that there was a neat park just minutes away, and maybe a job at the refinery.

On January 16, a group of "Drys" from Fairmount, Maywood, and Mt. Washington met with the purpose of barring anymore of that Saloon business at Fairmount Park. Called the "Law and Order League," it was organized to basically bar liquor anywhere, i.e., total prohibition of all alcohol, and they would succeed.

On May 14 Missouri Governor Folk's commission stated,

> "We believe that it is in the interest of good government that no saloon license be granted outside an incorporated town where there can be no police protection. The county judges know also that a legal petition for the Blue Township is impossible. Not only should they refuse to consider a saloon for Fairmount Park, but none should be considered from Sugar Creek, Cement City, Leeds, or any other point in the township outside the cities."

In a few years, the 18th Amendment, the prohibition of alcohol, would be eliminated even the cities, but not really.

Regardless, Fairmount Park opened early this year. On May 10, thousands rode out to the suburban oasis of fun a.k.a. "The Park in the Woods" and the "Home of Picnics". Many came to skate in the new skating rink, said to be the largest open-air rink in Kansas City. At 7 pm a rainstorm inundated the park, causing all the people to crowd the cars, returning to the local metropolis.

One poor lad didn't make it back to the metropolis. The streetcars leaving the park were filled to overflowing. Perched on the step of an over-crowded trolley, 16-year-old Carl Ruehle, ignoring his father's warnings, kept leaning forward as the fast-moving streetcar sped from Fairmount Park to downtown Kansas City. He was enjoying "catching the breeze," he told his worried father. Tragically, his coat caught a fence. He was pulled under the streetcar and killed instantly.

For management and the rest of the park's opening day visitors though, rainstorm or no, opening day was deemed a wonderful success.

Management decided balloon racing was going to be the main free attraction this year. The first contest was on May 16. Again it was a rainy day, but the race went ahead at 3 o'clock in the afternoon, across from the bathing beach. A local man, L. M. Bales, won by defeating a professional from France named Professor Antoine Gasper, the winner being determined by who could reach the highest altitude.

Fishing was a big draw. Poles and bait were available for a small fee. Most people could catch six or seven good-sized fish in just a few hours, mostly crappie, bass, and blue gill. Makes you wonder about the smell of some of the trolleys heading west.

Professor H. O. Wheeler's band performed, and stayed all season. Writing a lot of his own numbers and marches were his forte.

This year's improvements included beautifying the bathing beach, and two new concessions. Kalinsky's plantation troubadours and a new giant teeter, and Cusenbary Springs had a new roof built and an electric pump installed.

Memorial Day for all the parks was a big deal. 43,000 people visited Fairmount over the two-day holiday, and 2,000 went swimming. The fireworks display across the lake kept the people safe from the Roman Candles, skyrockets, and set pyrotechnics. The Winnings and Wright Comedy Company was in the theatre and the talk around the lake was about the man who caught a 32-pound carp.

After three balloon races won by Mr. Bales, attention turned toward fireworks and getting a jump on the Fourth of July. On Sunday, June 21, a huge display of the usual stuff, plus some specially designed for the park.

This year's theme for the Fourth was the siege of Tripoli. A town was built that was to be destroyed by fire across the lake from the bathing beach. H. O. Wheeler's band closed the day by playing the STAR SPANGLED BANNER. 30,000 people passed through the park for the Fourth. Because of clouds, only 700 went swimming. Many danced in the pavilion, but Fairmount was the most popular. Electric had a good crowd, even though it cost 10 cents to enter and 5 cent car fare. Skating was popular at Forest and Carnival parks, where skating contests were constantly being held. All parks had vaudeville and fireworks.

On July 12, a two-mile race on Fairmount lake by several swimmers featuring Carl Kunz, whose claim to fame was swimming from Lawrence, Kansas to Kansas City, the prize being the Championship of Missouri.

On July 19 under the heading "An Ideal Summer Hotel", a photo shows a two-story rustic building with a wrap-around porch filled with tables and a sign, "This Park Private". I quote, "A building of the home-like type, a lawn of grass that's even and soft as velvet, a group of trees that throw a shade enjoyable these days..." etc etc. This year is the fifth anniversary and is newly remodeled with new management, the owner, W. F. Smith, also owns much of the park. The rooms were large and airy due to the many trees. The food was excellent, with weekly rates from $3 to $5.

Also on the 19th, balloon racing returned, while the bathing beach broke a record by having 1,200 swimmers. Balloonist L. M. Bales, KC champ, took on Calhoun Grant from Providence, Rhode Island. The last balloon race of the season was held the first Sunday in August and was the best this year, won again by Mr. Bales of our city, against Terry Raymond of Chicago. Park Management also announced that the bathing beach would be open to ladies of all ages every Friday morning from 10 to 2. A qualified swimming instructor was provided.

The free main attraction on August 8 -9 was "Daredevil Evans", who was two generations ahead of Evel Knievel. Across the lake from the bathing beach, a 50 ft-high ramp was built by a bunch of union carpenters. Daredevil Evans jumped the ramp with a bicycle, while Wheeler's band played and fireworks exploded, twice a day for two days at 3 and 9 pm. The next weekend Fairmount had Graham the Human Fish who ate lunch and drank milk underwater in a glass tank.

Electric had a gasoline powered balloon. For the drama, a large tent was erected by the monkey cage and guarded 24 hours a day, even the employees weren't told what was going on. On August 21, two men from Omaha, Charles Bayadorfer and George Yager, opened up the tent and pulled out a lemon-shaped bag of gas powered by a small gasoline engine. Bayadorfer climbed in and took off, much to the relief of Mike Heim, who was responsible. It flew for a while but fell out of the sky at 37th and Brooklyn. After a few repairs it flew back to the park. Management at Fairmount took notice.

Although Mr. Rockefeller gave 4.5 million to charities this year, President Teddy Roosevelt was not impressed. On July 23, the US Circuit Court of Appeals in Chicago had found favor with Standard and the three judges ruled Standard innocent of the charges. President Roosevelt called the ruling a "gross miscarriage of justice", and directed the Attorney General to retry the case. He also brought Frank B. Kellogg, a hot-shot idealist attorney, who not only failed to destroy Standard, he won the Nobel Peace Prize in 1929 for outlawing war in 1928, another failure.

1908 was the year of the "Great Race", as in the movie of the same name, which starred Tony Curtis and Natalie Wood. Starting in February at New York City and criss-crossing the US, then following the Trans-Siberian railroad track through Czarist Russia to Paris. Won by a Thompson Automobile, built in Buffalo, New York. Standard furnished, free of charge, all the gasoline along the entire route, stationing depots every 50 miles.

Chapter 16: 1909

A few words need to be said about a group of people who helped the many local amusement businesses prosper. Local 31, called the Roustabouts then, Stagehands now. The parks need the union and the union needed the parks, because although already invented in 1902 by Willis Carrier, a/c was not in the totally enclosed theaters yet, so most closed in the heat of the summer. In the summer, many Local 31 members worked in the parks, from selling ice cream to running the rides. They also did the carpentry, painting of scenery, and the lighting about town. Today the union is still making things like concerts, conventions, and many other activities in both Missouri and Kansas possible.

It's a fact that a Republican helped save Sugar Creek. In February, Governor Herbert Hadley, a former prosecuting attorney, the first Republican in Jackson County to hold that post, came down on the side of Standard, preferring fines and regulation to throwing the multi-million dollar Standard Oil Refinery out of the state, and there would be more calls for ouster in the next few years by a bunch of myopic judges.

In March, the city of Independence got a great deal from Standard. Every month the city used two tanks full of fuel oil to power the electric plant. The city signed a deal with Standard to buy the stuff for $18 a carload, down from $48, or 55 cents a barrel, a cut of 60%, despite the fact that the Missouri Supreme Court had just voted to ouster the Standard Refinery from the State.

In early May the talk around the county courthouse was that Fairmount Park's management would again petition for a liquor license, the idea of a bunch of citified drunks roaming the countryside around the park did not set well with the locals. But management had other ideas, sell water.

While the local dries were about to march on the county court, and that was just about everybody, full page ads in all the local media warned of the dangers of drinking city water. It seems that alum added to the city water is not good for you. Alum is used even today because the stuff attaches itself to bacteria in the water and harmlessly sinks to the bottom. But the water from Cusenbary Springs has no alum or any other human interference. As mentioned before, Cusenbary Springs history goes back to pre-history. The Indians thought it had certain powers, and after they were run off it was a great place to have a picnic. Today there are still wagon tracks visible.

The assault began on Sunday, May 16, on page A-3 of the Journal:

The don'ts about your drinking habit

Don't drink filtered water.
Don't drink distilled or boiled water.
Don't get the soft-drink habit.

Drink "CUSENBARY" a pure spring water. Five gallons in a jug, 50 cents, or a case of 12 1/2 gallon bottles, $1. Phone 707 East.

The capacity of the pump was 1200 gallons per hour and was said to "arrive from unfathomable depths of quicksand. I was told as a youth that Dr. Fred Hink and Mayor R. J. Roper both sold water from the spring when they were just starting out on the road to capitalism.

Opening day for the three parks was Sunday, May 23. Carnival Park was already gone. Electric Park featured Alligator Joe from Miami and his Sea Cows, claimed to be the only ones in the world in captivity. Forest Park added a 175' x 90' swimming pool from two to twelve feet deep.

Fairmount went with free vaudeville and balloon races. Heading the bill was Rand's Dog Circus, thirty canines that barked up a storm. One of them could walk a tight-rope. A Japanese wire-walker, Meyers & Mason Comedians, and a local man who was a baritone. Vaudeville proved to be so popular that carpenters built extra bleachers to accommodate the extra crowds. No one complained about free vaudeville. If you became bored, there were a dozen other things to do. The lake was full of hungry fish and the summer of 1909 was going to be hot. To prepare, several carloads of sand were added to the beach.

In June, the main features were more freebies. Zimmerscheld's Orchestra was added to take up the quiet time between the vaudeville acts. The new features this week for the vaudeville were Huffell & Hiffell, vocals and soft-shoe artist, McClean & Simpson, Comedians, but the featured attraction was a guy named Arthur Browning, who was supposed to be the best "Buck and Wink" dancer in the U S of A.

On the lake, also free, were boat racing, the main feature being a contest of two miles, winner getting a silver cup. Big deal. Drawn to the races were a couple of studs from the farm. William McPike from Warrensburg and C. L. Gardner of Hannibal. After that some locals raced shorter contests that took less endurance. Buoys were strung across the lake to keep everything in order. After the boat races, swimming contests of half a mile and quarter mile were held for the locals. To finish the month free balloon racing was again employed, the winner getting a large silver cup. L. B. Bales of KC again took home the prize, beating out R. V. Porter of Minneapolis. Vaudeville featured new acts every week, from a Japanese man named Tom who juggled while walking a tightrope, to the usual dancers, singers, and comics.

The big advantage that Fairmount Park had and was emulated by Electric and Forest, was water. Fairmount had a spring-fed lake, the others had large pools, and the water wasn't always clean, if you know what I mean. That's why the "PARK IN THE WOODS" had such a draw on the city folk.

This year's Fourth of July was on a Sunday, which meant a long weekend. At Fairmount, the balloon race scheduled for the celebration had to be cancelled because one of the aeronauts was injured in the line of duty on the day before, so the lake became the main attraction. Because of the popularity of triculating around the lake, forty more boats were added weeks before and that still wasn't enough. Early in the afternoon there was a line waiting at the boat house for people with a boat out to bring it in, park management promised to buy more boats.

Swimming contests were held in spite of the large number of swimmers and boats, one of the advantages of having an eight-acre lake.

At Electric Park, the main attraction of the fireworks display was a likeness of President Taft in the sky, along with vaudeville. Poor Forest Park, while still very popular, had only a couple of Fourth of Julys before it returned to a forest.

On July 18, a new freebie was announced at Fairmount Park, weekly fireworks every Wednesday evening for the rest of the summer. Starting at 8:30 between the first and second vaudeville show, the area across the lake would erupt like the Fourth of July.

The following week's free attraction was a lady named Millie Zeino, female aeronaut. She was to cooperate with Zeketo, a daredevil who was another free attraction. His gig was to dive off a 75-foot high tower into a net set up next to the vaudeville stage, and he did this two times a day. But on Sunday he and Millie put on parachutes and jumped, gently falling to the deep part of the lake.

The free vaudeville bill was the usual fare: Rose Elliot, singer and dancer, Grogean and Maurer, musicians, and Collins & Le Moss, comics. On the lake, several boys will participate in a 150-yard and 300-yard race, first prize $25 per.

On the last Sunday in July, balloon races were back. L. M. Bales, the balloon champ of the park, raced R. H. Winstead of Indianapolis. Bales won again.

Management was very happy. The swimming contest and the cash prizes did what they were meant to do, attract people to the lake.

In the first ten days of August, more than 12,000 people paid to go swimming. Free balloon races, weekly fireworks, vaudeville, a band, and swimming contests along with a lot of picnics ended the season, and no one drowned.

Chapter 17: 1910

It's a big year for me. Grandma Novak gets pregnant and goes back to Europe to have my Mom, also named Anna. Giving your children dual citizenship was popular back then for those who could afford a year's pay. Since a laborer in 1910 America made about $1,500 a year for a 50 or 60 hour week, not everyone could afford it. Reasoning could have been that the talk about town was that this refinery job might not pan out and Grandma may have had thoughts of going back to the Austro-Hungarian Empire, not seeing the great tragedy that was about to unfold in 1914.

People who did were my Grandma and Grandpa and my eight-year old father, who settled in a coal mining town in Pennsylvania this year. The only thing my dad ever said about life in Europe was that he always had holes in his shoes and his feet always got wet, after coming to America he said he never had holes in his shoes again. In fact, he would grow up to be a rather dapper dresser, and win a new auto in 1927 at Fairmount Park.

In 1910 the population of the US was 92,000,000, with 14 million being foreign born. After a four year study the US Immigration Commission recommended restrictions on immigration, especially unskilled labor.

A new manager, Graham Reidy from Chicago, was making a lot of changes at Fairmount Park. Where once there were penny concessions now there were flowers and walkways. The picnic grounds were enlarged, the beach and bath house were also being expanded. 30,000 fish from Arkansas and southern Missouri were stocked in the lake; Wall-eyed pike, crappie, bass and perch.

Balloon races and vaudeville were again a part of Fairmount's free attractions. Opening day was on May 22. Bales again won the balloon race, and for his efforts won a gold watch. The free vaudeville had four performances each day, two in the afternoon and two per night. The opening act was LePearl and Bogart, singers and dancers, Curry and Reilly, funny people, then there was a short intermission so some of the crowd could go out and spend some money. Followed by Johnny Russell, a comedian, and McGrath, he walked around on his hands a lot, and juggled. The day turned out to be cloudy and drizzly so most of the many patrons stayed under one of the many shelters, like the dance hall which was elbow to elbow.

At Electric Park the big attractions were Philippini's Band and five vaudeville acts. The band played various types of music on different nights, Wednesday was ragtime, Fridays Wagmarian and Saturday, the popular stuff of the day, like

"Come Josephine in My Flying Machine", Mother Machree, Down by the Old Mill Stream or Let Me Call You Sweetheart.

A 100-foot dive from the roller coaster called, "The Scenic Railway", by Professor O'Hearn, was the feature at Forest, which had an earlier opening in April, getting a jump on the competition. The park also featured a Dutch cafe and free vaudeville.

Towards the end of May while the Earth passed through the tail of Haley's Comet and some predicted doom, my mother Anna was born in Europe.

Fairmount's balloon races continued along with the free vaudeville. The First of June brought the Paddle and Camp Club to the lake. The paddle club had been around for a long time, their headquarters was on the Big Blue River, but it seemed that all the people with the new-fangled motor boats were pushing them out. So they made a deal with park management to use the lake for their regatta. Silver cups were given for a 220-yard singles, 220-yard doubles, 100-yard mixed doubles, and 440-yard war canoe race.

While this was going on the "great Libertari" and his band played, and a few opera singers and entertainers entertained, after that vaudeville returned. One novel act was a guy who drew pictures while telling stories.

Vaudeville was strange; a young comedian named Johnny Russell appeared early in that capacity, but must have bombed. On June 29 he reinvented himself as "Reckless Russell," and he must have been hungry. Quoting from the Journal:

"After a swift bicycle ride down a steep incline, Russell propels himself about 50 feet straight in the air, while the bicycle crashes 40 feet to the ground. Then Russell drops, but his stopping point is a water tank filled to a depth of four feet with water."

Forest Park's daredevil was a guy from Belgium who slid down a 1,000 ft cable starting from 185 feet in the air to the ground without a net.

Since last year airplanes had been trying to get off the ground in most cities across America. Everywhere, it seems, but here until the Fourth of July at the Elm Ridge Racetrack, used for horse racing, located at the end of the Troost and Wornall lines. Charles S. Willard had been attempting to take off all weekend, on Friday he failed to get into the machine before it took off. The box kite with a motor hit a rock wall; it was the first time ever that an airplane tried to take off without a pilot. Repairs were made and by Sunday a Curtiss built aeroplane was ready to fly. Unfortunately it was windy and the thousand people who paid 50 cents to come out and see it were not disappointed because while repairs were being made there were motorcycle races held on the one-mile oval track. The machine on Sunday finally got off the ground. The goal of the early aviators was to "make a circle," or a 360 degree turn, landing where it took off. The 40 horsepower machine did it, making the circle to the cheers of the crowd, rising to just 60 feet tops and traveling at about 40 miles an hour. Next month Overland Park had its own aviation field.

On the Fourth, Reckless Russell was still very popular and wrecking bicycles well into July. Electric fans were added to the Dancing Pavilion and round by round reports of the Johnson-Jenkins fight in Reno were broadcast in all the parks. Johnson won. With the same old dancers, dog acts and comedians, the fireworks display was said to have been the biggest in the history of the park. But most of the action was just outside the park.

An unlicensed beer garden was set up just west of the park on property owned by Charles Lohes and administered by "Daddy Thomas". The rent was being paid by former inspector Pendergast. Neighbors had been complaining all summer so finally constables Ray Dickinson and Bert Hart busted them, confiscating three wagon loads of beer, bottles of Champaign and whiskey. Included in the trip to the pokey was a carload of women, everything going to the Independence lock-up. At the time there were 600 legal watering holes in Kansas City.

On July 10, Cement City had a large fire, destroying the only wooden building. Damage was estimated at $50,000. The blaze was fought by 100 employees using two 3 1/2 inch hoses with water being pumped by a steam engine. The plant was shut down for about a month.

Towards the end of July tragedy struck Fairmount Park Lake when 17-year-old William Wilson drowns. Just three weeks before, while swimming in the Blue, he cramped up but was saved. He promised his mother that he would not swim again. The moral of the story is, "Never break a promise to your mother."

The remainder of the summer at Fairmount was spent having fireworks two or three times a week, swimming, and the usual vaudeville. What was unique was the four-balloon balloon races. Four balloons bumping into one another while they ascended into the clouds, if there were any. They started from the bare spot across from the bathing beach where the fireworks were also deployed. $500 for first place, $100 for second, $50 for third. Most first place prizes went to Mr. Bales.

The last of dozens of picnics held this year was by S & H Green Stamps. While Rockefeller was giving away millions of dollars, the government was closing in.

Chapter 18: 1911

"I had a letter from Nellie saying she was going to quit teaching in Independence and go down to Sugar Creek. They offered her a large salary. I told her not to fall in love with a bohunk but if she fell in love with a Standard Oil magnate to nab him."

-- Harry Truman, in a letter to Bess, May 3, 1911

This year fishing and boating in the "lake in the woods" was allowed a month before its May 20th official opening. Ladies accompanied by gentlemen fished free, and all night fishing was permitted. A new manager, Thomas Taafe, was re-doing the park again, making it even more attractive for the city folks: steel hull boats and seven acres of picnic grounds, for a total of 20, for picnicking; brick fireplaces with cut firewood, neatly stacked, to cook or heat coffee, made picnicking easier. Dutch food was being served in the cafe at the hotel and the dance hall had a new floor. A 360 degree sidewalk has been built, going all the way around the lake. And there was beer.

Sugar Creek was becoming a growing community that was being recognized as having some legal influence. In the days before total prohibition of alcohol there were two camps, the Wets and the Drys. For the last three years Fairmount Park was located in the Mt. Washington community with 3,000 inhabitants, and was as dry as the Sahara, but was not an incorporated city. In January C. T. Lynch applied for a liquor license for the "Sugar Creek Precinct". Recently the county court had redistricted the precincts, moving the line from Mt. Washington to the west of the park. Fairmount Park was legally now a part of Sugar Creek, which was wetter than the lake, and was also unincorporated. The decision was made by Judge Hugh C. Gilbert, who said, "I for one granted the license with my eyes open and with full knowledge of what was going on. If placed in the same situation again I believe I would do the same thing." The judge had been on the bench for three days.

One of the local leaders of the Let's All Get Sober Movement was the good Reverend Serivener of 578 Arlington Avenue, pastor for the Mt. Washington Methodist Church south. He was not amused; by the time he heard it was too late. He came to Sodom, i.e. Sugar Creek when he heard about the new saloon, not knowing it was at the park. Upon inquiry, he was not happy at all, and vowed that the Drys would be back next year.

Besides a park Sugar Creek also got a new road, following the bed of the old railroad, now Sugar Creek Boulevard, to Gill Street, then to Fairmount Avenue, now Sterling. For years it would be called Rock Road, the work done by men who had fought the law and lost or were in the wrong place at the wrong time. They also improved the road to Cement City.

Sugar Creek School had its graduation on June 13, being the last school in the county to close for the summer. Mayor Jones of Independence gave the commencement address. The all-girl 8th grade class consisted of Lauretta Bukley, Susie Nagy, Mary Murray, Elva Thatch, Norma Dye, Helen Wesner, and Hazel Hackett. Obviously it was in the days before truancy. After the ceremonies a play, "The Heart of the Hero", was put on by the 7th & 8th grades, all under the supervision of V. A. Davis, principal, who will be in his third year of that job next year.

Back in the nation's capital, time was running out for Standard and the tobacco trust. A trust was actually a monopoly. In Standard's case there were actually 19 different companies that answered to 26 Broadway in the Big Apple, Standard's address and headquarters. At the time Standard's companies controlled 80% of all crude oil, owned half of the railroad tank cars, 80% of all domestic and imported kerosene, sold 300 million candles a year, 90% of all lubricating oils and had a navy of 78 steamers and 19 sailing vessels. The big question was how to divide up the empire. When the court's decision was announced Mr. Rockefeller was out playing a few holes of golf. He casually told his gold chums "Buy all the Standard Oil stock you can. You'll make a fortune," and he was right. The next day Standard's stock went up almost $5, too $680. Some people didn't make that much in a year. The Supreme Court gave Standard six months to dissolve and the stock market turned bullish. Ironically 1911 is the year that gasoline replaced kerosene as the most sold petroleum byproduct, which was once discarded.

The Elm Ridge racetrack was having better aero planes as the technology quickly improved. Balloons, a man who flew in the air with the aid of a huge kite, and aero planes, were the attractions in mid-May. It would have been a great weekend for flying, but a steady wind kept the planes grounded on Friday, and patrons were not happy, paying from $1 for a seat or 50 cents to stand. A small riot broke out, the pilots, not the wind, were blamed. Angry paying customers stormed the aviators' temporary living quarters, not realizing or caring that flight in a heavier-than-air machine would have a 20% mortality rate between Kitty Hawk and World War I. Most casualties caused by trying to make a living or breaking some kind of record, the altitude record at that time being 11,000 feet. On Sunday the wind was fairly calm and the planes took to the air, one flying over the picnickers at Swope Park. After circling the park a couple of times, he tried to find a place to land and show off his machine, but there were too many big trees. Auto, aero plane races, and huge balloon ascensions. The afternoon was filled with hecklers yelling, "No Fly No Pay!". To top off the day there was a race between an aero plane and a motor car. The auto won.

Back at Fairmount Park for Decoration Day, a four-balloon balloon race turned into near disaster when one balloon caught fire and another got away from the mooring crew, ending up in Susquehanna. Summer in the parks of Kansas City again was full of new stuff. Forrest was getting a sky-drop. Electric had a bathing beach, and Fairmount a new dressing room. All had Vaudeville. New acts were constantly coming through town because of a thing called a circuit, which was controlled by people with money. Swope Park was now very popular, there was already the beginning of a boom, thousands of people sometimes crowding the place. Everything there was free, except for transportation.

Fairmont started a new policy, if a person purchased an admittance to the bathing beach, which could be bought at the entrance, admission to the park was free, saving a person 5 cents if you were going to swim anyway. The bathing beach was also enlarged, free lessons were again offered in the mornings, and racing was popular. Water polo between teams of various athletic organizations was held. The area across from the bathing beach was roped off and off-limits to boaters, making for some excellent fishing.

On Sunday, June 18, an aeronaut jumped from a balloon and landed in Crisp Lake. It wasn't part of his plans, the balloon getting free and he figured a small lake was better than a large tree. It was a fitting end to the balloon racing for now.

The week before the Fourth of July brought the Whittaker family to the park, high-diving specialists. Mr. Whittaker made what he called his "Dive of Death", leaping from a 90-foot tower into a 10 ft by 15ft tank 5 ft deep, his better half and son made some spectacular dives of their own, but not from 90 feet. Their act was the grand finale after the vaudeville, usually around 10 o'clock at night. The German Garden had music from 2pm until midnight.

Everything in our story wasn't always fun. John W. West got his pocket picked while trying to help his mother onto a Fairmount Park bound streetcar. The perpetrator was described as a young man in his 20s, nicely dressed in a suit and straw hat. He lost $16.

The Skydrop at Forest was the first new ride in the three Kansas City park in two years. It was a 125 ft tower with four arms and parachutes. The patron was hauled by wire to the top then gently floated to the ground. The ride opened on the Fourth of July, just in time for the park to go out of business. In addition to the new ride, Forrest's last Fourth featured four acts of vaudeville. Professor

Reinhart dove off the highest part of the roller coaster, and the biggest and last fireworks ever at the park. Sadly, it was the last Fourth of July for Forrest. Electric had a huge fireworks display, so did Fairmount, along with balloon races, and they all had vaudeville.

At Fairmount Park, 14-year old Marrie Collier from Kansas City, Kansas, swam beyond the danger line and drowned in 15 feet of water. Not knowing the identity of the young lady, all women were ordered out of the water and to dress, leaving only one locker locked, thus revealing a number, to that was a name, a precaution taken for a tragedy such as this.

On a positive note, the number of people killed on the Fourth by all sorts of explosives was down to 13 nationwide, and 260 injured, due to a crackdown in 50 major cities, including KC. In 1909 43 people were killed, with 700 injuries. This set an appeal for authorities to do something. Giant firecrackers were the main culprit.

Between the Fourth and Labor Day, Fairmount Lake was the scene of a reenactment of two major Naval engagements, the first was a battle between the Monitor and the Merrimac of the Civil War, and the Battle of Manila Bay, as in the Spanish American War of 1898. Fourteen miniature dreadnaughts, six American and eight Spanish, seven with a motor, did battle on the lake starting at 9 pm. The original U. S. ships were under the command of Admiral Dewey, sinking all Spanish ships and blowing up a fort, all reproduced in miniature. Loud reports, the smoke and the light from the flashes of gunpowder, turned the lake aglow. A Spanish fort was blown up as a grand finale, and the Spanish flag fell, replaced by a huge American flag.

It was about this time that word came down from 26 Broadway on how the Octopus would be dismembered. The government had only told Standard to break up, but it didn't tell it how to do it. What was needed was competition, so the biggest, Standard Oil of New Jersey, became Exxon. Standard of New York became Mobile. Standard Oil of California became Chevron. Standard Oil became Sohio; Standard Oil of Indiana became Amoco, later to be BP. Once released from the umbilical cord, the different corporations excelled, adapting new technologies. No longer were they required permission from on high to spend over $5000 for improvements or $50 for a private donation, to like a hospital or school.

On Friday, September 1, the court order came into effect, the oil trust was legally dissolved. There was much confusion on the New York Stock Exchange, where no shares of Standard were to be had, and nobody knew what they were worth. The previous session the stock sold for $634 a share. There was much speculation, which ran from $300 to $650. They never missed a dividend payment, not even during the Great Depression.

For Labor Day, Fairmount feature "Daredevil Monte" and his double parachute leap, one man, two chutes. Forrest ended the year with a confetti fight, promised by management to be more fun than the Mardi Gras in New Orleans, obviously a statement made by people who have never been to Mardi Gras.

Baby Anna Novak and my grandma returned from Europe.

Politically this year, President Taft had a great idea he called the World Court, where nations could air their grievances in an attempt to avert war. This is one main reason former president Teddy Roosevelt broke with Taft and in 1912 ran on a Progressive ticket, allowing Woodrow Wilson to win. Had Taft had his way, possibly the war to end all wars (WWI) could have been avoided, or at least delayed.

Born this year in Sugar Creek who would be the city's third mayor, Rudolph Joseph Roper (also known as Rudy/R. J.). He would grow up to be a real class act. I can still remember him driving around town in his new Cadillac convertible, wearing a Panama hat and smoking a big cigar. He would be the first non-company mayor. Elected for the first time in 1941, he served for 30 years. Any opposition was sorely handicapped; Rudy sold beer.

Chapter 19: 1912

This year is best known for the Titanic disaster. It is also the year that my grandfather, grandmother, with my 10-year-old dad, left the coal mines in Pennsylvania, arriving in Sugar Creek during a time of crisis. Since Teddy Roosevelt launched his war on the trust, conversation around town was, What will we do if the refinery is closed. Because it was a possibility, and some people liked it here in the suburbs, with a neat amusement park and no cops or politicians. Didn't need 'em; no crime, also no laws and a school.

On May 15, a meeting was held in the school building about the current crisis with the ouster thing. A reporter from the Journal was there for the action and the following article appeared in the paper

SUGAR CREEK TO SELL BONDS
Citizens Don't Fear the Standard Oil Ouster

Owning to the fact that the school board of Sugar Creek felt some hesitancy to marketing the $12,000 bond issue voted a month ago to build an addition to the present schoolhouse. Because of the state's ouster of the Standard Oil Company, a meeting of the taxpayers was called last night. The taxpayers were unanimously in favor of floating the bonds and building the school addition. The oil refinery controlled by the Standard Oil Company at Sugar Creek is the principal industry of the village, and the school board feared that if the state carried out its ouster proceedings against the Standard, there would be little need of an addition to the present school building. It was suggested that a petition be sent to the governor requesting him not to destroy the only industry of Sugar Creek, but this action was not taken.

No one said, "Let's go back to Europe."

After twenty or so years, the earthen dam at Fairmount Park lake was leaking. Several generations of muskrats had burrowed into the foot of the dam and had their young ones. If the dam broke, all of the wooden houses and business along Sugar Creek would have ended up in the Missouri River. A cement dam was eventually built.

In June a great promotion took place. Robert G. "Ocean to Ocean" Fowler was given a week to make a lot of money. He got his name by being the first person to take off in Los Angeles, landing in Jacksonville, Florida after 60 hours of actual flying time. The thirty-year-old Fowler had been flying only ten months when he came to Fairmount Park.

The machine arrived at the park in pieces, once assembled on Sunday, June 2, everything was ready at the athletic field, again Roper Stadium. Everything but the wind. Without it there wasn't enough area for the Wright Brothers-built airplane to take off, so they pushed it to an adjoining "meadow". It must have been a goodly distance away, because by the time that the plane flew over the park it was already 800 feet in the air.

After doing a couple of 360s around the park he gained altitude and headed west toward Kansas City, at 1500 feet and 45 MPH. People at the park took to the high ground and were able to watch the whole show downtown, KC being only 30,000 feet away.

His first encounter was with the 3,700 fans at Exposition park, where the Kansas City Blues were locked in a duel with the Milwaukee Brewers, both of the American Association league. In the bottom of the 12th inning, the score was tied 4-4. The Milwaukee pitcher, Salpnika, had started the game many throws ago, as was the custom in those days. There was one out and the Blues had a runner on 2nd and 3rd. Fowler and his machine, making a pop-pop-pop noise freaked out the pitcher, and he tossed his next pitch into the grandstand. The crowd went wild as Rockfield, the second baseman, strolled home, winning the game 5-4.

Soon Fowler was over downtown, and a crowd of 3,000 craned their necks to see what was making the noise, Fowler tried to communicate with the people on the ground, and they to him, but noise from the machine prevented that.

After a 45-minute flight the frozen Fowler returned to the meadow, only a few feet from whence he started. After warming up, the first thing he did was to telegraph his mother in San Francisco and inform her that he hadn't been killed yet.

He wasn't the first aviator to fly over the business district. That honor goes to the late C. P. Rogers, who died a few months before in Longbeach, California, when his airplane came apart in the high wind. The previous October he was in town to accomplish this feat. He was quoted as saying, "Downtown KC is a dangerous place to fly because there is no place to land in case your engine conks out." Fowler's Wright-built plane wasn't the only one there. A second plane, built by Glen Curtis, was also at Fairmount. The two planes differed in that the Curtis used flaps, a much better design. At the time the Wrights and the Curtis's were in and out of court over patent laws.

Including Fowler, there were four pilots in his entourage: Bud Mars, Thornwell Andrews, and Nelson Nelson, who was in Atchison, Kansas, recovering from a broken arm; 'twas a dangerous business. The remainder of the week was spent flying every afternoon. On Wednesday Mars took the Curtis plane up for the first time. On Thursday, tragedy almost struck. Andrews had the Curtis up doing bombing runs on targets in the lake using oranges. While 1000 feet above the lake, on one of his runs, a storm/winds blew through. The fragile machine was tossed around like a kite, but he managed to land it just east of the athletic field, quite a ways from where he took off, and hit a fence. The Wright plane was also tossed around, and had to be held by six men, after being tossed into a tree, but not damaging it. Saturday and Sunday both planes went to the air at the same time, doing S's and 8's, racing and dog fighting. After this successful engagement, Fowler flew to Omaha.

The aeroplanes weren't the only attraction. The great Carver Horse Show warmed the crowds up, the main attraction was a young lady who dove a horse into a large tub of water from 40' high. The crowds were so large that cars ran every two or three minutes. Along the way people waiting for a trolley had no luck. Extra cars were added, but still they came. There was also bathing, boating, free vaudeville, picnic grounds, German garden, music. The Carver show was retained through the Fourth of July.

Between the air show and the Fourth of July, balloons returned. There were also many picnics. On Saturday, June 29, the Passenger Agents Association (they were an early version of a union) had their 20th annual picnic at Fairmount. At noon on Saturday, over 200 agents (the people who sold railroad tickets) locked their doors to the customers for a day and headed to the park on special trolleys.

The ladies were already there frying chickens and other delicacies, also plenty of liquid refreshment. Before chow, 50 picnickers tried to ride a burrow that was tied to a big tree, but all were thrown, some hard, and some into the flowers. Then dinner, while being serenaded by a brass band and some vocals. After that several speakers told them what a great job they were doing. A baseball game was held until all the balls were lost. Agents as far away as Chicago, St. Louis, and Wichita were in attendance.

The Fourth at Fairmount was very popular, thanks in part to the trouble that Forest Park was in, cash flow. Carver's horses, along with the high-diving ladies, were still the main attraction. Vaudeville wasn't' on the program. Everything went pretty smooth; 35,000 crowded the park. All-night fishing was becoming popular, staying up all night fishing, cooking coffee over an open fire and frying fish and bacon for breakfast. Might as well make money at night.

A lady broke her leg getting off the merry-go-round. She was 50 years old and had always wanted to ride one, but was apprehensive. So on the Fourth, Mr. and Mrs. Barrett rode out to Fairmount. To get up her nerve, she rode the camel. He warned her, "It'll throw you sure, Ma." She replied, "If you're scared, you don't have to ride. Watch me." She rode the camel three times at 5 cents per. After camel riding, she then rode the Merry-Go-Round. After the ride stopped, she stepped off backwards and broke her leg. The park doc set it, it was the only accident. The siege of Tripoli was the night attraction on the lake, along with the usual huge fireworks display.

While the majority of town was at the parks, on the river was where the real action was. The steamship Saturn had been running excursions up and down the river since spring, going as far down-river as Cement City. On the Fourth, the cops put an end to the orgies, gambling, drinking, prostitution, and the "debauching of young girls," etc. Since the vice squad knew about the perversions for some time, they couldn't get the county or city courts to do anything about the situation. So Chief of Police Griffin took it upon himself and sent two officers down to the Main street docks, where the Saturn was docking. There they stood by the gangplank, warning anybody that took the excursion that day would be arrested when the cruise was over. No one went, a large, angry crowd did gather, and the boat tooted its horn, but did not leave the dock. The Chief further stated that, "The Saturn would not in the future be allowed to operate." All this without a court order. For a couple of months the Saturn had been plying the waters between Kansas City and Cement City every hour on the hour.

After the Fourth, things were copasetic until the end of August. Forest Park had lost its lease, the owner of the property, Mrs. I. W. King, whose husband was in the real estate business, decided that they could make more money selling the property in lots as the city was growing to the east.

The fireworks began when the Jackson County Negro Association wanted to hold their annual picnic there. In the past, they had been meeting at Shelby Park, which had closed. Led by Leon Jordan, Sr., and Fortune J. Weaver, the latter a real estate dealer, the association had already handed over $1,500 as a down payment to lease the park for Negroes only. The locals were rather angry; there were even threats to dynamite the park. Racial tension was expected. The Association agreed to move the picnic if Mr. J. H. Koffler would just give them back their deposit. Independence had offered the use of its fairgrounds.

It went to the courts. The first judge, a Democrat, said no, but the second judge, a Republican, said yes. So they brought in another judge, a Democrat, but he said, "No." But Mr. Koffler didn't want to give back the $1,500, so the picnic went ahead without a license. On September 30, just before Labor Day, the cops arrested Mr. Koffler. Justice was swift in those days, and Judge Clarence A. Burney promptly fined Mr. Koffler $100. He said that he wanted to appeal and was released on $17 bond. The festivities continued until September 24 without any trouble.

On October 15, after ten years of fun, Forest Park was dismantled, and the $195,000 worth of amusement park stuff was sold to a carnival supply company for $5,000, some of it to live again, some not.

This year Fairmount Park closed after Labor Day, September 2, and all of Kansas City Labor converged on the park, after a parade Downtown starting at 9 in the morning. From 15th and Woodland to Grand, south to 18th, and on to 8th Street, thousands lined the streets. The parade was led by a platoon of police, then the firemen, followed by the speakers in horse-drawn carriages. The Grand Marshall of the parade, James J. Larkin, the head of Local 31 Theatrical Stage Employees Union (the stagehands), followed by the heads of four other unions, which was followed by three bands. Bringing up the rear were the bartenders who would come in handy at Fairmount Park. Once disbanded they boarded special trolleys to Fairmount. Speeches, athletic events, along with the other park attractions like balloons, vaudeville, etc, etc, were enjoyed by more than 25,000 people.

Back in Europe, the first Balkan war was a template for things to come. The kingdoms of Montenegro, Serbia, Bulgaria, and Greece attacked the land claimed by the declining Ottoman Empire, i. e., Turkey. After a few weeks of combat, Macedonia and Trace were divided up by the Balkan Alliance. In 1913 the victors would turn on each other for the second Balkan War. The third Balkan War would be a doozy.

Chapter 20: 1913

It is the last year of peace for a large part of the world. There was a second Balkan war, but it was also the year that brought us the concept of the forward pass. Ragtime music was in, along with dances like the Bunny Hop. Woodrow Wilson is elected president with less than 50% of the vote because of a split in the Republican party. Congress and the president signed on to the income tax... 1% for anyone making over $3,000. In their wisdom, they exempted themselves from paying.

In Sugar Creek, things were looking bleak, the problem was Elliot W. Major, 28th governor of Missouri (1864-1949), a Democrat from St. Louis. In March the Missouri State Senate and House of Representatives passed bill no. 516, also known as the Casey bill, written by State Senator M. E. Casey and Representative John F. Thice of Independence, whose district the refinery and 600 citizens resided. Governor Major, at last years' Democratic party nominating process, defeated a local man who would have made a much better candidate, William Cowherd. Cowherd was very popular locally, but the votes were in the bigger St. Louis area. Even the Independence Examiner got into the act of massaging the Governor's arse. In an editorial, "Here's to Governor Major", on March 20, the newspaper eulogized on what a wonderful and honest man he was. They lied. In defending the Standard Oil plant in Sugar Creek, they in effect said that just because Standard Oil is a bunch of crooks, that was no reason to destroy the town.

And what a neat little town it was. Located in a hilly valley bordered on the north side by the Missouri River and the refinery, about a mile or so south was one of the best and most successful amusement parks in the nation. Running from the refinery entrance several blocks north a dozen business prospered. And it was all threatened by Governor Major. Over half the 600 residents worked at the refinery. The town existed only to serve the employees and their kin. Everyone owned their own home or were paying for it. The only hotel, "The Standard", catered to single employees, most of whom wanted to own a piece of the American dream, your own home to raise "The Greatest Generation", as they were now being born.

P. M. McAvey, owned the Standard Hotel/restaurant, located three blocks south of the main gate. His business depended entirely on the number of men employed at the oil plant. There were also six general stores, three saloons, a pool hall/barbershop/eatery, another barber shop, a drug store, three coal-and-feed stores, a lumber yard, a church with two more churches on the way, and a new $25,000 school house. There was also a physician.

"I have been in business here for years," said J. F. McMains of the Sugar Creek Mercantile Company. "I built the building and my total investment is about $15,000." He was also going to lose $1,000 a month in sales if the refinery went belly-up. Mrs. L. W. Bollinger, wife of the Postmaster, located in the drug store. She was also the owner of the business, said, "We have a prosperous little village here. Most of us own our own home or are paying for them. To take the oil industry away from us will be to drive us away from surroundings that are dear to us. Yet we will have to go if the refinery is closed.

W. G. Dye, who runs a grocery and general store said, "I came to Sugar Creek busted. Now I am pretty well fixed and would like to stay that way. Of course I would have to move with the rest. Sugar Creek would turn into a frog pond. The Journal reporter called it a "lively little town".

Socially, Sugar Creek was a breath of fresh air from a bunch of silly laws like you can't drink beer and play pool at the same time. To prevent this from happening on March 26 a delegation from Kansas City, Sugar Creek, Independence, went to Jefferson City to talk to Governor Crook. Among the VIPs were Judge Allen Pruitt, Bernard Zick, Jr., Olney Burrus, Judge G. L. Chrisman, and Judge R. D. Mize. They all left by train from Kansas City and all were Democrats.

The judges made their argument from a legal standpoint, mainly that the elimination of the Standard Oil Company in the state would leave Missouri in the hands of another monopoly. Others argued that the destruction would cost the state a lot of tax money. Finally the people of Sugar Creek's representatives were allowed to speak. William Pavey, employee of the Standard at Sugar Creek, resident and taxpayer: "It spells ruin for us. There are seventy of us who have bought homes and what little we have is invested in them. Shut down the company and we will have to begin life over again." He continued, "We have just completed an addition to our school house, thereby issuing $12,000 in bonds. Send the Standard out of the state and there would be one room of the 8 in that schoolhouse needed, and those left in the school district could never take care of the bonds."

Edward Lynn, John Walker, George Hackett, and James McMain, all from Sugar Creek, told the same kind of story. McMain is a merchant and it would wipe him out, he told "his highness", "If this bill does not become law, my stock of goods I could move elsewhere. But my real estate and my buildings would be worthless." Mr. Hackett said that he had been working at the refinery since he came here. "The savings of a lifetime are invested in a $3,000 home in Sugar Creek. It would be a hard line to start over again with my family of seven children." His pleas gained him a street named after him. B. F. Larkin, who is a farmer and sells his veggies to the town, said, "There is no doubt in my mind the removal of the refinery would mean the wiping out of Sugar Creek." The governor had made his mind up a long time ago, as he was Attorney General before and had helped to initiate the suit against Standard in 1908.

Waters/Pierce was a St. Louis based distribution company without a refinery. Missouri had been divided down the middle. Standard didn't go into St. Louis, and W. P. didn't dare try to compete with Standard. The Governor and the W. P. Oil Company wanted to buy the Sugar Creek refinery, but Standard said no, and purchased land in Wyandotte County, Kansas, and prepared to dismantle the Sugar Creek plant and move the operation across the state line, leaving Missouri with only one oil company, but no way to make gasoline which by 1913 replaced kerosene as the most manufactured component of crude oil.

This was not the kind of outcome expected by the federal anti-trust laws. Standard's attorneys petitioned the State Supreme Court for a rehearing. The company also promised to enlarge the capacity of the refinery if permitted to stay.

The town did get a break when a fire broke out in a combination pool hall and lunch room, owned by Sherry Simpson. At 8:30 in the morning of April 4th, a fire started in the flue pipe of the kitchen area. It was feared that the whole business district would be destroyed, as there was not a brick in town. To the rescue came the Standard Oil fire department, saving the day. Besides destroying the pool hall, the adjacent building was damaged. The properties were owned by the Standard Warehouse Company, no connection to the big refinery. Loss was estimated at $2,000 but was covered by insurance.

Amongst all the turmoil Fairmount Park opened officially on May 4th. Admission was 10 cents. But as last year, fishing was allowed as soon as the ice thawed. Balloon races were again going up, a contest between balloons from St. Louis and St. Joseph was billed as "The Race of the Saints." A cabaret was built and the boats got a new coat of paint, picnic tables were added to the picnic area. The vaudevillians were now working in an outdoor theater, and the German cafe was still being called the German cafe. That would soon change.

Electric Park had made many improvements, too. A new ride called the "Ben Hur Roller Coaster." Two cars full of patrons ran along parallel tracks racing each other, powered by gravity and the weight and movement of the passengers.

On Sunday, May 4, Kansas City's newest amusement park opened to the water lovers. DREAMLAND, located along the tracks that took people to Fairmount Park along the Blue River. 500 boats and canoes were rentable. A 6,000 square ft. dance floor was constructed. McGain's 12-piece orchestra played. Concessions were to be added later. There must have been a lot more water flowing to the Missouri River via the Blue than there is today. Because of a drought in the summer, the enterprise was a flop.

This spring started out wet east and west of the Mississippi. Hundreds drowned. Opening day at Fairmount Park was practically washed away. It poured all day. New rock on the packed walkways were washed away. It was a good day for the fish in the lake, as there were no fishermen.

After a few weeks of intense rain, the 18-acre lake was again in danger of breaking the dam and flooding downtown Sugar Creek, fires, floods, and political pestilence threatened a piece of the American dream.

In between the cloudbursts, balloons took to the air. But it could be dangerous. On May 11, an aeronaut named Henry Sparks jumped prematurely from 200 feet. It was not high enough for his parachute to fully deploy, and his demised was saved by electrical wires that broke the fall, finally hitting the ground with a thump in front of the refreshment stand, missing all six thousand spectators. Later that day Teddy Clark, 12 years old, jumped from a moving trolley and received possible internal injuries. He just lived a few blocks east of the park; he must have been heading to Kansas City.

In early May the Supreme Court of the State of Missouri foiled the Governor's plans by agreeing to a rehearing of the Standard Oil's ouster. The Standard didn't really comply with some of the provisions, while Price/Waters did. They were just screwing with the state or were just showing complete apathy on the part of the company.

The eighth grade graduating class of 1913 at Riverview School was Charlie Mallinson, Jr., and Mary Spicer. As a soldier in WWI, Charlie would get gassed and died of his injuries in 1923. Thursday the middle-school kids put on skits. Friday night was the time to receive the degree, which was as impressive as a high school degree is now, as most kids didn't finish high school. Getting a job as soon as possible was more practical.

The school board had just adopted a new rule that all teachers had to live in the town of Sugar Creek. Mr.Hinkle of KC, the principle, didn't want to move, so he didn't renew his contract, and was immediately hired by the Independence School District to be principal of Ott School. H. J. Liggett was then hired to fill the vacancy. The grade school had four teachers. Miss Green was a new addition as the town was assured of survival. The other grade school teachers were Miss Edna

Marsh, Miss Mamie Farrell, and Mrs. Edith Pritchett, who, in the 1960s, taught Sugar Creek kids how to play the piano.

Thanks to the copious amount of liquid sunshine, Fairmount Park's lush grass and beautiful flowers had never looked better. Because of the acreage, lots of new activities could be included, like tennis and handball courts. The tennis courts were clay, but the handball courts floors were made from cement, the first in Kansas City. It was called "Western Style". Swimming lessons were given free in the mornings by Professor H. C. Wilson, former instructor at the New York City's swimming club in Manhattan. 10,000 baby fish were hauled from the government fish hatchery in Nevada, Missouri, via railroad tank car, and dumped in the lake from the railroad trestle that crossed over the eastern part of the lake, used to transport oil east.

On July the Fourth, the people of Sugar Creek celebrated their salvation from the clutches of Governor Major, whose main goal in life was to become the Vice President of the United States. In an article titled, "Sugar Creek Was Glad," the Examiner sent a reporter to cover the celebration in Sugar Creek, and filed the following:

Sugar Creek's celebration Saturday night of the Standard Oil decision of the Supreme Court was sane enough to satisfy the most exacting apostic of "sanity" in celebrations. There was an almost entire absence of noise. But none the less the people felt profoundly grateful for their deliverance from the disaster which threatened their homes, especially when they remembered how delicately their fate was poised in the balance for several months.

The three saloons of Sugar Creek voluntarily closed Saturday night, and the proprietors went up to the school house and helped to serve barbecued meat and soft drinks, such as lemonade, to the crowd. This was on the south side of the school house.

On the north side there was a "feast of reason and flow of soul." The crowd numbered about one thousand. A stand had been constructed on which the Third Regiment band from this city played several airs.

John F. Thice, City Attorney, representative of the legislature from this district, was made chairman of this meeting. Mr. Thice worked hard in the legislature to save Sugar Creek. Before he became an attorney he was for several years an employee of the Standard Oil refinery. In a brief introductory talk he drew a picture of the Sugar Creek of the near future, with a fourth-class city government, its own mayor and other city officers, and streetcar service extending from the Fairmount Park line.

J. G. Paxton was introduced. He said, "I wept with you in your sorrows, and now I am glad to rejoice with you in your good fortune." He reviewed some of the work that was done to save the refinery and the town from destruction.

State senator Michael E. Casey, of Kansas City, told how the bill which bears his name was carried through the senate and finally lacked only the Governor's signature to become a law, but was vetoed by the governor, thus leaving the only hope for the company and for Sugar Creek in a modification by the supreme court of its decision, which modification finally came.

E. C. Hamilton said that, "Now that the heavy cloud had drifted away from over the town, the time had come for the people to devote more of their attention to educational and social development. He said they had already made a good start in their fine $30,000 school building.

And then after three cheers had been suggested by the chairman and been given by the crowd, the exercise closed with a display of fireworks. The grounds were decorated with bunting and pennants and lighted with electricity. Many people from Independence attended.

Also in attendance were my three-year-old mother and my 12-year old father. The town would live and so would I.

Many picnics were again held at Fairmount Park, like the one for the Montgomery Ward company's family and friends, all 5000 of them. Being held at a different location every year, July 20 was Fairmount's turn, this being the seventh year. Many of the concession stands were leased by the picnic committee a "competent orchestra" played. A 55-person minstrel show was attended by 3,000. The dance pavilion was taken over for three hours. A baseball game was played on the athletic field between the "Fats and Leans". The umpire, A. J. Giron, manager of the clothing department, called the game in the fifth inning in favor of the Fats, 9, Leans, 0, in the middle of the game when one of the "Leans" vigorously argued a call. At the time the Leans were ahead 11-5. The Lean causing the altercation was last seen being chased by a pissed off bunch of skinny guys.

There were twenty-two athletic events with $600 in cash prizes; all this on a very hot day. A hospital tent with nurse was never needed. The picnic put $3,000 in the park's bank account.

This was a record year for large, corporate-type picnics at the home of picnics. Like the Grocers' Association picnic, that drew 20,000, Railway Passenger

Agents, Irish-American Athletic Association, the Railroad Club, and many, many more.

10,000 attended Labor Day at Fairmount Park because of the 100 air temperature, many went straight from the cars to the bath house to the water. By 4 pm it was standing room only. For the first time automobiles were allowed inside the park. There were so many that some had to park in the picnic area. Because of the heat the bathing beach and some concessions stayed open an extra week.

This was a time when husbands divorced their wives for sneaking a cigarette. One could travel practically anywhere in the world without a passport, and a person could take money from one country to another without any problems. That was about to change. The people of Sugar Creek won their battle, but because of years of working with carcinogens like benzene many, like my father who worked there for 36 years, would die of brain cancer and other health problems. The Price/Waters Oil Company was promised competition by Standard. Try to find one of their stations today.

Chapter 21: 1914

It was a good year here; it was the worst year so far for the world since that megalomaniac Napoleon was alive. In 1914 the megalomaniacs were ruling the earth.

Kansas City got a new and controversial major league baseball team called the "Kansas City Packers" of the newly-organized Federal League. The other teams in the league were the Indianapolis Hoosiers, the Chicago Whales, the Baltimore Terrapins, Brooklyn Tip-Tops, Buffalo Buffeds, Pittsburgh Rebels and the St. Louis Terriers. The league was only to last two seasons, the Packers going broke. Some of the teams made it into the National or American leagues in 1916. But not the Packers.

A week before Fairmount Park officially opened, the bathing beach allowed 56 hearty souls to take a dip. When it did open, on May 10, as in years past, improvements were made. Like a canvas cover over part of the beach to create some artificial shade. The bathing beach was enlarged and re-sanded again, and thousands of new bathing suits were available. A pavilion was built adjacent to the beach where ladies could get their hair dried and combed by pros. Tubs of iced spring water and new picnic tables dotted the picnic area. People with automobiles were encouraged to park in the park, with names like Auburn, Buick, Chandler, Chevrolet, Cole, Franklin, Humpmobile, Hudson, Maxwell, Moon, Oakland, Regal, REO, White. Ford, and many more. And they all had dealerships in Kansas City. A large stage was built in the German cafe, and higher-class acts were promised.

First to try and fulfill that promise of high-class entertainment was "Miss Myrti Howard" and her international trio, singers of the latest hits and trotters, i. e., professional dancers. The latest in trotting being the Hesitation Waltz, Maxixe, Turkey Trot, Kansas Shiver, Texas Tommy, and a dance called the Tango, banned in Europe because it was considered too risqué by them, them being the idiots who will be responsible for the killing fields of Europe in a few weeks.

Electric Park opened with a dog show. Mr. Hine, the owner of the park, was a dog lover and the President of the Kansas City Kennel Club. This was the first dog show in town to have a national exposure, 400 dogs, mostly from back East, were entered. The show was under the direction of the American Kennel Club. The two judges were a doctor from Chicago and another guy from Connecticut. One of the contestants, Pe-chi-li, was insured for $1,500. Who cares who won.

The Opening Day crowd at Fairmount numbered 10,000. A special gate had been added to the entrance so autos could now enter like at a drive-in theater, at 10 cents a head. Miss Howard and her group made a great impression. Before they left in four weeks, they had changed the way people in Kansas City danced, all now doing the latest dances. The lake attracted 350 people all day, but as soon as the sun went down only those fishing were left. After the crowds went home, the ground around the rides were covered with buttered popcorn.

On May 20, Earl Tuck of Independence and a young lady were riding on the Merry-Go-Round, and both fell off, he injuring his leg. Since he was a professional balloonist who sometimes would jump out of a balloon with a parachute, they had probably been to the saloon. Decoration Day drew 70,000 to the three main parks. Swope Park drew the biggest, 40,000 people. There were white picnic cloths spread throughout. The zoo was popular, and autos littered the grass. Children were everywhere. Fairmount and Electric both had 15,000. There were no accidents at any of the parks.

After the holiday, a change of managers was made at Fairmount Park. The president of the Fairmount Park Amusement Company, W. F. Smith, was in poor health. So Everett Wilson, formerly of the Grand Theatre downtown took his place. His first act as manager was to offer prizes every Wednesday in the dance pavilion. Prizes to be given away were a diamond ring for the lady, and a gold stick-pin for the gentleman who could most gracefully interpret the many new dances brought to our Big City by "Myrtie Howard and her International Trio in Society and Novelty Dances", now in her third week.

Myrtie's last day was June 7, a Sunday. Attendance was 20,000, the largest crowd so far this season. 2,500 people went swimming. Lines were long at some concessions, some people giving up. 250 autos parked practically anywhere they wanted. The new feature in the German Cafe was A Night in Old Heidelberg, a musical with seven women and five men. Altitude balloon racing, diving contests, and free vaudeville on the open-air stage. Featured were Hazel Walka, girl violinist, Elliot and Fassett, comics, Harrison Jones, cartoonist and whistler, with McRay and Simon, singer and hoofers, and Bennett's orchestra backing it all up.

Montgomery Ward company employees had such a good time at Fairmount Park last year that they decided to do it again. 20,000 employees, family of employees, friends, and moochers turned out. Over $5,000 was spent on this years' picnic, more money than last year. Next on the list is the annual Railway Passenger Agents' and Proctor and Gamble.

On June 29, the idiots got their chance. In a town called Seriavo, an idiot shot and killed another idiot, the heir to the Austro-Hungarian Empire, or what was left of it. Nobody around here cared. The only friend he had in the whole world was the Kaiser of Germany. Unfortunately, the Kaiser was a bully. Because of that, around 50,000,000 people were about to die. 10 million were about to die violently, and 20 to 40 million would die from the virus which was caused by the war.

Now, to take care of Price-Waters. Soon after the year began, Missouri had its first gas war. The Standard dropped its prices for gasoline 6 cents a gallon by the Fourth of July to 10.9 cents. Heating oil and Naphtha (a cleaning solvent) had also plunged in price per gallon. A barrel of oil was $1.75 for Penn State crude, to 70 cents for the stuff with a lot of sulfur.

The Fourth at Fairmount was quiet this year. No loud fireworks of any kind were allowed in the park. At night, the fireworks display was entitled "The Earth on Fire". For the first time this year all the boats and bathing suits were rented. People were turned away at the Dance Pavilion. In the German Cafe, the evening show featured Bennett's Orchestra and a host of talent. A balloon leap almost turned tragic when an aeronaut was whisked away before he could jump in the safety of the park. He rode the thing out as it traveled north with the wind, landing safely across the Mighty Mo in Cass County.

Time was running out for the Wets. One Saturday night in June, three drifting Mexicans were drinking in the Cement City saloon. An argument broke out and after closing at 12 o'clock; four shots were heard. The shooting was unusually brutal, as the victim was first shot in both legs, then as he lay on the ground he was shot in the shoulder and finally one to the temple at close range. No one knew the victim or his name, and the two perpetrators split. He was taken to the Independence Sanitarium, where he died of a bullet to the head at 4 o'clock Sunday afternoon. The Dries had a martyr to the evils of alcohol.

The early Prohibitionists weren't just preachers. Men had been taking a nip or two at work, which was okay until you included a machine of some sort. There were accidents where alcohol was involved in the workplace, and the practice of drinking on the job was discouraged. In 1890 the Anti-Saloon league got started. They were the more moderate of the two factions, the other being the mostly Protestant churches. The Catholics were more tolerant. The Prohibitionists wanted a total banning of alcohol, even 1% beer. The Anti-Saloon League didn't care if a person drank, just not in a place like Moe's on the Simpsons. The local Dries mobilized, trying to shut down any saloon not licensed by the county, which would include Sugar Creek. Because of last year's decision to keep the refinery, a new saloon had come to town, making the total four. Independence had nine, all around the Square. The Dries sent 200 women around and got 800 signatures in favor of a referendum to ban the sale of alcohol outside of city limits. The Wet vs. Dry vote was set for August 24. What the Dries needed was another martyr, and they got it. On Friday night, August 7, at Fairmount Park, Harvey Gillespie, a very Dry Sunday school teacher at Mt. Washington Christian Church, politically active in the Dry cause, was assaulted with a knife by a pissed-off drunk. The assailant took off but was recognized as a member of the Wets, not just because he was smashed.

Back then, politics and politicians revolved around the question, "Is he a Wet or a Dry?" At the polling places, women with cameras took pictures as they voted.

"Vote Early and Vote Often" was a way to make some money. Police were at every location. 40 women Dries were sent to Sugar Creek. The Dries won by 105 votes, but there were problems, and the Wets accused the Dries of irregularities in the voting. The Dries accused Nick Phelps, a county marshal with headquarters in Sugar Creek, of harassing the Dry workers. The election was over, the Dries won. There were seven arrests, and many other problems. Some men didn't like having their picture taken. One woman with a camera had acid poured down her back. Doctor Tryman treated her and took her home in his automobile.

George Rodman, one of the saloon owners in Sugar Creek and representing the three others, hired an attorney and went to court. The vote in Sugar Creek was 165 to 90 for the Wets. Mt. Washington was 367 Dry, 102 Wet. On the day of the election, 500 ladies in the Independence area signed a petition claiming to love their Wet men more if they would give up drink. The Wet men then passed around a flyer "We love you dearly, we love our home, we love our children. We cannot as men regulate fashion, but if you will give up the tango, the silk skirt, the shadow gowns, the tight skirt, and other degrees of fashion, we will vote to cut out the saloon. If not, we will all go to Hell." The leader of the Dries in Sugar Creek was the Reverend L. K. Kubus, the minister of the Sugar Creek Methodist Church. Roy Mallison was a Blue Township judge for the Dries. In Sugar Creek, the Dry judges were R. L. Bennett, F. A. Lee, Henry Lee, and the clerk was Frank Burkhart.

In July the clocks ticked down to Armageddon in Europe. Fairmount never had it so good. Record crowds filled the park. It was like a free auto show every day. The Kansas City Fireman's picnic was a little unusual, since someone had to be on duty. It was a two-day affair. Both days, hundreds of firemen, their family and guests, invited or not, took the day off.

Oklahoma oil was now being pumped to the Sugar Creek refinery, so an oil glut existed. On July 11, Jesse Jackson, 17, from Mt. Washington, drowned while swimming in the deep part of Crisp Lake. Dr. Gillmore was called from nearby Fairmount Park, where he is the park Doc. It only took him 15 minutes, but it was too late. Jackson was swimming with about 70 other mostly boys when the tragedy occurred. At that time, Crisp lake didn't have any cabins around it, but there were a lot of tents set up around the lake in the summertime.

While the Austro-Hungarian Empire was declaring war on Serbia in late July, the Jones Store employees, all 15,000 of them, closed up shop at noon and were given squawkers and horns to blast their way to Fairmount Park for their annual company picnic. Everything was free. A truckload of food was stationed on the picnic grounds, including 100 watermelons. Baseball games, swimming and foot races were held. Cash prizes were given. It had been a good year for the Jones Store, and many new employees created the largest and most successful Jones Store picnic yet.

A historian writing about the first World War said, "To understand it was like trying to put together a picture puzzle with some of the pieces missing and some that don't fit." At this time there were 20 kings, emperors, and a couple of czars, and some were related. Edward (England), William (Germany), and Nickie (Russia) were cousins, all related somehow to Queen Victoria, and they looked a great deal alike. So the war was a kind of family feud. America just wanted to stay out of it. Besides, everyone got along pretty well here no matter where you came from. America at the time had the 17th largest army in the world, but thanks to Teddy Roosevelt a pretty good navy. At Fairmount, the last thing anyone cared about was a war. Balloon races and parachute leaps from 2,000 feet were again attracting large crowds.

The parachute of a local lady aeronaut, Maggie Myers, was caught by a gust of wind, and instead of landing in the lake landed in a tree just outside the park, by the Independence Avenue entrance, caught on a limb which broke, sending her 50 feet to the ground. Doc Gillmore patched her up. A few weeks before, she was injured at Swope Park, same deal, tree.

The hot, wet, humid summer helped bring out the lushness of the park in the woods, yet also allowed the crowds to grow, as this was the most financially successful year in park history.

It wasn't a Merry Christmas to all the Wets employed with the county. They were fired and replaced by Dries.

HOTEL
COTTAGES
BOWLING ALLEY
GREENHOUSE
BOAT HOUSE
BEER GARDEN

FAIRMOINT PARK (1917)
(E.A. HWY NORTH *
CARLISLE TO WILLOW)

AUDITORIUM
PICNIC GROUNDS
BATHING BEACH
ATHLETIC GROUNDS
HORSE RACES
ZOO

91

State Shoot at Washington Park (above)

141. Fairmount Park, from Independence Avenue, Kansas City, Mo.

Bathing Beach at Fairmount Park, Kansas City, Mo.

The Beach, Fairmount Park, Kansas City, Mo.

Bathing Beach at Fairmount Park, Kansas City, Mo.

Al Carlisle and family enjoying their father's lake at Fairmount Park.

Fairmount Park, showing Lake, Kansas City, Mo.

At Lexington Avenue and Ralston
(Photo from Al Carlisle)

The Bandstand at night at Fairmount Park

Fairmount Park Cafeteria at night – Notice the flags and the band

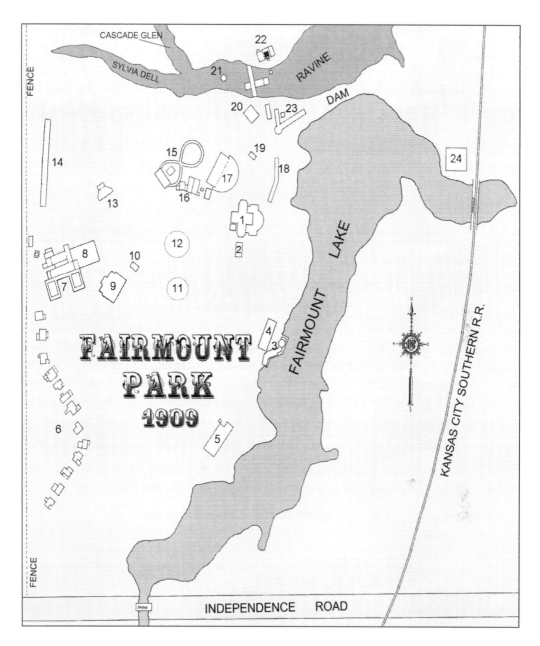

1. Cafe	7. The Fairmount Hotel	13. Band Stand	19. Photos
2. Dining Room	8. Soft Drinks	14. Horse Sheds	20. Billiards
3. Boat House	9. Dancing Pavillion	15. Toboggan Slide	21. Cusenbary Springs
4. Concessions	10. Coneys	16. Concessions	22. Power House
5. Skating Rink	11. Merry-Go-Round	17. Auditorium	23. Bathing Pavilion
6. Cottages	12. Circle Swing	18. Bath House	24. Ice House

Electric Park (above) and Carnival Park (below)

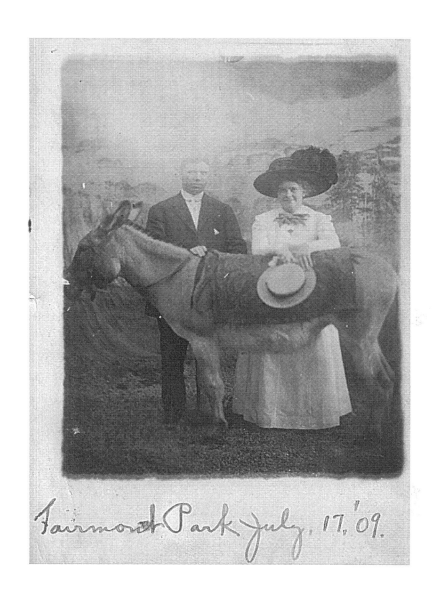

Fairmont Park July 17, '09.

The following pictures are from the collection of Raymond and Peggy Goucher, taken by an amateur photographer in 1907:

The boathouse (above) and the beach (below)

The Bandstand at Carnival Park (above) and the Natatorium at Electric Park (below)

Chapter 22: 1915

In Europe, as 1914 turned into 1915, things were not going well for the evil empires, Germany and Austro-Hungary. In short, they had already lost the war but as yet didn't know it. The Germans had failed to take Paris by going through small Belgium, which fought harder than the Prussians had assumed, which allowed the British to send 80,000 troops; the French and British (mostly French) stopping the Germans at the battle at the Marne River, thus giving the Ruskies time to attack Germany, giving it a two-front war, something they knew they couldn't win. The Austro-Hungarian people, with ten times more subjects, attacked little Serbia. Serbia, being two-thirds Slavs, was thought to be a push-over. Some genius general sent the Austro-Hungarian army through the area where the Serbian army practiced artillery. So the Slavs just waited, then KABOOM. Several whole divisions of Austrian troops ran, not walked, back, leaving their dead, wounded, and weapons.

The Dries won. On October 30 last, the saloons in unincorporated areas like Sugar Creek of Jackson County were supposed to close. The saloons in Sugar Creek refused on the grounds that they had paid their county liquor license for six months, expiring in January of 1915. George Rodman, one of four bar owners in Sugar Creek and the most outspoken, was arrested. Tried and found guilty, his attorneys appealed the conviction on the grounds that the petition drive that started this whole mess was never verified. In the meantime the saloons were allowed to operate thanks to Judge Johnson.

The liquor licenses were due to run out on January 5, 1915 so all the bars, even the ones in the city of Independence, which was incorporated, were closed. Two weeks later, Judge Johnson again allowed the saloons in Sugar Creek, Levasy, Lee's Summit, and Cement City to reopen. The Dries were angry but the saloons in Independence were gone.

The saloon owners in Sugar Creek were George M. Rodman, also known as Mike, man of the hour; Mike Bine, Bert Scott, and M. M. Emright. When the judge made his decision a loud cheer went up in the courtroom and everyone hurried to open their business.

One of the problems now faced by the working man of Independence was where to cash a payroll check as the saloons were gone. Since working six days a week was the norm, most industries, like Standard of Sugar Creek, payday was Saturday evening, the banks were closed so the former saloons of Independence functioned as banks, exchanging checks for silver and gold-backed paper money.

Not one of the five banks in Independence would stay open. Sugar Creek Saturday night was a hoot.

In Jefferson City, things they were a-changin'. Where once legislators ran from the Dry constituents, they now had to actually listen because of the popularity of the anti-saloon feelings. One area especially troublesome to the Dry people was along State Line, which was lined with hundreds of dives. Since Kansas had total prohibition since 1888, Missouri border bars were a necessity if the juicers of Kansas needed something to wet their whistle. The object of the dries was to, by state law, prohibit liquor sales within 1/2 mile of the Kansas line on the Missouri side. These do-gooders were definitely serious.

The city of Independence passed a strict liquor law with a huge loophole. No liquor could be sold or bought in the city limits of Independence but if you bought and paid for a bottle of hooch legally in Kansas City or Sugar Creek, it could be delivered by commercial carrier only. Once delivered you could legally share it with your friends.

Another attack was on the drug stores. It was illegal for a drug store to sell a bottle of whiskey without a prescription from a doctor, a practice that had been ignored. An attorney for the dries sent a letter to all the drug stores in the area reminding them of the law; sales stopped.

As part of the legal stuff, saloon owners had to have the signature of the residence living near the business. This was no problem in Sugar Creek, Cement City, and Levasy. Lee's Summit stayed Dry. A threat made by the Dries was a promise to prosecute the owners of said bars if the state Supreme Court ruled in the Dries' favor. They were a vengeful lot, for people whose hero, Jesus of Nazareth, turned water into wine.

Near-tragedy struck Sugar Creek 8 pm Friday night, January 29. The Wyandotte Furniture Co., owned by R. L. Bennett of Independence burned to the ground, this time the Standard Oil fire department stayed put. The second floor had eight apartments, occupied by men employed by the refinery. A cottage was also destroyed. The origin was in the apartments, luckily a nearby lumber company was spared.

On April 1, a jitney began running between Independence and Sugar Creek. A jitney, being any motor driven vehicle used to haul paying passengers, in this case a big Buick. W. C. McDonald took over the route just established a couple of weeks before by A. J. Young, whose automobile broke down for good. Leaving from the Independence Square in front of Robert's Department Store at 6:45 am, the route being Maple Avenue to Union Street, then to Independence Avenue, west to Fairmount Avenue (Sterling), north to the refinery, after which he parked in front of the Sugar Creek post office, leaving on the half hour. Five at a time for a dime. He ran until 7 pm, thus a possible $12 a day. Jitneys were already running from the Square to Cement City, Oak Grove, Blue Springs, Grain Valley, Buckner, and Kansas City.

On May 6, a German submarine sank a 700-foot luxury passenger ship called the Lusitania. 126 Americans died, including at least three millionaires. President Wilson wanted peace at any price. Ex-President Roosevelt and many others wanted war, but it would take many more insults against our county before the pacifists saw the danger.

On May 17 Fairmount Avenue from Independence Road (now 24 Highway) to the refinery was coated with oil. No longer was it a rock road.

On May 30, my mom's fifth birthday, Fairmount Park finally opened, the delay due to several improvements. A new bath house large enough to accommodate 300 people, new bathing suits with "FP" on the front were for rent. They were never washed, just hung out to dry (yuck!). My mom's second favorite ride, the Jack Rabbit, was put in operation, located on the north side of the park, just northwest of the Lexington/Ralston intersection. It was a figure-8 ride costing five cents, six rides for a quarter.

Closing the saloons at Fairmount became an obsession for the Dries. On Sunday, June 20, a "remonstrance" (a petition) against the sales of booze at Fairmount Park was held at all the churches in Independence. Dry representatives were stationed outside with petitions for signing by "the flock," urging the county government and anyone else who could help close the saloons at Fairmount. Help came from Mike Pendergast, the same one who was just a few years ago selling illegal hooch out of a rented house adjacent to the park, his big brother ran Kansas City. Now county liquor inspector, he voted no. Out of the 600 or so liquor licenses submitted to the county, mostly from KC, Fairmount is the only one refused. His reason: "I refuse to recommend the issuance of a license to Mr. Niswanber (of Kansas). I do not believe the park is a suitable place for a saloon. It should be kept a place for people to take their families, and if liquor were sold there they could not safely do this. This will be my attitude as long as I am license inspector. I took this position without considering the question of the sufficiency of the license. In short, he was going to give the Dries the carrot and whack them with the stick.

For the Dries, Fairmount was just the first step in turning the whole world Dry.

Just before the Fourth of July drew a great picnic at Fairmount Park. The Shriners were formed in 1872 in New York City. Two Masons thought their organization needed fun. They got their idea from a costume party in Europe attended by one of the founders. Dressed like Arabs, they drank and had an awful good time. The Arab thing has carried on to this day. Membership is open to anyone, no matter what their race or religion. On July 2, 7000 members and guests filled the park with their presence. One of the purposes of the gathering was to allow 25 candidates to cross the hot sands of the desert, Fairmount having plenty, upon which time they belonged, making them eligible to board a train soon headed for Seattle and their national party. Officially called the Annual Session of the Imperial Conclave, there were fezzes everywhere. The Kansas City Ararat Temple, in spite of the dark clouds and chance of rain, didn't let it dampen the spirits. 200 braved the cool water to take a dip. There was boating, dancing, sack races, peanut rolling. There were delegations from Marceline, Moberly, Sedalia, Boonville, Excelsior Springs, and Leavenworth. Two trains were chartered for the 200 local and 400 members from St. Louis. Parades, banners, a tango car equipped with a dance floor, a piano, and a Victrola and the Shriners weren't dry. Today, Kansas City has about 5000 members, best known for their antics at Fourth of July parades. But the Shriners have 11 children's hospitals in the US, and more overseas, paid for by the Shriners, their circuses, dances and generosity.

The Fourth of July at Fairmount was more subdued than years passed. No vaudeville. The cafe was still called "German", but that would soon change. On Sunday, July 4, and Monday, July 5, the following were things to do in Kansas City:

Swope Park, boating, picnics, golf, menagerie, and a municipal picnic and flag raising with a band concert, all free.

Baseball: The Federal League Packers were in its last year. They played St. Louis at Federal League Park, 47th and Tracy.

The Sells-Floto circus, at 17th and Indiana.

The steamer Chester, boarding at First and Main.

Electric Park: Mulicnhauer's Band, captive balloons, sea beach bathing, dancing, fireworks, and fifty other attractions.

Fairmount Park: Balloon ascension, boating, bathing, dancing, fireworks.

Boating: Blue River and 15th Street

Americanization Exercise, Central High School

Lincoln Electric Park (colored), 19th and Woodlawn Avenue

Independence City Fairgrounds, trotting races, picnic

German/Catholic societies, Wright's Grove, 50th & Genesee

The ad was paid for by the Metropolitan Streetcar Railway Co. It gave directions how to get to every location by streetcar.

Following the Fourth at Fairmount, Professor Oscar R. Gleason brought his talents to the park. His claim to fame was his ability to tame any horse, no matter. Ads were placed in all the local newspapers for all the out-of-control horses to be brought to the park to be broken by "the horse whisperer". After this attraction, park attendance cooled considerably. Though still popular, someone was running out of money.

In Independence, things were getting tough for the Wets, who refused to knuckle under. Julius Erickson was charged with selling one bottle of beer. The jury was hung. A new trial was being discussed. Road houses were a big problem for the Dries and police, some of whom were wet. They sprang up everywhere, in houses, barns, basements. There was a $50 reward for any rat if he or she turned one in. Barrels of beer and whiskey were being smuggled in after the street lights went out at 12 o'clock from Kansas City, probably coming from Mr. Pendergast.

In Sugar Creek and Cement City, dram shop liquor licenses were granted to the five saloon keepers. There was no protest as one, the Dries didn't want to get beat up, two, the only hope for shutting down the Sugar Creek saloons will be in the courts.

Chapter 23: 1916

For 11 seasons Charles D. Carlisle had owned the wet half of Fairmount Park. Born in Newton Falls, Ohio, the year the civil war ended, he graduated from college at Mt. Union, Ohio, in 1886. A year later he was on his way to Arizona to get rich in the mining business. He stopped in Kansas City, Kansas, to visit his uncle, a judge. Judge Carlisle talked him into giving KC a try, and he prospered. He made the most of his first job with the Chesterfield Feed and Grain Company. He married the boss's daughter, Maude Chesterfield, and when Alfred Chesterfield passed away he took over the business.

He didn't just own the water, he was responsible for the beach, boat house, fishing, and the boats. Every Sunday he would load up the family in his new electric auto, and his wife would drive out to Fairmount to pick up the receipts of the week. Since the electric auto only had a range of 20 miles per charge, and the Carlisle's home being ten miles away, occasionally they ran out of juice. That could be a big problem because his kids always rode along. Going to an amusement park that was owned by your father had its perks; they would have been treated like royalty. Hot, dry summers were the most profitable. It wasn't all profit, though. Every spring money was spent to restock the lake with fish, buildings had to be improved and painted. Boats and bathing suits wore out, people stole fishing poles. A caricature about this time of Carl, in a Who's Who of KC, shows him dressed spiffy, riding a pig to market. Carl was cut from the same cloth as other great American entrepreneurs, like Carnegie and Rockefeller, only he diversified. Besides Carlisle Feed and Grain and a lake, he invested in race tracks, the riverboat Chester, and a retail feed store located near Kentucky Road and Blue Ridge Boulevard. Unfortunately, he would also invest heavily in the stock market.

The other half of the park, on the high ground to the west, was owned by a corporation, management usually not lasting over a few seasons, with new stuff every year. The Goetz Brewing Company of St. Joseph held the lease. The Cusenbary family owned the land.

Prohibition of alcohol passed in an election several months ago, eliminating all saloons outside of Kansas City in Jackson County. Sugar Creek's argument was that the Wets had won 160 to 90, so leave us alone. It was not to be.

The proprietors of the saloons stayed open despite threats. On January 8, John Kerr, one of the early founders of Fairmount Park, a self-appointed do-gooder, troublemaker, and a member of the Jackson County Law Enforcement League, went to the Jackson County court to complain that the saloons in Sugar Creek were still open, despite all the hard work done by the Dries. Things did not go well for him, and he was informed by Judge Miles Bulger that there was nothing he could do and suggested that he take his cause up with the Grand Jury in Kansas City. He would die in 1928, still a Dry. When questioned about the charges, Mr. Rodman of Sugar Creek replied,

"A great deal of fuss is being made because we still have our rooms open, which we have a perfect right to do so long as we cut out the sale of booze. We expect to sell soft drinks and put in a lunch counter and maybe pool tables, which I think we have a right to do, so long as we don't violate any laws."

He spoke for all four former saloon owners. Sugar Creek was a great place to sell beer, lots of Catholics.

Despite their standing, things were not going well at all for the bar owners. M. Enright and his bondsman, H. J. Helms, and Walter Gray, were being sued by Mrs. Orbie Bryson, widow of George M. Bryson, who died of alcohol poisoning on November 7, 1915. She was asking $3,000 and she would get $2,000, which was paid by the Schlitz Brewing Company, as nobody else had that kind of money.

In March the trial of the Sugar Creek Four, the former bar owners, was held in Kansas City. They were found guilty of selling alcohol without a license, and each fined $500 and given six months in jail. Apparently they got off, because three weeks later they applied for four licenses for pool halls in their old buildings. A local woman carrying a baby testified that she witnessed liquor being stocked in said location. The courts decided not to grant the license. No more pool halls. What's next, smoking? Yes, smoking. "Papered Tobacco" (cigarettes) were soon barred from any county building, along with pipes and cigars. The legal sale of alcohol was stopped, but consumption wasn't. Bootlegging was already becoming a great business.

Even Kansas City wasn't immune from the alcohol Nazis. Inspector Mike Pendergast knew that his job was secure, as it came from Jefferson City, the appointment approved by the Governor, probably repaying a debt. There were 550 saloons in Kansas City having to renew the city and county licenses, then called a dram shop license, every six months. Mike grew up in a saloon, his big brother Tom owned one. That's how they started in politics. Both were good with their fists, especially Mike. Years before, a prize fighter was passing through town and got drunk in Tom's bar. He claimed he could whip anyone in town. Mike was called and beat the tar out of him. In 1916 Mike had an auto, a driver, and two or three deputies. They were supposed to make sure no unlicensed saloons were open. It was a good way for him to make some extra money. Distributors backed some of the saloon owners, and that was very illegal, but it happened. The thing that could kill a saloon in Kansas City was the neighbors. If they complained, you were in trouble. On the other hand, no one wanted his house burned down.

No beer or any kind of alcohol will ever be served at Fairmount Park again legally. A month before the grand opening of the new Fairmount Park, the gates were opened on Easter Sunday, April 16, for the people of Kansas City. Thousands strolled the park in their Easter best. Lots of money had been invested for 1916 and management wanted to show off.

Fairmount Park opened for business on Sunday, May 21. A lot of neat things had been added to the park this season. For the first time, water from the spring was pumped through pipes to various parts of the park for human consumption. Wagons on wheels were pushed about the park selling various goodies. The German Village was now called the Fairmount Inn, thus no more German anything. An all-women's orchestra played good old American music.

Fairmount Park pioneered in the new technology of motion pictures. A large studio, for the making of silent films, was built. The enterprise was called "The Fairmount Feature Film Company", starring Fatty Lewis, played by Arthur Killick. For the crowds they performed a skit, "The Bright Lights Dimmed". The Overland Park Aviation Field also had a feature film company, neither lasted very long.

Also new this year was a "Children's Play Ground", guarded by responsible adults, giving mothers an opportunity to take a dip in the lake. New metal boats were replacing the wooden kind. A large, gasoline-powered metal boat patrolled the 18-acre lake, manned by lifeguards. It was a water patrol.

Management had changed. Samuel Benjamin, last year the manager of Electric Park, was hired to run the amusement side, and Gabe Kaufman, the assistant manager at Convention Hall, was hired by Mr. Carlisle to manage the lake, until his sons would be old enough to take on that responsibiligy. A newly remodeled and enlarged men's bathing house served as his office and living quarters, on the second floor. He was to spend many seasons at Fairmount Park. During the winter he managed the Orpheum Theater; many park employees were drawn to Fairmount from the other entertainment businesses in the KC area.

Also new this year were concerts in the Amphitheater, dancing in the Dance Pavilion, music by Coleman's orchestra, Hillary Hall filled with weird sites, something called a "Suffragettes' Kitchen", and automatic baseball courts.

Threatening weather in the morning didn't keep the crowds away. The sun shone brightly in the afternoon, and by 7 pm an opening day record was surpassed again. A four-balloon race was held in the afternoon, with parachute leaps into the lake, all filmed by the Fairmount Feature Film Company. Because of cool weather there was no swimming. The boats and the fishermen had their way with the lake. Still, 20,000 paid a dime.

Swope Park was also open. Both streetcar lines were at capacity. 12,000 enjoyed boating and fishing, golf, zoo, picnics, or the 20 or so horses carrying kids around a pony track northeast of the zoo.

Another enterprise by Mr. Carlisle was the Steamship Chester. Many groups chartered Chester this week. Among them were the Woodmen of the World, No-Name Club, I. A. B. Outing Club, and the Kansas City Board of Trade. When not engaged, the Chester made two trips a day up or down the Mighty Mo, shoving off every afternoon at 2:30, band starting at 2:00. Evening band, 8 o'clock, sail, 8:30.

The Reverend Billy Sunday was at Convention Hall for all of those in Kansas City who needed it.

The rest of the summer's entertainment at Fairmount stayed pretty constant. Instead of changing acts every week or two, people were booked long term. Earl Flynn and Nettie McLaughlin performed plays until August in the former German Cafe, where good old fried chicken had replaced sausage and sauerkraut.

Since Artillery Battery B of the local Missouri National Guard was called up to add to our firepower of our war piss-ant with Mexico, Fairmount Park furnished patriotic entertainment. On June 18, called "Preparedness Day", Hiner's American Legion Band played Patriotic music while the 3rd Regiment of Kansas City drilled and played soldier. Next year it would be for real.

The Fourth of July had a record-breaking crowd of 44,000. It must have been packed. Balloon races, the water, the fireworks, but not all the people of Independence went to Fairmount. Picnics large and small were everywhere. Most business didn't bother to open. The largest picnic was for the Latter Day Saint's Sunday School, held on Enoch Hill. Foot races and baseball took up the whole day. At the fairgrounds, six horse races were witnessed. K. C. Anderson's horse caused a pile-up. Fortunately, no one was hurt but the horses.

This was an election year, with a primary to be held on August 1. On the evening of Monday, July 24, an open air meeting was held in Sugar Creek. Henry L. Jost was the main speaker, followed by Dr. Morrow, Alexander Graham,

George Reinhardt, A. C. Southern, James Compton, J. Allen Prewitt, Harold Spencer, R. S. Stone, and O. H. Gentry.

The day before the election, two well dressed men in a new auto pulled up in front of the home of B. E. Cook, 705 Maple Avenue, Mt. Washington. A Democratic-Progressive election judge. Mr. Cook was at work. Mrs. Cook answered the door. The men told her that they were from the election commissioner's office and asked for the two boxes of ballots, as there had been a mistake in the printing. She refused, as a county sheriff had delivered them. The men left the porch and stood by their auto. Mrs. Cook's phone rang, a man identifying himself as Jim Gilday, County Clerk, said it was okay to give the men the boxes, and she did. They also tried in Sugar Creek, but failed, because they didn't have a phone. The boxes finally turned up at a Pendergast Democratic judge's residence a few hours later. The Pendergasts were just showing off.

A dead body was found in a tank car at the refinery, a half-empty bottle of whiskey by his side. He died from inhaling fumes; the whiskey probably helped. Getting a stiff out of a tank car with a 16-inch opening proved to be a problem.

The Riverview School graduated its High School Class of 1916, Sugar Creek school being the last to close in the county. Two young ladies, Nora Lee and Suzie Nancy, were it. Nine graduated from the eighth grade. A play put on by the underclassmen, began the ceremony, followed by a Commencement address by the Honorable William Bland. A. S. Hurt handed out diplomas. The teachers were Margaret Chorn, Alma Johnson, Geanne May Rhoades, Lottie Worley, and Betty Edmondson. Two more teachers will be hired for next year's kids. Initiation that all students at the Riverview School had to tolerate, especially the new ones, was being drenched with water by the upperclassmen, Riverview School equaled water. Unlike today, there were no child molesters in Sugar Creek. Today, they're protected like some endangered species.

Now that they had defeated the Devil Rum, the Christians tried to fill the vacuum. The room above the bank was turned into a Sunday School. It was the idea of the Reverend James Fuller, Pastor at the Mt. Washington Christian Church. They brought in a piano and proceeded to hold classes at 9:45 AM every Sabbath. Among the invaders were Mr. and Mrs. Rich, J. A. Boulware, Ernest Raynor, H. Furguson. Anyone interested were asked to bring their Billy Sunday hymn books, people without one being either an atheist or a Catholic, thus beyond hope for Salvation. Where the Devil now resided was Cement City.

On September 27, two Mexicans were killed in a six-inch dirk knife versus pistol. Both lost. A drunken argument led to the incident. When Constable Henry Chastain arrived an hour or two later, he found a dead man in the road full of bullet holes holding a bloody knife that looked like a very sharp letter opener. The man with the pistol was found bleeding to death, also in the road, about 50 feet away. Seems as though they were playing cards and drinking, both former employees of the cement company.

The Labor Day holiday at Fairmount Park was the end of the season. Sensational Rich, said to be the highest trapeze performer in the world. In the Fairmount Inn, Miss Leslie Carter, America's Divine Emotional Actress, performed the role she wrote and made famous. By the time the park would open next year, the U. S. of A. would be gearing up for

WAR.

Chapter 24: 1917

Born in 1884, Harry Truman was a pretty good farmer, living in Grandview, Missouri. He was a smart farmer, rotating his crops and leaving some ground fallow.

In Germany unrestricted submarine warfare to strangle England like England was strangling Germany was announced. If this wasn't enough, even for a pacifist like President Wilson, a telegram from some idiot named Zimmerman in Berlin to the Mexican government, proposing Mexico attack America, and when Germany wins the war, Mexico would get back Texas, Arizona, New Mexico, and any other state they wanted. They also suggested that the Japs might like California if Mexico didn't want it. The problem for the Kaiser, who may or may not have known what a big mistake this was: the British were reading all the German cables, and gladly passed it on to Washington.

At the time, the US had a pretty good Navy, thanks to President Roosevelt, but the Army and Marines ranked 17th in the world in manpower, behind Portugal, who was 16th.

Back in the real world, the local economy was booming. Cement for protection and to walk on was in great demand in Europe, but what was in real demand was gasoline. The stuff that was once junk is now gold, because of its high compression rate; very flammable. The fumes blow up great. That moves pistons, that move propellers and wheels. Like airplanes. At the beginning of the war, the British and French had 1,500. By the end of the war, 175,000 had been produced. 116,000 were destroyed. The US produced 50,000 trucks by the end of the war.

100 men were hired in 1917 at the Standard Oil refinery. Work at the refinery was dangerous. Besides the threat of fire, a lot of new construction continued. On January 11, 34-year old Charles Bryant, while making new stills, fell off a 30-foot scaffold, falling head first to his death. Charles was one of many newly hired men who once lived in Kansas City, moved to Independence with his wife and two kids for a job, as Standard was becoming the largest employer in Kansas City. Afterwards, his family was destitute and Standard would not accept responsibility. The widow had no recourse but to sue. She won $10,000. The cheapskates didn't want to set a precedent for the next casualty.

In February, Samuel Y. Thompson of Sugar Creek was killed by a large sheet of iron being hoisted to make a storage tank. Again the jury found the company negligent.

All this activity called for better transportation to this area, electric lines were proposed. One called for the extension of the Fairmount Park line, which would do Independence no good. Mayor Ott and others proposed a line from Independence to Sugar Creek. It was to be called the Court Creek Electric Line. Very little money was raised.

The wildest was a proposal by P. P. Balfour, boss of the Portland Cement Plant. He suggested and Mayor Ott and City Engineer H. H. Pendleton agreed that a tunnel was possible. The line to be used was already 1/2 mile into the Bethany limestone, moving at 20 feet a day, 40' wide by 15' tall. Its main use would be for sewage, since the city of Independence was using septic tanks. The cost of a sewer line was in the millions of dollars, which would bankrupt the town.

While the saloons were closed for a long time, Tom Berislavich and John Nowak received from the court permission to open a pool hall in Sugar Creek. Sibley, Courtney, Atherton and Cement City were also granted permission. The carrot to the county was the tax, $15 per year per pool table.

Sugar Creek merchants A. I. Mossie and H. Kamensky were fined $75 each for selling cigarettes to minors. They both claimed to have been set up by the newly formed Sugar Creek branch of the Women's Christian Temperance Union. Some of the members were C. Murray, C. Davidson, President, Mrs. Jensen, Vice President, Mrs. Burwar, Secretary, Mrs. Anmen, Treasurer, Mrs. George Mallinson, Press Secretary, Mrs. A. Mallinson, Flowers, Mrs. Hurt, Sufferage, H. Black, Propaganda. Little Miss Pearl Mallinson was the piano player. They had their work cut out for them. The goal of the International WCTU was to ban alcohol all over the world; they were obviously delusional; like the French are going to give up drinking wine. They also didn't care for tobacco in any form.

On Sunday, April 8, after putting in a hard day shoeing horses at Portland Cement, Andrew Chiles of Mt. Washington was driving home through Sugar Creek. This being the first weekend after the declaration of war with Germany, a small crowd of men were stopping every car that passed and making the drivers salute the flag. Since few of the men could speak English, Mr. Chiles refused, saying that he was a patriot and didn't need to show it to a bunch of drunken immigrants. In broken English they demanded that now he had to kiss the flag. Again he refused, whereupon the crowd pulled Mr. Chiles out of his car and proceed to beat him, knocking out four teeth, and breaking a jaw and a few ribs. They then threw him down a 15 ft. embankment into the Sugar Creek creek. Arrested for the deed was Franz Jones, 25, a newly hired boilermaker at the refinery who was new to the USA, and two others. At trial he was fined $1,000.

His interpreter was Steve Kolby. Afterwards, two bars in Sheffield lost their license because their labels were on the gallon jug that induced the patriotism.

Fairmount Park opened for the season on May 20. Only 7,000 showed because of rain. The beach was closed, but everything else was running. Because of the booming local economy, $100,000 was invested by Sam Benjamin, who was again the manager. Among the new attractions were six monkeys who drove and raced miniature racing cars. 100 craftsmen were still busy putting the finishing touches on the park.

Among the many new features were tennis courts, playgrounds with swings, Spin-the-Top, Indian Frolic, a photo studio to take a picture with that certain someone, penny parlors, shooting galleries, and a large ice cream pavilion, a miniature railroad, and the Canals of Venice. The park also boasted a new merry-go-round with organ, the Whip, the Human Puzzle, an enlarged dance floor, a circle swing, Hilarity Hall, the Jack Rabbit ride, and Ferris wheel. There was even a special restroom for mothers to do the diaper thing. The lake had a new 20 passenger boat, along with the usual stuff, like chicken dinners, Homer Montfort and his band, a parking lot for 1,000 autos, and 4,000 new bathing suits.

On Decoration Day, May 30, the Sugar Creek Park Skyline Addition lots went on sale, located just outside the north, or back, entrance to the park. Etrucius Smith owned the area and divided it up for sale. Lots were priced from $200 to $500, $100 and a buck a week for a very long time. That's how many of the houses that are there now got there.

The season didn't go completely without a certain amount of drama. A young man who claimed to have been injured by a trolley brought a frivolous lawsuit against the park. The accident had occurred two seasons ago, while waiting for a car at the park depot. He claimed that because of the inability of park management to control the crowd, he was pushed in front of a car, hurting his leg.

On July 1, a man of 29 drowned in the lake under mysterious circumstances. At 4:00 p.m. that Sunday a couple from Kansas City, Kansas, rented a boat. At 7 p.m. the lady dove into the lake, clothing and all, leaving her purse in the boat. The man rowed about 15 feet to the deepest part of the lake, and also dove in, clothes and all. The lady was saved by lifeguards. The man grabbed the grass that grew on the bottom of the lake and held on until he drowned. When pulled to shore, he had a death-grip on the grass. Soon a copy-cat suicide by a 20 year old man in Cement City and a Sugar Creek girl happened. They both just walked into the Mighty Mo, leaving just their shoes and a few personal items on shore; suicide being a long-term solution for a short-term problem.

118

Fairmount Park was still the home of picnics. One of the better took place just before the Fourth of July, paid for by the Gideon Society, the Bible in the motel people. The picnic was given for the traveling salesman, the very creature they were trying to save. First prize in the pumpkin pie eating contest went to Miss Ruby Walden of Independence; her prize was a 24 lb. sack of flour. Mrs. R. H. Bainard , who came in second, won an aluminum kettle. J. J. Riley won the pop-drinking contest, Mrs. P. F. Riley, won a sack of flour for being married to the homeliest man. She said, "I can use the flour, but I've seen a lot worse here today." An old man's fiddlers' contest was won by Captain Ewing of Armourdale, Kansas. Old Soldier Spencer of Ft. Leavenworth won second. Both were survivors of the Civil War.

Both Electric and Fairmount broke attendance records for the Fourth of July. At Electric 50,000 had turned the turnstile by 10 pm, and it was still clicking. Lines were long for everything. Rhonda Royal's Elephants were the main attraction. At Fairmount the crowds were so large that an employee called the cops claiming the crowd was out of control. Constable Arthur Metzer took the call and thought that a riot had begun. He hopped in a couple of autos full of local and county police. When they got there, the crowds were jovial.

Because of problems, Electric changed the water every Sunday night, making for a cold swim on Monday. Not so at Fairmount. With a crowd of 46,000 the spring-fed lake stayed warm and fresh, which was the most popular place to be this Fourth. People waited for wet bathing suits, which carried little bugs.

After the "War in Fireworks" on the Fourth, every Sunday and Wednesday was a war of pyrotechnics. The locals would have sat outdoors every evening and watched from their porches.

As the season progressed, the popular park became again the Home of Picnics. These included the Traffic Club, Proctor and Gamble, Kansas City Street Railway Co., Court of Honor, Kansas City, Kansas Chamber of Commerce, Irish Americans, Loose-Wiles Biscuit Co., Masonic Blue Lodge, Women's Christian Temperance Union, Woodmen of the World, Catholic Societies, and all the chapters of the Eastern Star. The Homer Montfort band played Labor Day, Monday, September 3. Balloon races, triple parachute leaps, athletic events, games, races, and prominent speakers.

A report by the Superintendent of the schools outside of Kansas City in Jackson County, which included Sugar Creek's Riverview School was interesting. There were 8,806 pupils, mostly white, 258 teachers, mostly women, in 116 schools. Average daily attendance was 6,000, meaning that there were a lot of sick kids, especially on sunny days. 9,000 cases of tardiness, 71 truancies, and 447 corporal punishments. Men teachers were paid the best, $101 a month. Women teachers received $60 a month.

The Commercial State Bank of Mt. Washington was having a run of bad luck. Right after the Fourth of July, three men drove to the bank, which is now a vacant building at 9525 Wilson Road. One stayed in the auto, leaving it running, while the other two, in the bank, locked the president and cashier, Mr. A. R. Perrin, and his assistant, Miss Jessie Martin in the safe after pointing handguns at them. They left heading towards Independence but they had come from Kansas City. The locals knew what was going on but didn't intervene, the three getting away with about $1,000. On Friday afternoon, November 23, one of the three walked into the bank by himself with two big, unloaded pistols. This time Mr. Perrin was prepared. After giving the robber the money, he started shooting up Arlington Street as the moron ran. Next door there was a grocery store. In it worked W. J. Penden, who was a deputy constable under Arthur Metzger. He ran from the store and captured the 23 year old, who was from Kansas City. When asked his profession the man said, "Bank robber," and admitted to robbing the bank back in July. Justice being swift back then, on the following Monday, Judge Latshaw gave him 30 years. The man also spoke with a German Accent, which didn't help.

Fires at the refinery were caused by technologies new to the oil business. On November 5, five of the new stills being of that technology, started a fire. Damage was estimated at $50,000. On December 15, twenty stills blew up, attracting sight seers from as far away as Kansas City, flames shooting up more than 100 feet that seemed to touch the low-hanging clouds. The streets were packed with people who stood in 39 degree temperatures. The trouble started in the afternoon when the pipe sprang a leak; for hours the fire was kept under control till finally, about 10 pm, KABOOM! followed by continuous booms as every still, one after another, blew up shooting flames in the air. George Moffett, boss man at the refinery, estimated damage at $50,000 and said that production would not be affected. The firefighters were brave, magnificent and well trained. As the stills exploded they went about their business professionally. No outside help was needed and no one was injured. A still wind and the cold night air helped keep the fire away from the tank farm, which could have been a disaster. People living on Park Street removed items of value from their homes. The threat seemed so great.

In late summer a rumor came through Sugar Creek that a huge electric plant was to be built on 118 acres between the Standard Oil Refinery and the Portland Cement plant. The reason for the multi-million dollar project, said to need 3,000 employees, was due to the threat of agents of the Kaiser on the Eastern Seaboard. Nothing, of course, became of it.

Since 75% of the breweries and saloons in Kansas City were owned by German-Americans, the prohibition people jumped on it. Claiming by consuming beer, you were helping the enemy; how un-American can you get?

The war was going bad for both sides. Because of the British blockade the Germans were starving and it was just the beginning. No longer did anyone cheer the war. Cartoons of men still fighting in 1950 appeared. Because of some idiot French general, the French armies rebelled and were no longer capable of attacking. Many were shot. The British and French wanted only American grunts, and no rank higher than Captain, wanting to use Americans as nothing more than replacements. President Wilson told General Pershing we would fight as a united Army and the Limeys and French didn't like it.

Local boys wanted to go and joined Company C & E, an artillery unit. Thanks to leaders like Captain Harry Truman, most would come home alive.

Chapter 25: 1918

Because President Wilson didn't want to anger the Germans America was ill-prepared for war, and it would cause a lot of problems. Ex-president Theodore Roosevelt said it all in an open letter to the Kaiser.

Dear Bill,

We have been at war for nearly a year and have not been able to hurt you yet. And the prospects are that you are perfectly safe as far as we are concerned.

The President is merely a coiner fatuous rhetorical platitude.

The Secretary of war is an imbecile.

We are in the throes of a coal famine, owing to incompetence.

Our soldiers are armed with telegraph poles for cannons and broomsticks for guns.

Everybody is a slacker but me.

Yours,

Theodore

Soon after the first of the year, several local army officers were granted a five day leave from Camp Doniphan, now Ft. Sill, Oklahoma: Captains Sermon and Allen, Lieutenant Bundschu, and a former Corporal, soon to be Captain, Judge, Senator, Vice-President, and President of the United States of America, Lieutenant Harry S. Truman. The rest of the local boys in camp would be rotated home over the next few months.

The local coal shortage was offset thanks to the Standard Oil Company of Sugar Creek, which made sure that all the schools and the hospitals had plenty of coal, due to the fact that Standard could buy all the coal it wanted, coal selling for $6.40 a ton. Households were allowed one ton a week but were encouraged to burn wood.

Also locally was the problem of transportation. Standard Oil, with 1,200 employees and still hiring, drew from Independence and Kansas City for manpower. It was the same with the cement plant, getting to work presented a real problem. The only way to get to Cement City was through Sugar Creek, which had a county road. But that ended at the confluence of the Sugar Creek creek and the Missouri River. From there it was almost two miles of mud, dust, or ice, depending on the time of year. The county fixed the road. Next Mayor Ott of Independence proposed an electric line between the Independence Square and Sugar Creek. The Kansas City Railway Company wouldn't invest the $50,000 for the enterprise. The mayor suggested that they, being the citizens, and businesses of Independence do it. Standard Oil gave $5,000. Other businesses and individuals gave from a few thousand to $100 being the minimum. It was an investment, interest was paid at 6% over ten years. $40,000 was finally raised, coming up short, and the line was never built.

The Sugar Creek River View School graduating class of '18 consisted of three girls, Mary Burkhart, Edith Campbell, and Elva Thatch. The eight grade promoted five: Wilbur Bickley, Irene Mallinson, Elma Erickson, Frances O'Connell, and Mary Latimer. Commencement ceremonies were held in the hall over the Sugar Creek bank. While the rest of the students, all 150 of them, sang patriotic songs, a few days later. Thanks to the influenza (the first of three or four waves just now starting to cause massive casualties on the East coast) there wouldn't be much school next semester.

Every ounce of energy seemed to be going into the war effort. Crime dropped and you better not get caught driving your automobile on a Sunday afternoon.

Fairmount Park opened on Sunday, May 19. The place was redone and painted, the work having started in March. Several new concessions had been added, including a new ride, "The Captive Airplane", four full-size airplanes of the day, going around 360 degrees with a gasoline motor propelling the thing. Very popular, but it took up a lot of space and was noisy.

Even entertainment was influenced by the war. "The Four Minute Men" gave patriotic speeches not just in the amusement parks but in the movie theaters and every kind of entertainment, like they did all over the country. Fairmount Park did its bit for the war effort. Friday, May 24, was Red Cross day at the park. Blue Township, which included Independence, Maywood, Mt. Washington, and Sugar Creek, had a quota of $40,000 to raise. To help, park management gave all money collected on that day to help meet that goal. Young ladies from the area volunteered to dress like Red Cross nurses while collecting dimes and nickels. The swimming hole wasn't yet open. Church groups and Sunday School teachers were encouraged to bring their students. Businesses were encouraged to work half a day and allow employees to attend.

Boy Scouts were used as gophers for odd jobs, like the newly organized Boy Scout troop from Sugar Creek, organized by A. S. Hurt, Superintendent of Riverview School. The Reverend B. D. McGowan of the Sugar Creek Methodist Church was their Scout Master, Shelton Huffman was his assistant. Scouts were Howard Huffman, Carrol and Carl Stinnett, George and Joe O'Renick, Fred Creviston, Wilbur and John Bickley, Daniel O'Connell, Theo Carver, Harry Lee, Sam Kamenski, Lewis Porter, Bradford Evans, Forrest Barkdale, Lee Evenger, John Mayernick, Evan Turner, and the man would bring thousands of babies into this world, including myself, future Dr. Fred Hink.

Standard Oil and Sugar Creek purchased $63,000 worth of War Bonds. Men too old to fight (32 and over) were sent door to door in every city in America. If you gave you were put on the "good" list. If you didn't, maybe because you didn't support the war or lack of money, or didn't open your door, you went on the "bad" list and were considered a slacker to be called upon in the future by someone more patriotic and less pleasant. In other words, intimidation. It worked. No one wanted to be called a "Slacker".

About this time Miss Pavey, the lady who approached Sam Benjamin, manager of Fairmount Park for a donation, and got a whole day of receipts, started a Red Cross branch in Sugar Creek. The local ladies were invited for a patriotic program above the bank. A play and a speech entitled, "Food Conservation and Women's Part in the War" was given by the state chairman, Mrs. Walter McNab Miller, who was probably impressed by the $63,000. Pearl Mallinson gave a piano solo to close the meeting. As it's part to keep the men at the front happy, millions of cigarettes were given by the U. S. government, free, to the Red Cross and the Salvation Army. The Red Cross sold theirs, angering many of the grunts. The Salvation Army gave theirs away, sometimes even going into the trenches, bringing much admiration from the troops.

Winnwood Beach, just North of the River, off of Chouteau Trafficway, was now open and would stay open until the late 1960s. It had very little impact on Fairmount or Electric Park's popularity until the late 1920s.

On several occasions Electric Park's popularity caused it to ran out of tickets during the weekdays. Along with an indoor and outdoor pool, Lenge's Military Band played two concerts daily at 2:00 and 8:00. Vaudeville was the main attraction this year and many class acts made their appearance. Because of the war and a strike, many women were now running the trolleys, called "Conductorettes". On the Fourth of July they were put to the test as 50,000 attended both Electric and Fairmount Parks, band concerts and fireworks were the usual fare. The war was brought home via pyrotechnics.

The place to be was Swope Park, where a huge celebration unfolded after five weeks of planning. A day of patriotism began at 10:30 in the morning, when the Seventh Regiment of the Missouri National Guard led a parade from the zoo to the flagpole, followed by Boy Scouts and flags from the Allied nations. Bands played as 10,000 foreign-born citizens and patriotic societies marched in revue. The Daughters of the American Revolution carried flags from the past, the War of 1812, 1861, 1898 and flags of all the American Forces. 11:30 was the Pledge of Allegiance. At noon another parade was held by the former citizens of the Allied countries. Represented by England, France, Belgium, Italy, Slavs, Greece, Syria, Armenia, China, Ireland, followed by patriotic societies and newly-minted American citizens. At the end of the parade a picnic was held near the new music pavilion, while bands from the various cultures played native music. At 4:00 in the afternoon, lectures and the reading of the Declaration of Independence, speeches, band music, and singing lasted till dark. There were no fireworks.

Picnics and Patriotism was the theme for the remainder of the season at Fairmount Park. The Knights of Pythias and the Irish American picnics were just two of many in August.

The final attraction was Professor B. Peri's "Patriotic Allied Ballet and Carnival", which included a masquerade and confetti war. Park patrons were invited to participate. 250 people were in the ballet. A huge stage was built for the players in the center of the park, with special lighting. Before every performance there was a parade through the park, accompanied by Montfort's All-American Band. To encourage park patrons to dress for the masquerade, prizes were given for the most original single costume, the best costumed couple, and the most strikingly costumed group.

Fireworks went off every Sunday and Wednesday night. Scenes like, "Blowing the Kaiser Off the Earth," the Fox Trot Acrobatic Clowns, Jeweled Fan, Aurora Borealis, the American Flag, and the Battle on Land and Sea, all accompanied by Monfort's All-American Band.

The final picnic before Labor Day was held by the Knights of Pythias, on August 25. A picnic for family and friends was followed by games. Foot races for boys and girls, men's' peanut race, women's potato race, boys' shoe race, men's pillow fight on a wooden beam, tug of war, nail driving, and a fat people's race. Soldiers were in attendance; all sang songs into the evening and continued to sing on the trolleys heading back to Kansas City.

In 1918, 619 men were hired at the Standard Oil Refinery. One of them was my dad, John J. Olinskey. Another was his partner in crime, John "Pee-Wee" Pavola, One day when I was about ten and dad had a few beers, he told me how he and Pee-Wee Pavola and some other local delinquents disassembled a wagon and re-assembled it on the roof of a feed store on Halloween. A few days later, on November 1, he was hired as a water carrier at the refinery for 29 cents per hour. Standard Oil was a great place to work. In August the company offered a retirement plan, giving money to people after they reached the age of 50 for women with 30 years continuous service, and men 55, with 30 years' service. Also offered was disability insurance for anyone with more than ten years who was hurt on the job. If you didn't have ten years in, it was "See you in court."

The influenza closed the schools until November 13. The influenza killed few children or old people. Traced to pigs in Haskell, County, Kansas, at Camp Fungston, it was called the "Spanish Flu" because Spain, at the time, was the only country in the world not at war and had a relatively free press. The Spanish Flu effected the strong and came in waves, the first being mild. As it mutated it became more deadly, killing an estimated 675,000 Americans.

On a brighter note, after 1,564 days of killing, the war ended at 11:00 in the morning on the eleventh day of the eleventh month, now Veteran's Day. 53,000 Americans died of wounds, and 250,000 were wounded in only 200 days of combat and 13 major engagements.

Near Verdun, France, on November 11, was Captain Harry Truman, in command of Company D, 129th artillery, 35th Infantry Division, made up of men from Missouri and Kansas. He was a good officer and would be the Commander in Chief when Corporal Hitler blew his own brains out.

The celebrations started at 3:00 in the morning here, when every whistle and bell in the world started ringing and blew and rang all day. The Independence Square looked like Santa-Cali-Gon gone mad. All businesses closed. Prisoners were let out of jail. Rifles and pistols cracked. Parades were everywhere. Tin cans were dragged behind autos and bicycles. No one knew it, but the Roaring Twenties had just begun.

Chapter 26: 1919

One of the new sayings of post-war Europe was, "Shot while trying to escape," and it will be used a lot.

In January, President Wilson was in Paris for a peace conference. Upon hearing of the death of President Theodore Roosevelt, one hell of a good man and a pretty damn good president, Wilson merely smiled. All of the belligerent countries on the winning side were there. They won the war, but would lose the peace, the reason, six words: France, Italy, Wilson, England, Greed, Myopia. In England sixty-five thousand men suffered from "shell shock" caused by years under artillery fire, and would spend the rest of their lives in and out of hospitals, mostly in.

America had a similar problem. 200,000 men were seriously wounded. Many, like Charles Mallinson, would soon die of wounds. He was gassed. It is estimated that taking care of the wounded would cost more than the war. Veterans were paid between $65 and $100 a month in disability. Lots of government sponsored vocational programs were made available to the disabled.

Another problem, on May 3, the 129th Regiment entrained in Kansas City at Union Station. After the parade the uniforms were discarded, or sold cheap. Many non-veterans paid a dollar for a uniform, and dishonored them by going on crime sprees. After World War II, this problem was solved. Every discharged veteran's uniform received a patch called a "ruptured duck". Most everybody wanted one. Today, on eBay, a WWI uniform sells for $1000 or more.

To accommodate the coming boom in automobile traffic, road expansion and repair became the job of Jackson County. The first order of business was to repair the rock roads with a thin coating of oil to hold the rocks together and kill vegetation. Much of the rock was provided by the county Workhouse, prisoners breaking big rocks into smaller rocks. Twenty three men were hired by the county for the job, the job being to spread the gravel to repair the existing roads, eight more than last year.

Ed Smith was assigned to repair the Sugar Creek roads, while J. C. Farran was responsible for Mt. Washington. The men were paid $100 a month. The job lasted from April 1st until it snowed. Last year's bill to the county was $12,000. There were 400 miles of rock road in Jackson County.

In March the county court took an automobile ride from Sugar Creek to Cement City. All agreed that something had to be done. Bids were requested. A local crook with political connections, W. M. Spence, who had never built a road, came in cheapest at $32,000 to grade and rock the two miles by eighteen feet. Unfortunately, he ran out of rock, and to make it to Cement City he had to knock off several feet in width, so the road got skinnier the closer you got to Cement City, to the disappointment of the many who were counting on an easier way to get to work. Still the county began clearing for a road to connect Cement City with Atherton and the ferry at Liberty Landing. Two things the road was good for was dumping bodies and parking autos in the Missouri River. On May 12, Larry Lynch, and employee of Standard, saw something in the river. It was an automobile. He pulled it out and notified John Hayward, law enforcement officer. In August the body of a lady was pulled out, and later they also pulled out an automobile full of bullet holes. The car had been shot up by the Kansas City police.

The Riverview School graduating class of 1919 again had three; Elizabeth Hink, Helen Campbell, and John O'Connell. Col. E. M. Stayton, former commanding Officer of the 110th Engineers, spoke of World War One. Thirteen students advanced to the high school. Among them were Doc Hink and Dora Kominsky.

Fairmount Park opened on Sunday, May 17. One of the people who would have visited the park in 1919 was Walt Disney, born in 1901 in Chicago. When he was five, his family moved to a 48-acre farm near Marceline, Missouri. In 1910 he moved to Kansas City. During the war, because of his youth, Walt enlisted in the Red Cross and drove an ambulance in France. When the war ended he returned to Kansas City, where his older brother still resided. He worked for Kansas City Film Ad Service. Later he would start his own business, fail, and move to California, in 1923. He would, in the future, create Disneylands all over, i. e., super Fairmount and Electric Parks, memories from his youth.

Again this year, new amusements were numerous. There were 30 new concessions. Located on the north side of the park was "The Mammoth Mountain Speedway", claiming to be the longest ride in America. Several cars on tracks were hoisted to the top, which was 60 feet above the ground or so. Then gravity took over, the cars going up and down in a 360 degree circle, ending the ride on terra firma. Admission, 10 cents. Also new on the north side, behind the auditorium, was Puzzle Town, which featured games and rides like the Spinning Top: rotating in a counter-clockwise direction, like a large 33 1/3 record, it was a fight between gravity and inertia, inertia winning, throwing everyone off. The Crystal Maze was moved inside Puzzle Town.

Opening Day was the biggest ever, according to Sam Benjamin, manager. Many young men were seen in uniform. Some were real soldiers. The dance floor was enlarged, making it Kansas City's biggest. Haley's Orchestra was back with the addition of several new members, so was Montford's All-American Band. This is the same dance floor where Red Skelton will ply his trade in the near future. Both the Mountain Speedway and Puzzle Town had lines from 2:00 to 10:00 pm, sometimes a block long. The ponies for the kiddies was popular, games of chance like hitting "the baby" with a baseball could earn someone a box of matches or a ham. Once the weather warmed, around the first of June, Mr. Carlisle decided to open the beach for swimming at 6 am. Before the sun came up people were in the lake, luring even more picnics and money.

Also in June, was the wedding of Captain Truman and Miss Bess Wallace at the Trinity Episcopal Church, still on Liberty Street in Independence. Miss Wallace was a very popular bridge player, a game later played often at the Truman Home. She was also very active in the local Red Cross. Captain Truman's best man was Captain Theodore Marks. The church was decorated in local flowers. The altar was covered in daisies, pink hollyhocks, and pale blue lark-spur, which is poisonous if consumed. When asked where he was going to honeymoon, he replied, "North."

This is the year Mt. Washington received a gift, Mt. Washington Road, now Winner Road. Starting at Van Horn (Truman) Road, it ran along the trolley tracks by Washington Cemetery, adjoining the Kansas City road (Wilson Rd.) at a cost of $20,000 a mile.

The Fourth of July was hampered by rain, delaying the fireworks, and ruining many picnics. It was the safest in years. Hardly anyone hurt themselves and the fire department had nothing to do. The reason? No booze. But there were signs that things would change. In New York City people were having too good of a time to be sober.

At Electric Park fireworks, band concerts, and the Mid-Summer Review; vaudeville with acts like Miss Vera Howard, the Dancing Violinist, an act with more talent than you're bound to ever see on American Idol. Mr. Jack LaFollette, songster, Randall & Randall, some song, some dance, plus the sea beach and natatorium.

Because of the rain, the fireworks at Fairmount were delayed until Sunday, July 6. The Veterans of Foreign Wars held their first picnic. Longview Farm had a horse show. Association Park held boxing matches. Two actors pantomimed the boxing match between the world champion Jess Willard and Jack Dempsey in front of the Kansas City Post offices. A wireless hookup from Toledo Ohio allowed the actors to pantomime the fight blow-by-blow as it was happening.

Dempsey won in the fourth round, and would hold the world champion title until 1926.

The steamship Majestic made two trips from Downtown to Cement City and returned. The reason for not going any farther downstream was because of the huge horse-shoe then in the Missouri River. Swope Park had the usual stuff, including a World War One military trainer airplane, flown by a couple of WWI veterans. The plane would take off and fly around the city, dropping coupons. Sadly, the plane caught fire and crashed near a refreshment stand. The pilot was pulled out of the burning plane and rescued, but the mechanic, who was throwing the coupons, was killed.

There were a lot of strikes in 1919. Railroad, coal, Standard Oil of Sugar Creek. Mr. Rockerfeller was the richest man in the world. A share of Standard Oil stock cost over $700, six months pay. The trouble started in June, when the company announced the organization of an industrial relations board for its three refineries, Sugar Creek, Whiting, Indiana (near Chicago), and Wood River (near St. Louis). The object was for the employees with sixty days on the job to elect representatives. In effect, it was a union. Some of the concerns these men would face were hours of labor, wages, employment and working conditions, housing, domestic economics, living conditions, safety and accident prevention, sanitation, "health-works practice", method economics, and anything else the 1,600 employees could think of. There would be monthly meetings and an annual meeting chaired by the president of the company.

On June 16, most of the 1,600 employees of the Sugar Creek Refinery voted on 36 candidates. Only twelve were voted in. Water boys or anyone under the age of 21 had no vote.

In May, the 800 laborers requested a 7 1/2 cent raise, to 57 1/2 cents per hour, the union rate in Kansas City for laborers. On August 1, while George Moffit, the boss, was in Chicago, the employees struck. It was a wildcat that included helpers, water carriers, and men who worked the stills. With that, no gasoline was going to be made.

They met over at the bank building, and dispersed for homes in both Sugar Creek and Independence, and Kansas City. Groups of men were seen discussing the strike. August 2, a Saturday, the strikers met again above the bank, overflowing into the street. At 11 a.m., while the crowd milled about, a striker announced that Harry Hoffman, county marshal, had announced that the county would hire 100 men to guard the plant during the strike. W. L. Ware, business agent and strike leader, declared to the crowd, that if more than 100 men showed up, they should stop them.. The huge crowd approved. Only 30 men guarded the plant, with nothing to do. There was no violence.

Mr. Moffit replied that yes, inflation had raised the price of food, clothing, and just about everything else, by 78%, but the wages had increased by 138%. Besides, he argued, the union laborers in Kansas City worked 8 to 9 months out of the year, due to the weather, whereas Standard's laborers worked 12 months out of the year, allowing them to make more money. He also didn't offer any compromises. The company knew that kids would soon be going hungry.

The employees were now ignoring the advice of the Industrial Relations Committee, calling it a creation of the company, radicals were temporarily in control.

It wasn't long before there was dissention among the men. Many were tired of the strike, many went looking for new jobs. The refinery was shut down, the men who were the skilled laborers, carpenters, brick layers, etc., couldn't work because it was against union rules.

On Saturday, August 9, a vote was held above the bank over whether to continue the strike of Local 303. There were only 302 men who voted, out of 860, meaning 558 didn't care or were tired of the whole mess. The men were called by name and dropped a secret ballot in a box. When the votes were counted, 208 voted to continue the strike, 94 to go back to work. The next day Mr. Moffit again said that the company would not compromise. The payroll for the plant was $111,000, twice a month.

On Saturday night, August 16, at 11 pm, the strike ended. This time the vote was a lopsided 209 to go back to work, 23 to starve. The following Tuesday they returned to work. After a talk by a Mr. Gill (Gill Street), from THE UNITED STATES DEPARTMENT OF LABOR, he advised the men to go back to work pending a hearing of the Industrial Labor Relations Committee.

On August 29, the committee voted to give the men a 10% raise, or 40 cents a day, or 5 cents an hour. On hearing the news, Mr. Moffit replied that he had been given permission to increase the wages by 10% in Chicago. But the strike vote was taken while he was on a train heading back to Kansas City. In other words, had he flown in a Boeing 737, there would have been no strike.

Changes were made. Instead of just 12 members picked by employees, the company also picked 12 to present its interests in any further problems. One of the first things the committee did was to give approval for a company-wide magazine called the Standolind.

Meanwhile, back at Fairmount Park, Sunday and Wednesday had fireworks. Every night presented a different war hero's likeness. The first was French General Foch.

Every weekend day was potentially a record at the gate. In July swimming events were held in the morning. In the afternoon and evening Nancy Best Ruffner, an interpretive dancer took the stage at the bandstand. Homer Montford's All-American Band played off and on all day into the evening. On practically every day there was a good-sized picnic, like the Woodmen of the World, Retail Grocer's Association, and the Irish-American Society, all annual picnics for Fairmount Park.

Homegrown chickens were the main course. Fried, boiled, roasted or stewed. The hot weather of August packed the lake with swimmers. The noise of machines and laughter could be heard from a kilometer or more away.

Labor Day proved to be rather interesting this year, because of something called the Plumb Plan, the brainchild of a troublemaker named Glen Plumb. The railroad union had 20,000 members in 80 locals in the area. They ran the trains, that were usually on time. The Plumb Plan would turn the railroad over to the government, and the employees, so that the trains would never be on time again. The railroad union was for it, the Federation of Labor, or AFL, had its doubts. The split came because of the Plumb Plan. At first, two parades and picnics were a possibility because of the animosity. The parade part was worked out, but the railroad people went to Electric Park and the AFL to Fairmount, where 48,000 played and 2,000 more listened to speeches denouncing Bolshevikism, and debating the Plumb Plan, which lost.

Electric Park had the Commies, but there were only 500 including the unfortunate wives and children, or 1% of the Fairmount crowd. These were the radicals, and they were for the Dumb Plan. But it failed in Congress and everywhere else.

Even by today's standards, Woodrow Wilson was a poor president. On September 6 he stopped in Independence on his whirlwind tour of the Wild West, supporting his League of Nations. Soon he would have his fourth stroke, the first in 1896, then in 1906, and one in Europe earlier in 1919. His train pulled out from Independence at 7 am on his way for a parade and speech at Convention Hall. Very few people were there to shake his hand. One was Mrs. L. B. Elfea, who lived nearby. She said he looked fine. His next two strokes, one on the train, would do him in, and his league. His wife would soon be president.

The Sugar Creek Riverview School's second building got its start in August when a $50,000 bond issue was voted in, 67-0. Excavation had already begun, and will include a lunch room, auditorium, workshop in the basement, and I will throw a brick through a window and rob the science lab.

The do-gooders shut down all the pool halls in Sugar Creek. They'll get theirs.

The Standard Oil Band of Twenty-Five gave its first concert for Christmas. Mr. E. J. Cox is the leader. Mr. Moffit gave a pep talk and said there would be a concert twice a month. Mr. Moffit seems like such a nice man.

Chapter 27: 1920

"Beer is living proof that God loves us and wants us to be happy."
— Benjamin Franklin

"Here's to alcohol, the cause of — and solution to — all life's problems."
— Homer Simpson

On January 16 the Volstead Act, or 18th Amendment to the Constitution of the United States, became law. No alcohol consumption. The trouble started in 1862 when President Lincoln taxed liquor to raise money for the Civil War, thus making it legal. During President Grant's scandals the liquor people played a part, making the early Dries mad, with good reason. Making decisions while drunk doesn't always work out.

Since most teachers were ladies, and ladies didn't drink, children were taught in the school that alcohol led to sin, or worse. The Dries became numerous, especially in the rural areas, Methodists followed closely by the Baptists, were the most radical anti-alcohol. It became a duel between the country and the large urban mentality, or between the few and the many, the dries being inspired by Lenin, who did it with a few thousand followers.

Because of compromises the law was as full of holes as a "No Hunting" sign. First, three of the groups that opposed liquor got to keep theirs. The clergy got its wine, industry still produced industrial grade alcohol, doctors and pharmacists had access. A patient could be prescribed a pint of good whiskey every ten days, it would prove to be financially lucrative for all three.

Legally, a person could make the contraband but no one could sell it. Sears sold mail-order stills that produced a gallon a day for $7. The Dries got their opportunity with the Declaration of War in 1917. Because it took food to make beer, wine, and other spirits, the manufacturing of these commodities was temporarily suspended until the end of the war. The Dries and the people whose job it was to enforce the law naively thought that because Americans were, for the most part, law abiding citizens it was just assumed that everyone would just stop drinking because everybody would comply, only 1,500 Federal agents were hired to regulate 110,000,000 people, many of them hard-core alcoholics. The groups that supported the law 110% were the Ku Klux Klan and guys like Al Capone, the Dries were now in league with the devil.

The men coming home for the war were asked to vote on Prohibition, and the voted over 90% against it.

Fairmount Park opened on May 16, a cloudy, cool day. Too cold to swim, but with "New Attractions Galore" and "No Advance in Prices."

Fairmount's new attractions were the "Maggie Murphy" and the "Double Whirl." Electric Park's crowds were huge, between 25,000 and 30,000. Both Electric and Fairmount turned to Vaudeville. That was a sign of good financial times for the parks. Every couple of weeks the acts would change, mostly by changing lady dancers. Called, "The Fairmount Revue," a company of eleven headed by Earl Flynn and Eddie McLaughlin. They played the winter season dancing at the Orpheum theater where they were regulars, all vaudeville. There were two shows a day on weekends, 5:30 and 8:15, weekdays at 8:15.

The bathing beach opened on Memorial Day, George McMinn was Mr. Carlisle's manager. He slept on a cot on the second floor, above the men's dressing room, in the winter he also worked at the Orpheum, a member of Local 31 Stagehands. New sand, diving boards, and bathing suits awaited, along with new picnic tables, ovens, and free ice water.

There would be many picnics, some planned, some not, some large, some small.

The following was found in the Missouri Valley Room of the Kansas City Public Library. The author is unknown.

> "The dance hall, all open with the exception of the top ceiling, is the coolest place to 'step' in the city and deserves its large patronage. Haley's jazz orchestra has been engaged for the music and the management of the park states that this is the most expensive orchestra ever presented but Fairmount is determined to give only the best in every line and the way this orchestra can 'fox trot' or waltz makes even a 'non-performer' go through his paces.

> "James Kastetter has three rides, the Maggie Murphy, Double Whirl and Merry Widow Swing and is busy installing a new ride to be known as The Whirlpool. All of these rides are "putting it over."

> "Armer and Davis have the show 'The Honeymoon Trail' that is making lots of friends. Mr. Armer came here especially from Chicago for the installation of this attraction and the opening of the park early in May.

"R. C. Terrell has just finished putting a Silodrome and here races take place that are sure-enough thrillers and give the crowds all the gasps they want. Mr. Terrell also operates the Miniature Railroad.

"Ed Mayer is seen presiding over the Ingersoll Amusement Company ride 'The Mountain Speedway.' Congratulations Ed on getting away with the dough.

"Another Mr. Ed Maier, this time, has 'Over the Top,' another dandy ride that lets Ed wear 'the smile that won't come off.' But Ed naturally has a good disposition and most generally wears this smile. Mr. Ed Maier is the stage manager of the Grand Opera House here during the winter season.

"The Captive Airplane, Ferris Wheel, Shooting Gallery and Ten-Penets all belong to J. C. Hausamann, and you can always see an interesting number of people collected around these amusements.

"The Merry-Go-Round and Canals of Venice are owned equally by the Park and the Ingersoll Amusement Company and both manage to give good accounts of themselves.

"PuzzleTown, a park show, has been completely renewed, and 'you'd be surprised.'

"Henry Whitsell is captain of the cafeteria and 'drink emporium' and soda stand and 'believe you me' this is where the shekels are put away in the hot evenings, and Harry knows how to handle a crowd.

"R. C. Brown is voted the finest man at the park, by the younger generation at least. R. Brown has the best pony track ever put in at a park and has fifteen of the cutest Shetland ponies imaginable for the youngsters to 'take a spin around the park' and this is one place you can always find 'next.'

"The Whip riding device was to have delivered to Fairmount in time for the opening but on account of traffic congestion and shortage of cars this will not make its appearance in the park until July 4th, when it is 'absolutely promised.' Everyone likes "The Whip so we know this will go big.

"Last but by no means least, and perhaps should have started the list. Tyler and Howk and their string of fourteen concessions. These gentlemen are both well known to the Concession people the entire U. S. over and we have said a plenty when we just mention that all of these are doing nicely, thank you, and that there are many new ones in the lot. All the dolls, etc., used by these stands are manufactured by the H. S. Tyler Plant in K. C. George Howk is one of the most ardent supporters of the Showmen's Club of America and it was with his help that the organization was made such a complete success. But you all know George so 'nuf sed.'

"Mr. and Mrs. H. S. Tyler are the luckiest mortals. They are living right out at the Park during these summer months and have the only 'tent house' on the grounds. Just outside of the park is a large cottage colony where camping and outdoor life is enjoyed by Kansas Cityians, but this little tent owned and occupied by the Tylers is the nicest 'contraption' you can think of. It is a three room cottage, tent, with floors, windows, etc., and with the 'fly' over the top there is always air and consequently no stuffiness. Everything necessary for a well-conducted home is in this 'tent house' and Mr. and Mrs. Tyler can show their friends what real life is. The tent house is in a grove of trees, giving plenty of shade and Mr. Tyler drives each day to his factory in the city, leaving the car in the evenings right under the trees, a regular 'garage.'

"The special two days celebration will be put on by the park for July 4th and July 5th when the Martin Fireworks Company will present some new and novel features in fire.

"Mr. Sam Benjamin, who has managed Fairmount so successfully in the past few seasons is again at the helm and he can always be depended on to give the patrons everything new and different and is ably assisted by Mr. G. C. McGinniss, who is also the auditor. Mr. McGinniss was with Fairmount for two years previous to 1919 and then was away that season but is once more helping to take care of the fine big business Fairmount is doing these days. The picnic grounds have all been rolled and sodded and Mr. Benjamin has succeeded in booking a great many of the large picnics of the season.

"The children's playgrounds at Fairmount deserve a special mention. These are the largest and best equipped in the city, and everything for a child's pleasure, such as swings, sand piles, jumping rope, etc., etc., is here and this is one of the many reasons that Fairmount is chosen as picnic headquarters.

"Mrs. Walter Stanley's 'Over the Falls' is a real money getter and Mrs. Stanley is a charming and gracious addition to the cottage colony of Fairmount while Mr. Stanley is with the Wortham Show."

Al Carlisle tells me that he remembers some of these people. They were still at it in the late twenties. The rides, from time to time, changed their name, or with a different coat of paint, could be called, "new," but many were new, like the new Mountain Speedway ("Goes a Mile a Minute!").

The rain on the Fourth of July caused the giant, patriotic fireworks display to be postponed until July 17. On August 8, the Standard Oil of Sugar Creek refinery held the first of many annual picnics at Fairmount Park, "The Home of Picnics." Picnics, large and small, were the park's bread and butter. The largest was the Grocers' Picnic, over 30,000 came for the goodies. All the stores closed at noon. After a parade of forty bands and floats downtown, trolleys were boarded for the ride to the picnic at Fairmount Park.

Labor Day weekend was special in those days of unrest. Inflation was bad, unemployment was rising, and American farmers' goods were no longer needed in Europe, so prices dropped. The economy was headed into recession. To bring an end to Fairmount's most successful season, the park had the coolest Labor Day of Labor Days. Both the labor unions and the Kansas City American Legion posts met at Fairmount, the latter celebrating its second anniversary after being born in France.

After the two parades downtown, almost every trolley in town headed for Fairmount Park, loaded, and so was some of the people, as Prohibition was already breaking down. Motorists were asked to volunteer to drive the disabled veterans out to the park. Leading the parade from the Great Lakes Naval Base was the Great Lakes Naval Band. Pershing's own band from Camp Funston, now Fort Riley, Kansas, followed. Fairmount furnished several bands, and at the park they would all play from Tuesday till Sunday, many playing at the same time, till Sunday, September 12, the last day of the park's season.

Awaiting them at the park were some Army toys. One jumbo and two baby tanks, four 75mm "3-inch cannons," the same kind used by Captain Harry Truman and his boys, machine guns, and several tons of Army issued pyrotechnics. Tanks were set up by the twenty-six tank men, drivers and mechanics. There was a mess tent and a medical tent with a doctor, who was a captain. The commander of the First Battalion, Third Regiment, was Major E. W. Slusher. The tanks and grunts attacked the machine guns, who were well dug in. The machine guns also did a live fire, no one was hurt. The Navy took over the lake, blowing things up including some fish. Some Marines demonstrated a rescue mission, a recreation of "Night in Flanders, pistol flares, rockets, signal bombs, cannons, and small arms luminated the lake. When it was all over, manager Sam Benjamin was off to the East Coast to buy new park stuff for 1921.

Location, location, location, that's what the area just to the Kansas City side of Fairmount Park was. By 1920 businesses stretched west on both sides of the Independence road for over a quarter of a mile, and there was Mt. Washington just to the west of that.

Among the businesses were several grocery stores, meat markets, cafes, a garage specializing in Ford automobiles, a livery stand (cab stand), two drug stores, two hardware stores, a furniture store, a jewelry and optical store, a dry goods store, two coal yards, feed store, a lumber yard, a new motion picture theater, two barber shops, a real estate office, and in Mt. Washington, a bank called "The Commercial State Bank," the working capital was said to be $14,000. The president was M. J. Halpin, and whoever W. M. Halpin was, he was embezzling the money.

Technology that would soon change the way entertainment is enjoyed had its infancy at the home of G. S. Turner, Kansas and Pearl street, Independence. On a snowy night, January 13, about a dozen men met and formed "The Real Radio League of Independence." Among the members was Virgil J. McElroy. He was elected the secretary. They fiddled with a receiver and picked up signals from amateurs in Texas, Minnesota, Yonkers, NY, St. Mary's, Ohio, and Roswell, New Mexico.

Also in January the water in Independence started to taste a little oily. Standard was sued by the Independence Water Works for pumping the water directly into of the river a mile downstream. Standard's argument was that the water didn't belong just to the Water Works and if it couldn't drop its goodies in the Missouri River it would have to close, leaving 1,500 men without work, depriving the community of $200,000 a month in wages, depriving the world of 3,500,000 barrels of gasoline a year, and an investment of two and a half million dollars. A few weeks later, Standard was found to be the problem. But the real problem was taking the water directly out of the river. Liberty, Missouri, just to the north, had no problem. They had aquifers, 2/3 of the water in a river flows underground, only slower. In December Standard agreed to pay to relocate the Independence water intake upstream or pipe its pollutants downstream. The county finally agreed to allow Standard to put in a pipeline upstream.

A dry, hot summer up north dropped the level of the Missouri River four feet, below the intake of the Independence water company. Independence's ten thousand residents went without water for three days. A deal was worked out with nasty old Standard Oil, whose intake was still below the water level of the river. Standard, which had an excess of water, pumped its water into the Independence pipeline using its own labor and cost, saving Independence from becoming a ghost town.

Standard also paid to give adult citizens of Sugar Creek the opportunity to go back to school. About sixty people signed up to attend night school, Tuesday and Friday evenings in the Riverview School. Professor Harry Andrews from Northeast High School was hired by the Sugar Creek Board of Education. He was experienced in teaching the foreign-born the three "R's" and English. Many of the students had been highly educated in Europe and needed to work on their English. G. C. Chandler, a clerk at the refinery, was also a teacher. The motivation for many was to learn the language, important if you wanted to become a citizen.

For some time, the people of Sugar Creek, the village, wanted to become the City of Sugar Creek, meeting every Monday evening in the hall above the bank building. They were the Sugar Creek Improvement Association. On July 10, two attorneys had two different opinions as to whether it could be pulled off. One of them said no, because this area is too close to a first class city, Kansas City. John F. Thice, city counsel for Independence, said, "No problem." First, Kansas City is not a first-class city, it isn't even a second-class city. A few working days later, Attorney Thice, acting on behalf of the citizens of Sugar Creek, filed incorporation papers with the county court. Sugar Creek wasn't the only village/community that wanted to become a city. Many like Gilpen Town, Little Santa Fe, Courtney, Cement City, Fairmount, Mt. Washington, Maywood, Englewood, Wayne City, the list goes on and on, never made it. Standard Oil was worth a huge amount of money. Sugar Creek was falling apart. It needed improvements like sewers, running water, electricity, there were a lot of outhouses, the streets would wash out and Standard was tired of paying. The solution was, let the residents pay part of it. The refinery's tax money would come in handy. The refinery wasn't going anywhere; gasoline was in.

On November 14, the county court granted the petition for incorporation. Mayor for eight more years was H. R. Baughman, a supervisor at the refinery. City Clerk and Collector A. D. Woolridge, Marshal William Ginhart; Alderman First Ward, Frank Woodward; Alderman for the Second Ward would have been William Hollis, Jr., but he passed away at the Independence Sanitarium a couple of days before and was replaced by George Evenger. Third ward Alderman, Edward Lynn. Fourth Ward was F. H. Frisbey. Frank Ainsworth was the Treasurer. The first order of business was gambling. A petition was presented, signed by 165 local women who wanted all gambling outlawed, including punch boards, which were still legal in Independence. No gambling on pool, no booze,

140

no cards. Money was a problem. There wasn't any, as taxes weren't due until April. No one would be paid. The Board also appointed Frank Berkhart Police Judge; Dr. Charles E. Nixon, City Physician; City Attorney, Mr. Thice, of course. Regular elections will be held in April.

In December, Standard Oil employees were allowed to invest in a stock plan. For every dollar they invested, the company kicked in a buck towards the purchase of common stock, and gave them voting privileges. Buying a share might take a while, though, as the stock was $400 for one share.

Just before Christmas, Sugar Creek's River View School's $75,000 addition was opened to the public. The bond was originally $50,000 but it wasn't enough to finish the job, so they voted another $40,000, and were able to bring it in at $75,000. Entertainment was furnished by the students in the new 1,000 seat auditorium. Four classrooms, offices, and a gymnasium in the basement; it also connected to the first building. It will be open to the students after the holidays. The school employs ten teachers, led by F. M. Stephens, formerly of the Blue Springs School District.

Baby announcements like the one which spoke of the celebration over the baptism of tiny little Matty Butkovich, son of George, proved to everyone that Sugar Creek was still wet.

Chapter 28: 1921

"In Heaven there is no beer,
That's why we drink it here."
-- Popular Polka Song

In early January the new commercial bank of Mt. Washington, now located in Fairmount, closed. On the door was the following note:

This bank has been closed
by order of the banking
department of the state
and will not open until
further notice.

This was not good news to the 800 people who had entrusted their savings. The problem was Walter M. Halpin, who had taken $40,000 over a period of time, it's called embezzlement. Mr. Halpin also worked a bank in Melford, Missouri, a little east and south of Nevada, Missouri. Whenever anyone came in for a loan at the Mt. Washington bank, he also duplicated the loan in Melford, keeping half. I would imagine the word "lynching" was used by the crowd that gathered by the closed sign while the state and suckers tried to figure out what to do.

Dr. Gilmore was there, his job was chairman of the board, James Duncan, a deputy state bank commissioner from Kansas City, was chosen to sort things out. The bank was closed until mid-February. The town of Melford was fleeced, too, and never did recover.

The plan that was worked out was to sell stock in the bank and ask the customers not to make a run on the bank. They were also asked to sign a document stating that they would not withdraw more than 20% of their savings right away, and not to withdraw another 20% for six months and so on. The alternative was to lose everything, as there was no FDIC at that time. The bank was saved, and became Standard State Bank, now history.

On January 30, Mrs. Bertha Guinich of Sugar Creek was arrested by Sugar Creek's appointed city marshal, William Dindhart. Early in the day the marshal spotted a drunk carrying some illegal liquor. The guy said he could get the cop all he wanted. "Go ahead," said the marshal. He did, and Mrs. Guinich was busted. In her basement was three barrels of "White Mule," a kind of whiskey. She was immediately fined $500 and sentenced to one year in jail by Judge Fonda. This led to a 3 a. m. raid on a card game. Four men, Eli and George Mikulick, George

Stelenoch, and Mike Miller. $38 was on the table when they were so rudely interrupted. Didn't need a search warrant back then. Judge Fonda fined the men $11. This guy was a little too gung-ho.

Because of post-war deflation, Standard Oil of Indiana cut the wages of all its employees by 10%, effective February 16. The 1,800 employees were paid from $5 a day for laborers to $8 a day for skilled labor for an 8-hour day. Company men received from $160 to $275 a month. Everyone was affected, to make it fair. When announced, a meeting was held at Bryant Hall in Fairmount. Hundreds attended. Bricklayers, carpenters, painters, and electricians debated whether to walk or work. The Kansas City Builders' Trade Council favored a strike as the cut would put the various crafts below union wages in town. It would also set a precedent. Only 100 picked up their tools and walked. The rest went to work after a few days. Mr. Moffitt declared that if the remaining strikers didn't return to work by Saturday they would lose their seniority and be replaced. All but 8 were there Saturday morning. Standard's second strike again ended in the company's favor. Oil was $2 a barrel.

On Tuesday, February 15, the new city of Sugar Creek held its first election. On the ballot was adding 12 twelve electric street lights to the ten already in place. Kansas City Power and Light supplied the electricity; the city bought the poles and lights. The measure passed 82 - 34. This gave the city council permission to sign a 10-year contract for the power.

A jitney driver with a big mouth caused another booze bust in Sugar Creek towards the end of February. Boys were caught drinking wine by County Marshal John L. Miles. After questioning the driver, he took them to the house where one of the deputies bought a quart of wine for $1.25. Arrested was Pellegrino Rossi, and the owner of the house was also arrested. The wine was made from grapes grown on the property. 200 gallons was seized. The men were fined $50 each and some of the wine, which was really good, was given to the local hospital. The remainder was to be destroyed by being turned into human urine.

In February the local phone companies were consolidated by the Kansas City Phone Company. The Fairmount business district was the hub. Business lines were $4.50 per month, home phones $2.25; two-party lines, $2; four-party line, $1.75, great for nosy people. Extra phones, business, $1 per; residents, $.75, rural party line, business, wall phone, $2.50. Resident wall phone, $2. A desk phone was an extra quarter. Calls between Fairmount, Sugar Creek and Independence were free, up to three minutes. Calls to Kansas City were a nickel for the first three minutes.

Ballard Todd, 16, had a good job. Every morning he drove a Model T to the Sugar Creek depot to pick up the U. S. mail from the 9:30 Santa Fe train. On March 5, four Italian gentlemen in a large Chandler machine (all autos were then called machines). They forced young Todd off the road, brandishing 45s. They took two mail sacks and drove off, heading toward Kansas City. In the sacks, they thought, was the payroll for the Standard Oil employees. They were spotted by Constable Howard Ainsworth on his motorcycle. He gave chase but a few well-placed rounds from the 45's caused him to dump his bike and pray. Later that afternoon, rumor spread that the bandits, having missed the payroll by one day, were very angry, and now they were going to rob the bank of either Sugar Creek or Mt. Washington. Police were sent to Mt. Washington, but at the Sugar Creek bank there were enough deputized citizens with weapons to hold off the French Army.

The auditorium at the Riverview school was getting used regularly, with concerts by the Standard Oil Band playing marches and patriotic music. The Red Cross of Sugar Creek and Mt. Washington held a dance there Saturday night, April 2. 200 attended. A one-hour concert by the Standard Oil Band, followed by refreshments, followed by a piano solo for dancing, for the Standard Oil Band was forbidden by the company to learn any dance numbers. $90 was raised, a good time for a good cause, admission was 50 cents.

Many of the children attending the Sugar Creek school were underweight or malnourished. 125 of the 375 students were so diagnosed by the Red Cross, just the opposite of now. There was no cafeteria; children had to bring their own lunches. Some parents could only afford to give their kids an apple or an onion. The local Red Cross began providing milk to the children. At 10:30 every morning, milk was served along with two crackers. Those who had no pennies for the 1/2 pint got it free. Sounds a lot like poverty.

On a brighter note, the newly minted city of Sugar Creek held its first major general election in April. For mayor, Boehmer, Republican, refinery hot-shot, beat Charles Choat, Independent, by 141 votes. Lee Norman, Democrat, beat R. M. Davenport by 38 for marshal. G. W. Evinger received the most votes for councilman, and won a two-year term, Frank Woodward, second in vote-getting, received one year. Edward Lynn and F. H. Frisbee won the Second Ward. George Rodman received 107 votes, but it was not enough for a show. The first order of business was to dig a culvert along Carlisle Road at a cost of $200. The road was already called Carlisle because it led to Mr. Carlisle's lake.

It was brought to the attention of the county authorities that something strange was going on at the pool hall at Cement City. Upon undercover inspection, it was noted that the three pool tables had no felt. There were only three balls on the front table and the closest cue ball was in Sugar Creek. On payday, April 29, six county policemen entered the pool hall, guns drawn. Knives, cards, dice, and corn whiskey were found. 43 men were wasting their hard-earned money, but having fun doing it. 4 were arrested and fined $50 each. The pool hall was then shut down by Judge Fonda.

In May the city of Sugar Creek was wealthy. Land values in the town of 1800 were $5,000,000, thanks to the oil refinery. The total value of Independence with 10,000 people was $11 million. The city wanted running water and sewers now, and they could afford it.

Fairmount Park opened on Saturday, May 14. Record opening day crowds packed the park. Although the lake was not open to swimmers, the warm weather made it tempting. Picnickers were everywhere again. New tables, ice water, more fireplaces with firewood were furnished. More parking, new concessions, "101 New Novelties", Homer Montfort's band gave concerts at 2 pm and 8 pm. Electric's crowds were also large. They would have witnessed The Follies, a vaudeville show in the new Pasaic Pavillion, no admission. Oscar V. Babcock and his Leap of Death. The Alligator Boy in the Swimming Pool with 34 well fed alligators. In the evening, dining and dancing was in. "The Midsummer Frolics," music and cocktails in the Silhouette Garden with a jazz band.

On Decoration Day, when the beach at Fairmount opened, it was packed. Many just hung on the ropes separating the swimming areas from the boating and fishing areas. The beach had again been enlarged, with 75 boats and hundreds of new bathing suits, a new locker room, and several new diving boards of different heights. Because of the crowds, hundreds lined up.

On June 17 the Mason's put on a huge picnic for Kansas City's less fortunate children. Kids from Boy's Hotel, Children's Hotel, Evans Home, Interdenominational School, Spofford Home, Scottish Rite Home for Crippled Boys, McCune Home, Jackson County Girls' Home, and from Kansas the Chidren's Home, Life Line Mission, and Menonite Chidren's Home, all of Kansas City, Kansas.

The festivities started Downtown at 12:30. A parade by the Masons and the children ended by everyone driving out to Fairmount Park in private automobiles furnished by private citizens, that being a parade of sorts. Once at the park, the children were given popcorn, peanuts, Cracker Jacks, and lemonade, and free tickets for the many rides, with a concert by William Roy's DeMolay Clown Band at 6 p.m. Free ice cream and other goodies was followed by an auto ride back to town. They got everything except into the lake.

By now fifty organized picnics had been held, and there would be more than 100 before the end of 1921. The week before the Fourth, four picnics were scheduled: The Mount Washington Blue Lodge of Masons, Chapter of the Eastern Star, Good Fellowship Club of Kansas City, and the Employees of the National Zinc Company. In the children's playground, a large herd of trained Shetland ponies and a troop of monkeys had been added. The beach had never been more popular. At night, the band shell showed photo plays, cheaper than any vaudeville act, they being short silent films that started early in the evening.

The Fourth of July was picnic day. No balloon ascensions or vaudeville, which cost money. Sporting events in the lake and on the ball diamond took up the daylight. There was no room for big company picnics; they would have to wait. Paine's Fireworks Company provided the pyrotechnics. People were encouraged to view the display, free of charge, on the knoll east of the lake between the railroad tracks and Fairmount avenue. The coins they dropped may still be in the ground. Between numbers by the band in the dance pavilion, "Grottos" were held, a kind of treasure hunt.

After the Fourth there was a large picnic almost every day, sometimes two. One was by the unemployed Veterans of the Great War. By the end of the year, there would be 600,000 of them. In the end they would get screwed real good. The First of August brought gas balloon racing back, temporarily. A three-balloon race had to be cancelled because rats ate holes in the balloons. Labor Day at Fairmount Park again started downtown. 15,000 union men, representing 20 crafts and 80 unions, led by bands. First came the building trades, carpenters and plumbers, then the railroad people, followed by the industrial trades, amusement crafts (like stagehands), more bands, metal workers, printers, more bands, electricians marched last, followed by a band.

James A. Reed was the featured speaker, followed by hours of others. Meanwhile, the park put on a party. A tongue-in-cheek celebration of sobriety, as in John Barley-corn, the devil of alcohol consumption. Balloon races and fireworks were part of the corn festival, and would close out the season at Fairmount Park. Customers were encouraged to wear their country worst. Prizes were given to those who took the dressing down to extreme. Roving judges dressed as farmers gave out the awards. Upon entering the park, everyone was given a noisemaker of some sort, so all week the park was full of nauseating sounds, horns and bells drowning out the roving minstrel bands and serenaders. Various paper hats were part of the end of the season.

This year the beach part of the lake had over 125,000 paying customers, not including the boaters, fishermen, and midnight skinny dippers. It was a record. Cool weather caused the lake to shut down early, as expenses were high. Ever morning chlorine was sprayed on top of the lake. The laundry bill was said to be $1,000, plus people had to be paid.

Electric Park put on a Mardi Gras, with nightly band concerts and awards for the most grotesque costumes. There were confetti battles, and Hugo the Highdiver diving from a 100 foot tower into a small net. Electric Park was where the Negro unions held their labor day celebrations.

Not only did some of the Sugar Creek children suffer from malnutrition, they had the highest trachoma rate in the state. In 1913 legislation was passed to stamp out the degenerative eye disease which, untreated, turns eyelids inside out, cutting up the eye ball, causing blindness.

Backed by the Red Cross, on June 15, Doctor William H. Schutz, an eye specialist from Kansas City, talked to parents in the school auditorium. Because of the obvious problem, the whole town got behind solving it, which was caused and spread by dirty hands and faces, i. e., lack of proper hygiene. The mayor and city council signed on, along with the Sugar Creek Red Cross, the School Board, PTA, and the Sugar Creek Improvement Association. After four weeks of weekly exams, it was determined that out of the 242 students examined, 49 out of 242 students examined had trachoma and were in need of treatment. Ten needed operations. Cement city had yet to be examined, and there was fear that it may also be rampant there. The disease is no longer a problem, the last cases in America being in the early 1950s.

The election of Lee Norman, Sugar Creek Marshal, was questioned after he was caught in a sting operation at Fairmount Park. It had been reported to Major Miles, County Sheriff, that someone passing as a police officer was patrolling the park after hours and hassling the people spooning. Park security claimed ignorance. Park management said that it wasn't happening. Officer R. C. Phipps, deputy County Marshal, went with his girlfriend to the park. At about 1 o'clock in the morning, while spooning on a park bench, they were approached by a man carrying a badge. After apologies, the man with the badge was offered a $10 bribe by Marshal Phipps. When accepted, Officer Phipps pulled his pistol and placed Marshal Norman under arrest. Norman grabbed for the weapon and was shot in the shoulder. Before going to the hospital, he was identified as Marshal Norman, newly elected Sugar Creek marshal, out of his jurisdiction. After getting out of the hospital, he was arrested for impersonating a police officer and released on $500 bond, probably paid for by the city. He was finally acquitted by a jury after his defense cited a state law that allows small city cops to protect the land around said town. The county wanted to charge him with bribery, but nothing ever came of it.

1921 was not a good year for the area's major employers, Portland Cement and Standard Oil. First, after the Standard Oil strike, the company laid off about 600 employees. In July, Portland shut down for two months because of a glut of finished cement with nowhere to go. 200 of 300 were unemployed. In August, Standard Oil laid off another 400, bringing the workforce to between 500 and 600. The reduction wasn't limited to the Sugar Creek refinery, but throughout Standard Oil (of Indiana). At Sugar Creek, 80 of the 100 stills were shut down. Mr. Moffitt said every day now seems like a Sunday. Luckily, all my relatives remained on the payroll.

A $120,000 water and sewer bond was passed in Sugar Creek. Because even after the Standard Oil cuts, the town was still financially well off. The school was holding night classes for 24, mostly males. They were taught English and the basics of business. The school also had a new 40' x 70' gymnasium and basketball court. Movies were shown in the auditorium every Saturday. In the school, the main curriculum for girls was what then called the "domestic sciences". The boys were taught trades like shoe repair, besides wood shop.

In Germany, and American Army Captain of the occupation, asked a 4-year-old boy what he wanted to be when he grew up. "I want to be a soldier and kill the French," was his reply. On a brighter note, Harry Truman was going broke. He hawked everything on a Downtown Kansas City haberdashery, trying to compete with the big chain stores. He had a great location, Twelfth and Main, right across the street from two illegal saloons. One day Jim Pendergast walked in the store to encourage Harry to run for office. In Jackson County there were two factions, the goats and the rabbits. 1922 will be an election year, and Harry Truman is a goat.

Chapter 29: 1922

On January 1, 1922 there were four radio stations licensed with the Commerce Department, headed by Secretary of the Commerce Herbert Hoover. By the end of the year there were almost 600. Kansas City had four, Independence one.

WPE, later KLDS, was run by the Reorganized Latter Day Saints church in Independence. On Sunday, June 14, Elder E. D. Moore broadcast from the Stone Church from 8:00 to 8:45 p. m. There were only 200 receivers in Kansas City then, but the signal was heard as far away as Ft. Worth, Green Bay, Memphis, and Boulder, Colorado. Reverend Moore's message was "Main Street Religion" and was well received to the point that every Sunday evening there will be religious and gospel music coming over the airwaves. Arthur B. Church was the brains behind the station, and in 1927 he would change the station to KMBC out of Kansas City. The Kansas City Star also had a station. They broadcast live concerts from their offices.

The third station of importance was WHB, owned by W. M. Sweeney, also owner of an auto mechanic's school. A courageous broadcaster in a time of the Ku Klux Klan, he offered a lot of diversity in his broadcasts. Many of the better singing groups were African American. It was a time when stations with only a few hundred watts could be heard all over the USA. He broadcast African American, Mexican, and Hawaiian talent, including Protestant and Catholic Sunday services from various churches. Kansas City had two other radio stations, neither of which seemed to have much impact.

Tragedy struck students of Sugar Creek school on May 16, when six-year-old Augylene Detel stopped by little Alphonse Novak's house to swing after school. Lightning struck a tree, sending thousands of amps down the wire rope tied to a tire, killing little Augyene instantly. Alphonse lived, although he was left with a speech impediment that didn't allow him to communicate well in English for the rest of his life. Unless, of course, he thought that you were trying to get his cans or bottles, then he spoke perfect profanity.

The following day was the last day of school. Sixteen "Creekers" graduated (the nickname Sugar Creek residents had adopted for themselves). Two won a $5 gold piece. The Daughters of the American Revolution offered the prize to a senior boy and girl who wrote an essay on "Why We Salute the Flag." School let out at noon on that Wednesday. At 2 p. m. all students, teachers, and parents gathered at the schoolhouse and marched to Fairmount Park for their annual picnic.

Fairmount Park opened on May 13, a week before Electric Park. There were fifty concessions this year, many were new. Haley's Orchestra played in the newly-named Venetian Ballroom, complete with a crystal ball. Large shade trees, flowers, shrubs and many, many birds inhabited the park. The big, new ride was the "Auto Raceway," twelve tracks with twelve gasoline motor-driven midget autos. New diving boards were installed on the lake, but would not be used until "Decoration Day."

The following Saturday Electric Park opened at 6:00 p. m. A new ride, the $300,000 Giant Dipper, made a circuit around the park, having sixteen big dips, some more than seventy feet high. A new cafeteria was opened in "The Garden," chicken dinners were the specialty of the house.

The latest in ladies' swim wear was finally showing the knees.

Decoration Day at Fairmount featured Captain Hugo, who dove off of a 102-foot ladder into a small net twice a day, at 5 and 9 p. m.

Motion pictures were shown in the bandstand. It cost ten cents to get into the park, children under 12 free. There was also the back gate, that's where all the Creekers got in.

On June 10, 15,000 Oddfellows of Jackson and Wyandotte counties, and the women's auxiliaries, picnicked at Fairmount Park. The Oddfellows started in England in 1743 and crossed the big pond in 1819 or so. They got their name because it started as a kind of union for people with unusual trades. They, like the Shriners, try and help the less fortunate. A basket and blanket dinner was served at 6 p. m., followed by a concert of the Oddfellows Jazz Band. P. A. McIntosh announced that a "Corn Carnival" would be held by the Oddfellows Labor Day weekend at the park.

On one day there were eighteen separate picnics at Fairmount Park. The bathing beach was the main draw. Manager Benjamin said that there were 5,000 bathers every day of the week. Some arrived at 6 o'clock in the morning to take a dip, then cook a breakfast over the many fireplaces, wood and ice cold water were everywhere.

On the Fourth of July both major parks threw a party. At Electric Park, carpenters built wooden frames for "set piece fireworks" all the way around the perimeter of the park. Starting with six bombs, next a grand illusion around the water, an array of cascades and "spinners," "The Salamander", "World in Rotation," "American Beauty Rose", "Niagara Falls", a bell between a land battery and two ships to be sunk, and, sadly, the "Negro Being Chased by a 20-ft Illuminated Alligator".

Fairmount Park was packed on the Fourth. 40,000 + watched Fairmount's "set piece fireworks" display. People completely circled the lake, some of them 100 feet away from the water. 3,500 picnickers were counted by 5 p. m. People actually stayed out of the water to enjoy the activities on terra firma, like dancing.

The city of Kansas City banned the sale and use of any fireworks, because of the fires and mayhem sometimes caused by small sticks of dynamite. That didn't stop the sale and use of fireworks outside the Kansas City limits. This would have included the entrance to Fairmount Park. Only one serious injury occurred in the area and no fires, a big change from years past.

Sam Benjamin, manager of Fairmount Park announced that after the Fourth, until the close of the park, there would be a massive fireworks display every Sunday night. Sam's stock rose as he thought of new ways to promote the park. Four Shetland ponies were given away every Wednesday in August. Acts like the dozen or so attractive lady divers, dressed in the latest bathing suits, lady daredevil motorcycle riders circled in a cage. Flapper revues where girls with bobbed hair were allowed free entrance, and cash prized were given in the ballroom every Friday night. There was also the famous Choy Linghe's Troop of Chinese Acrobats.

On Thursday, August 10, the grocers held their annual picnic at Fairmount. 25,000 grocers, their families and freeloaders scrounged the park for the many freebies. The water was not the place to be. No one ever left a grocers' picnic hungry. Besides free rides and ice cream, the Miller Automobile Company brought some free samples for people to drive around the park. A hill climbing exhibition was popular. There were many games with prizes. And almost everyone received a one-pound sack of flour. Rationed during the war, the bottom fell out of farm prices because of the surplus of everything, sticking the farmer with products he couldn't give away, rendering some broke.

Labor Day was unusually mellow, although someone called the governor a name not in any dictionary at that time. Next year the new Fairlyland Park will steal Sam Benjamin.

In the 1920s Kansas City, with a population of 325,000, was a small version of Chicago, without the extreme violence. Open saloons, prostitution, and gambling were wide open. It was said that people would come from Chicago and St. Louis for a sandwich because it was the only place where you could buy a sandwich and a cold beer that was served by a completely nude lady for $1. The county around Kansas City, for the most part, abhorred that kind of living.

While Adolph Hitler was busy taking control of the Nazi Party, the Ill Duce took control of Italy. The guy who would bring their whole nightmare scenario to an end not of their liking was barely elected a 38-year-old judge. Held in the Democratic party primary, Harry Truman, now a major in the National Guard, won by 300 votes in a race of five, with him being the only candidate under the age of 50. Problems arose on Election Day in Fairmount where goons were reported to be headed to the polls in that direction, a common practice locally. Major Miles, county sheriff, got the word and sent two deputies to protect Fairmount voters from the Shannon machine's treachery; the rabbits were scared off.

Harry's speeches were pretty much the same. "A Day's Work for a Day's Pay," "No More Macadam Roads"... they were good for the Romans and the early Americans, but not today, today being 1922. It's oil and gravel. The whole county could be paved this way on the cheap. He didn't really like to give speeches to large groups of people. He preferred to hop in his Dodge coup, bounce around the county roads, and talk to the farmers. They were an easy sale. Later, he defeated the Republicans by 3,000 votes.

The Portland Cement Company of Kansas City built a school near Cement City for forty children of employees. It also had another murder.

No such trouble in Sugar Creek. On Tuesday, August 29, the businessmen and Standard Oil took out a full page ad in the Independence Examiner:

SUGAR CREEK NOW A CITY.
Comfortable Homes, Good Schools,
Up to Date Stores.

One of Sugar Creek's first businessmen, Harry Kamensky, came here in 1904 and still ran the oldest business in town, United Merchandise Company. He came to America from Poland in 1896. Another old timer, who had just sold his grocery store to his sons, was A. J. Mossie. The first thing they did was build a new brick 35x70' building. Sirloin steak, 30 cents a pound; chuck roast, 15 cents a pound; 100 lbs of flour, $3.85; twelve 3-lb cans of peaches, $2.75. F. W. Ainsworth ran the dry goods store and post office. R. L. Bennett owned the Standard Furniture Company: "New and Second Hand Goods Bought, Sold, and Exchanged. Also Undertaking and Embalming." Mrs. Rose Pitzer just sold her Standard Hotel and bought a general store and confectionary, complete with a soda fountain and all sorts of candies. Mate Butkovich arrived in Sugar Creek, getting out of Europe just before the war. He found work at the refinery, and built a home with a grocery and meat business. The town mechanic was R. M. Davenport. W. H. Palmer fixed shoes. Badger Lumber Company had many stores in the Kansas City area, one of the largest being in Sugar Creek. Other businesses were W. H. Coleman, grocery store, Standard State Bank, People's Hardware, and the Missouri Beverage Company. $100,000 worth of bonds had just been approved to hook up to the Kansas City Water District. Independence was downstream from Standard Oil, and the people of Sugar Creek didn't want to drink it thus they hooked up with Kansas City.

A joke going around Sugar Creek claimed that a man walked into town and inquired about the price of land. "200 gallons an acre," was the reply. The bluffs on both sides of the Missouri river teemed with stills, hidden by the rugged vegetation and vertical topography. City Marshal Lee Normon, a former employee of Standard Oil, was more concerned with the twelve mile an hour speed limit coming down the hill. But Lee had problems of his own. In November his wife sued him for divorce, claiming that he was taking more than just bribes.

Sports became an obsession with many of the employees. The many departments formed baseball teams, thus a plant league. Basketball courts were erected on plant property. The company furnished instruments and uniforms for a 30 piece band. Horseshoe tournaments were played even in the snow. Boxing was popular. Mr. Welch boxed 20 year old Pee Wee Pavola's ears. But Pee Wee would learn, and become a force to be reckoned with. They were tough men. Every issue of the Standolind included news about what was going on with the plant, its people, and the community, including this advice: Kansas City was no longer safe at night. A person might have to walk back from KC without a car. Standolind brought news about the many nice homes that were being built. The Beal residence on Chicago was at one time the nicest home in Sugar Creek. Many of the same names appear in the publication regularly. Either they were really popular or idiots.

1923 will bring another fun spot to Kansas City.

Chapter 30: 1923

In 1900 Sam Brancato, an Italian blacksmith, arrived in the United States. After the 1903 flood, Sam dug through the sludge. Besides a lot of dead cows, he found $300 worth of treasure, whence he bought a grocery store, and played the stock market real well. By 1920, he was a neat guy with a lot of money. He decided to build an amusement park out south to funnel his entrepreneurial juices.

He first proposed to build it close to Swope Park, but the locals were having none of it. He finally purchased 89 acres at 75th and Prospect Avenue. The next thing was to find the best man to run it. Sam Benjamin of Fairmount Park was he.

On June 9, 700 people, some friends, VIP and the 300 locals who also invested in the million dollar project, were given a freebie. The money was well spent. 40 acres of grass and trees were set aside for picnics and, like Fairmount, had free ice water. Parking for 10,000 autos, 5,000 feet of gravel walkways, refreshment stands, the Sky Rocket, a 5,000 ft roller coaster with 32 dips, the Whip, the Dodge-Em, the Butterfly, the Caterpillar, a big Ferris wheel, Fun Land, miniature railroad, children's playground, band concerts. The wooden dance floor, which had a capacity of 2,000 and was 118 feet by 300 feet, roughly the size of a football field, took a lot of trees. Pony track, merry-go-round, goat track, shooting gallery, billiard hall, and a swimming pool that was still under construction.

A week later, the gates were thrown open to the public. Management hoped for 40,000, but the 30,000 that showed still caused a traffic jam. The trolley line ended at 72nd street, and buses were provided from there to the park, unless, of course, you wanted to walk the three blocks. Sam Benjamin, general manager, said it would be several weeks before all of the finishing touches would be complete. As Fairyland's general manager, one of Sam Benjamin's jobs was to book picnics. After the grand opening of Fairyland, it was announced that the biggest and best picnic in town, being the Grocer's picnic, had been booked at Fairyland for August 9. 40,000 were expected, a major boost for the new park, the rat.

By then, Fairmount and Electric parks were already going strong. Improvements were being made in both parks.

Electric spent money, too. A boardwalk, patterned after Atlantic City, which includes the "New Follies". The picnic grounds were enlarged and electric heating plates for cooking were installed. New were a pony track for the kiddies, the "Big House", Sea Planes, and professional divers.

Fairmount's new manager was A. P. McGinnis. $150,000 had been spent on the park, most of it building a new roller coaster called, "The Big Dipper." At 5,372 feet of track, with a dozen dips, one 86 feet, in excess of 60 miles per hour. Not only was it the longest in town and called, "The World's Longest," it only took about a minute or two to ride. It was the most dangerous, and the lines were long. There was also a new Ferris wheel. The dance hall had been re-named the "Venetian Ballroom", featuring a mirrored ball that rotated, splashing beams of light through the dancers, 50 years before Disco.

Although Fairyland was taking picnics, there were plenty to go around. Also, Fairmount had been there for a long time. Some of the kids were third generation Fairmount Park fans, and loved the place. The lake was still the main attraction; it was simply the best place in town to swim or fish. Ride, swim, dance, boat.

Fairmount Park was still the "Home of Picnics." On Saturday, May 26, the park hosted the Kansas City Parent/Teachers picnic. To the students, this could be compared to the Fourth of July and Christmas. Kids started arriving at 7 a. m., but weren't allowed in the park until the adults arrived. The ladies arrived dressed in white dresses trimmed in red with large red hats which could be seen over the children's heads, or a kilometer away. The chow arrived in baskets lugged by ladies and gentlemen, also dressed in white and red. Free hot dogs, ice cream, popcorn and drinks were served until the kids had more than enough. Ropes divided off the different school districts covering the picnic grounds. At 9:30 the Boy and Girl Scouts, Girl Reserves, and Camp Fire Girls marched in revue at the athletic/ball field. Lunch baskets were served and by 12 o'clock noon, 25,000 people had entered the park and the day was still young. The trolley cars going back to Kansas City were going to be empty for a while.

After lunch, competitive events between the schools were held. Garfield and Norman schools tied for First. First prize was a trophy. Prizes for the individual boys for various sports included baseballs, bats, gloves, tennis rackets, belts, hats, Kewpie dolls and handkerchiefs. Mayor of Kansas City, Frank Cromwell, was the guest of honor and gave a short speech. Eight special street cars carried many of the picnickers. The parking lot was full. Boy Scouts were employed in the afternoon, matching missing children with their mothers, whether the kids wanted to be found or not. Manager McGinnis's employees counted a total of 60,000 tickets to enter the park. He also donated half the money collected at the gate after 6 p. m. to the organization, in hopes that they'd be back next year.

The weekend before July Fourth, the WWI Veterans held their annual picnic at Fairmount Park. The talk again this year was the so-called Federal Bonus. Missouri and several other states had already paid the men between $65 and $100. Many people were against it, including people in the government like Andrew Mellon, Secretary of the Treasury, and the third richest man in the United States, behind Rockefeller and Ford.

The summer of 1923 in Kansas City reeked of fun. Besides the three amusement parks, Electric, Fairyland, and Fairmount, there were dozens of lakes and streams that no longer exist. For the fisherman or swimmer, the two Blue Rivers actually had water in them, with fish. Golf was very popular locally. The sport started in Scotland in the 1400s. Claims that it was started by men with wooden clubs knocking round rocks in rabbit holes. The first US course was in Wheaton, Illinois, just west of Chicago, in 1893. From 1923 until 1930 Bobby Jones won 5 amateur US Opens, three British Opens, and five British Amateur, and 4 USA Opens. Swope Park links was the most popular in the city, the club having 500 members. In addition there were a dozen courses in and around Kansas City: Oakwood, Blue Hills, Mission Hills, Kansas City Country Club, Lockwood, Hillcrest, Meadow Lake, Ivanhoe, Milburn, Crestwood, and Shawnee Heights being the most recent to open. The word "GOLF" is said to be an acronym for "Gentlemen Only, Ladies Forbidden."

The Kansas City Athletic club moved into their new 22-story facilities at 11th and Baltimore in 1923, in a building that stood 263 feet high. The KCAC started at Fairmount Park around the turn of the century, and when the park closed in '02 they moved to the future location of Electric Park. In 1906 they moved again to Central Street, paying $60,000 for the building and grounds, and $16,000 for the equipment. The club's new kitchen was one of the finest and largest in town. The main dining hall seated 450 persons. There were six other dining rooms, seating between 40 and 400. Other athletic clubs across the country sent their emblems to be displayed. Represented were the following clubs: The Missouri Athletic Club, and the Athletic clubs of St. Louis, Los Angeles, Olympia, San Francisco, Minneapolis, Illinois, Chicago, Milwaukee, and Omaha.

Tennis's popularity was increasing, with public tennis courts going up all over town. Boating was popular. The most popular river was the Blue, at 15th Street, where the boat house was. Motor boats, canoes, and row boats crowded the Blue to the Missouri River.

But the most popular outdoor sport was baseball. Greater Kansas City was the home to 400 amateur and semi-pro baseball teams. Two pro teams, the Blues and Monarchs. Although illegal, Muehlebach beer built a baseball stadium at 22nd and Brooklyn Avenue by George Muehlebach, hometown Beer Baron. Called

Muehlebach Stadium, it opened on July 3rd and seated 17,500, and was the home of the Kansas City Blues.

Like San Francisco, New York City, Chicago, and New Orleans, Kansas City was considered a "wide-open town", which meant that if you were new to town and wanted to get a drink, you would just ask a cop. A dollar here would get you a cold, 12-oz draw of Michelob and a marijuana cigarette, served by a young lady dressed only in a thin sheet and who might just sit on your lap. The object: prostitution.

On the Fourth of July the three amusement parks had the usual fare, topped with a night of fireworks, and thousands attended, taxing the trolleys to the max. The baseball game at Muehlebach Stadium was sold out, but the most popular thing in town was the auto races. At the end of Troost, way out in the country, now called 95th Street, the Kansas City Speedway was built. The oval mile track had a wooden surface. Indianapolis was called The Brickyard. This would have been called the Woodyard, wood being cheaper than brick. 60,000 race fans were crowded into an area built to hold 40,000. The race cars had evolved from a two-seater (driver and mechanic) with a 180 cubic inch internal combustive engine (i. e. gasoline), to a one-seater with 122 cubic inches. A rule was that if a car didn't average 100 miles per hour in four laps, they were disqualified.

Among the notables was Barney Oldfield, 1878 - 1946. He started racing bicycles, drove for Henry Ford in 1902, where he was the first man to exceed 60 miles per hour. In 1910 he did 130 mile per hour in a Benz.

150 men in white cover-alls and hats worked as ushers. There were 25 food courts, selling mostly hot dogs. The 250-mile race began at 4:30 and ended around 7 p. m., but the parking lot wasn't cleared out until 9. Casualties for the Fourth in Kansas City were few. Independence was deserted.

On the first weekend after the Fourth the Jackson County veterans association held it's annual picnic at the Home of Picnics. The British/Canadian Bagpipe Band furnished the music, dressed in kilts. Jackson County was mostly settled early on by people from the South, mainly Kentucky, who brought with them their great love of horses. Among the Vets were forty from the local VA hospital, who were either crippled or blinded for life from their service in World War One. The program started at 4 p. m. with speeches from former commanders titled, "Boys in Gray Sixty Years Ago" and "Boys in Blue Sixty Years Ago," followed by entertainment and goodies. Many came with family and basket lunches. One thing the old Civil War Vets on both sides agreed upon was the fact that everyone had had the cooties. Many, many vets wore their old uniform.

157

Between the Fourth and Labor Day fireworks were reflected off the lake every Sunday night, 9 p. m. sharp. Some were given names like the City of Pyro, where a small city, nearly a city block long gets blown to Kingdom Come. Or a huge dragon named, "St. George."

Among the A-type picnics were the American Insurance Company, United Garment Workers, Irving-Pitt Manufacturing Company, Saline County Reunion, the Oddfellows, and Postmen of Greater Kansas City.

The Standard Oil Company of Sugar Creek held its first annual picnic. Much of the talk at the picnic would have been about autos and radios. Things like the sale at C. J. Warman Electric Company, just off the Square in Independence, where you could buy a $6.50 pair of red head-phones for $5.35, crystal sets for $4 or $5. Everybody needs "B" batteries, 3 for $2.65; spring aerial and stranded aerial wire for 75 cents, or a double-throw knife switch for 40 cents, besides the local chit-chat. Also would have been talk among the men about who had the best hooch. My mom and dad would have been there. Mom was thirteen and dad was drunk, like many (if not most) of the Standard Oil revelers. A good time was had by all, and there were few if any cases of the brown bottle flu.

Laborer's destination again this Labor Day was again Fairmount Park, in Missouri, and City Park in Kansas City, Kansas, after the parades. Senator James A. Reed of Missouri was the main speaker. His topic, the immigration bill that he had helped defeat this year. Among the many speakers, but far down on the list, was future President of the United States, Harry S. Truman. In Germany, Hitler would soon be locked up. Fairmount Park management shut the rides down while the speakers spoke to 6,000 gathered in the southwest corner of the park. Games of skill were rewarded by prizes from lollipops to tons of coal. A couple of days later the world's longest roller coaster crashed. Nothing too serious, Car Two ran into Car One, sending one person to the Independence Sanitarium and several others with minor injuries. The strangest thing about the accident is that no one sued. The ride was immediately closed, and so was the park.

In the town that Rockefeller built, at least his people still ran it, the mayor, Mr. Boehmer, was a plant supervisor and a Republican in a Democratic town, but he kept on winning, possibly because the citizens knew that if they voted him out the goodies might stop coming, for instance a new 50,000 gallon water tower was being constructed on the high ground in the southeast part of the city. Sewer lines were being installed throughout. New light poles were being added two at a time, as could be afforded at $65 per. By the end of the year, Sugar Creek had 41 poles. Water was running out of pipes under pressure by the end of the year, and bids were asked for the town's first fire truck. Taxes were set at 75 cents for every $100 of valuation. The refinery was worth a lot of money.

The City Hall chambers moved from the bank building to the new Snyder building a block south. Now there are Moose in the basement. By now the Sugar Creek School was no longer called "Riverview." The school graduated 15 this year. The Red Cross, along with much help from the Sugar Creek School, the City of Sugar Creek, and Standard Oil had completely wiped out the infestation of trachoma that had plagued the area. It was the first Red Cross district in the state to do so. The town reacted like it had won the Super Bowl. Meanwhile, the school auditorium hosted everything from concerts by the Standard Oil band to wrestling, boxing, plays and vaudeville. 1924 is coming, and it will be a bad year for future President Truman.

Anna Novak, a.k.a. "Mommy", at Fairmount Lake, 1923.

Chapter 31: 1924

At least four good things came out of Prohibition that we still have today. Number one, nightclubs, unlike saloons of pre-Prohibition days, they were called same because that's what they were. Since they legally didn't exist, there was no closing time. Two, mixed drinks; with real booze going for $8 to $12 a bottle, drinking it straight could be expensive. The smart thing to do was to dilute it. Three of the most popular were highball, with whiskey and 7-Up, vodka and orange juice, called a screwdriver, and rum and Coke. Three, soda fountains. Since alcohol was a sin, ice cream and soda pop were in. The soda shop lowered the drinking age as it was now the center of socialization. Four, beauty shops, since men no longer came home with beer goggles. Wrinkles, gravity and familiarity put the birth rate in America in jeopardy.

By Sunday, May 18, all three parks were open to the public. Electric began the season with a circus. It was a three-ringer with clowns, elephants, horses and aerial acts. Poodles Hanneford, world's greatest riding clown, was the featured attraction, along with Hall's Juvenile Elephants, and Swan Ringen, lady diver. Two shows every night. Matinee Saturday and Sunday, rain or shine.

On Saturday, May 24, the 15,000 students of the Kansas City Missouri schools, were treated to a picnic at Electric by the PTA. Though there was quite a wind chill, the kids didn't seem to mind. The temperature at 6 a.m., as the line to enter started to grow, was only 41 degrees. There was frost in St. Joe. The circus and entrance were free, but everything else cost money. This came as a big disappointment, so park management gave way. One free ticket to eight concessions, given randomly. Some big kids received tickets for the kiddie train or Merry-go-Round, while some children's tickets were for the roller coaster, much trading followed.

Fairyland's second season again saw Sam Benjamin the head honcho. The Crystal Swimming Pool was given two coats of white paint with lead. There was a new kiddie pool, from 4 inches to a foot and a half deep. A cafe had been added, enabling parents to keep an eye on their children, and vice versa.

The park's first major picnic was the Campfire Girls.

The trolley line had been extended down Prospect to the main entrance. Admittance was still ten cents, kiddies were free.

The work on Fairmount Park started on the first days of Spring, as painters, carpenters, electricians, and laborers prepared the park for its May 17 opening.

The carpenters and electricians worked on the new stuff, like the Caterpillar, a ride that moved up and down while flying around a track; King Tut's Tomb, The Mysterious Knock-Out, and a pony track. The kiddie playground was enlarged with new stuff to entertain. Among the attractions to get a new coat of paint were the Mountain Speedway, Over the Top, Canals of Venice, Captive Airplane, Puzzletown, The Whip, Miniature Railway, Ferris wheel, Fairy Swings, Merry-Go-Round and the Motor Dome. Fifty new boats were on the lake.

The disco ball in the Venetiani Ballroom was removed in favor of more dignified lighting. Music would be furnished by Ray Stinson's Orchestra. Last, but not least, were the hundreds of newly-built picnic tables throughout the park. The following people were responsible for the good times had by all visitors to Fairmount Park: President A. R. Goetz, Vice President M. L. Goetz. These men were the sons of M. K. Goets, a St. Joseph, Missouri beer brewer. Even during Prohibition they brewed Goetz Country Club Malt Liquor and Country Club Pilsner. J. C. Houseman was the Treasurer, G. C. McGinnis, General Manager; John Wunderlich, Public Relations, Carl Carlisle owned the water. Fairmount's first major picnic was the Jackson Count Oddfellows' eighteen lodges and twelve auxiliaries = 12,000 people.

The first week in June brought the Shriners back to Kansas City. The Shriners liked Kansas City; beer was cold and came in plain brown bottles to go. Lots of movie theaters, pretty girls, and three first-class amusement parks. Fairmount announced that Thursday, June 5, was official Shriner Day. Anyone wearing a fez or any Shriner paraphernalia was admitted free. Sam at Fairyland went one better, anyone with anyone that even looked like a Shriner was admitted free. He knew that once a Shriner came in contact with fun, price was no object.

At Fairmount the picnics at the "Home of Picnics" continued through June. A record of sorts was broken when a dozen picnics were booked for one day.

As the season progressed, the warm temperatures drove the people from the city to the parks and water, and soon it was time to celebrate the Fourth of July.

The three amusement parks, as was the custom, had the best fireworks in town, and thousands attended. While the Blues were on the road many attended the 250 mile race at the Kansas City Speedway. Many church congregations held picnics. Swope Park was full of people too cheap or poor to attend a real park, where you could spend a lot of money.

Independence, Missouri, finally got with the program and had a fine Fourth of July. At 10 o'clock sharp, the Boy Scouts held a parade around the town square. After Mayor Sermon gave a speech on the "American Flag", a double header followed at the high school campus. The second game was won by Excelsior Springs, beating Independence 9 - 2. Races for the girls and boys followed, prizes given, followed by political speeches and a D. W. Griffith movie ("Orphans of the Storm"); then fireworks. Taps was blown at 11 p. m. Earlier, the Chief of Police, John S. Cogswell, warned juvenile delinquents to discontinue throwing small bombs under or in the back seats of autos, as they drove slowly through town at 15 miles per hour, a tempting target. 1,400 autos were counted by somebody, probably a reporter. No fires and no fingers blown off.

At Fairmount, Sunday evening for the rest of the summer would be capped off by set-piece fireworks. The first were Barney Google and his race horse "Spark Plug", cartoon characters whose popularity still is with us as one, a very large number, and two, a search engine. Wednesday night would be Surprise Night: Mrs. H. L. Davis of Sugar Creek drove home in a new 1924 Ford Model T.

Towards the end of July Ford Motor Company held its picnic at Fairmount Park. Five autos were given away to employees, black Model Ts. Model Ts were called, "Flivvers."

A few weeks later Fairyland Park and the local Ford Dealers' Association opened the park free to anyone driving in a Ford. Prizes were given for the oldest Ford, the Ford coming the longest distance, fattest man in a Ford, tallest man and woman, most people in a Ford, prettiest woman, and largest family. Dealers participated in contests consisting of cranking, i. e., starting the Ford, slow race, tire changing, driving fast in reverse, and towing away any flivvers.

In late August the Fairmount/Mt. Washington communities held a parade and picnic at Fairmount Park. The parade snaked its way to the Independence Square, and then on to Fairmount Park. Soon after, Independence held a city picnic at Fairmount Park. 3,000 free admittance tickets were given to children.

Electric closed the season with "Auto Polo", which might have been the precursor to the "Demolition Derby".

Once again the Labor people of Kansas City picked Fairmount Park as the place to hold their annual picnic. A gentleman came all the way from Cleveland, Ohio, to make a pitch for Senator Robert T. LaFullette, Sr., running for President as a Progressive Socialist, a third party started in 1912 by Theodore Roosevelt. It went down hill after. The Progressive Party was pro-Labor and pro-Farmer. It was also a leftist organization with a bunch of peaceniks. LaFullette voted against going to war in 1917, mainly because Wisconsin had a large German population. He received 17% of the vote, but he didn't last much longer, dying in 1925 of a heart attack.

Fairmount closed at midnight on Sunday, September 7. The final group to enjoy the "Home of Picnics" was the "Knights of Pythias" and the "Knights of Khorassan" of Greater Kansas City, holding their annual picnic, after which the leaves would fall from the trees and the lake would freeze.

On September 1st, the Feds raided a drugstore at Linwood and Main. By now, Prohibition was a joke, and a Carnival atmosphere prevailed, attended by a thousand citizens, twenty deep. They hurled verbal insults as the Eighteenth Amendment of the Constitution of the United States of America was enforced. The local cops, whose job was crowd control, smiled at some of the insults, since it wasn't aimed at them. Cries of "I want my Coke!" followed by laughter rippled through the large, angry crowd. Sixty-seven half-pint bottles of prescription whiskey was loaded into the Federales' vans, along with the 18-year-old soda jerk, and two pretty good-looking Flappers who were drinking Cokes with added ingredients. Ten minutes after the raid it was business as usual, without mixed drinks.

On July 27, the Standard Oil Refinery at Sugar Creek held its Second Annual Picnic at Fairmount Park. The September Standolind Magazine had eight photos on five pages. The author was not the same fellow who put together the monthly plant gossip.

On that day, the people with the goodies started arriving around 7:30. Tubs of lemonade and tons of ice cream were furnished by the company. Employees brought the rest. Food prices, thanks to overproduction by farmers, were stable. Smoked hams, 12.5 cents a pound; hamburger, 3 pounds, 29 cents; bread, 9 cents; butter 37 cents a pound, and brisket 18 1/2 cents.

By ten o'clock the horseshoe pits were ready. Thousands of free admission tickets were given away, but the kids from the Creek didn't need tickets. They never paid anyway.

Various games and races were held on the athletic field by boys and girls, men and women. Virgil Lynch, the 14-year-old future Police Judge, won two contests: first by running in the sack race instead of hopping like everyone else, and the three-legged race. A trick was played on some women in the "Bottle Blindfold Race". Before the blindfolds were applied, the ladies stood facing dozens of empty beer bottles. After the blindfolds were on, the bottles were quietly removed while instructions were loudly given, and they proceeded to walk through what they thought were bottles, when there really weren't any bottles there. Everybody got a kick out of that. Then it was time for chow, followed by a baseball game, the highlight of which was when one of the sluggers hit a home run over the right centerfield fence, missing some swimmers and sticking in some mud, well over 300 feet. The Standard Oil Band gave a concert in the band shell. As the sun set on the horizon, the crowd dispersed, looking forward to the third picnic, which would be smaller.

It wasn't all roses. A week after the picnic George Moffett, the refinery's General Manager, announced a huge layoff. At least 250 men, 40% of the work force, would get pink slips. The reason given was overproduction, but Standard Oil was involved in another scandal, the Teapot Dome. Standard owned a large piece of Sinclair Oil, now under investigation. Shortly after the announcement 100 men, Standard Oil employees from Sugar Creek, crowded the City Council meeting, concerned about their jobs and the future of the city. They were assured by Mayor Bohemer that the company would not fire Creekers, as there were no unions and seniority didn't mean squat.

Judge Harry Truman was doomed. On Groundhog Day the "Regular Democratic Club of the Eastern Judicial District of Jackson County" endorsed Robert Lee Hood (a Rabbit) to run against him. Hood, for years, was Chief Deputy Tax Collector for Jackson County. Soon Judge Truman was approached by fellow "Goats" to appoint all the road overseers Goats. To do so would have gone back on his word. To his credit, he gave the Rabbits nine positions, the same as last year. The Goats got 36. Fairmount Park was accosted by the "Rabbits" on August 1st, a few days before the primary election. Judge Truman caught hell from Judge J. K. Wallace. Truman was called a crook, denying that he had a surplus. Truman ran on his record.

Meanwhile, Truman gave a speech just east of the Jackson County Courthouse, exactly where there is now a statue of him. He gave his usual speech of his accomplishments. In the primaries, the Goats beat the Rabbits, Truman winning by 2,000 votes out of 12,000 cast. The Rabbits hated Truman. In November the Republicans swept the county on Calvin Coolidge's coattails. Henry W. Rummell, banker and former Independence councilman, beat Truman, 9,679 for Rummell, 9,061 for Harry. Truman was most cordial after the defeat, sending a letter to Rummell congratulating him and offering any assistance his two years on the bench would be of any help. He would now just fade away.

Chapter 32: 1925

According to professional historians, 1925 is called, "The Year When Nothing Happened," because there was very little world strife. Corporal Hitler and his girlfriend, Rudolph Hess, were released from a cushy prison where the Fuhrer wrote a book dry enough to absorb half the water in Fairmount Lake. The Great Commoner died two weeks after winning the Scopes Monkey Trial, a debate pertaining to the evolution of species, between himself and Clarence Darrow, who was representing the American Civil Liberties Union. One of them was heard to say, "We didn't mean to kill the S. O. B." A Mrs. Darwin, daughter-in-law of Charles Darwin, commented about the trial, "I think men are beginning to make monkeys of themselves." Former Harry Truman was unemployed, but not for long.

Jackson County had 9,460 head of horses, 3430 mules, 19,800 milk cows, 16,300 hamburger/steak/roast cows, 15,690 sheep, 60,440 hogs and working around the clock for the last nineteen years, the 250 human moles at the Portland Cement plant at Cement City had dug five miles of tunnels and turned three million tons of limestone into powder. Prohibition of alcohol was a pain. There weren't many raids because to be busted in Jackson County there had to be a snitch. On February 7, three houses were raided, two west of Independence and one in Sugar Creek. The "Whitney Place" on Cunningham Road, when raided, four guys were found throwing craps, four quarts of beer, two bottles of whiskey were seized along with a hypodermic needle. A young lady and the drunks were taken into custody. Bond was $100 for the lady, 4 drunks, $300 each, two Whitneys, $1,000. George Patillo was visited the same night, because then cops could just walk in, catching George and a still. He denied knowing anything about the brass knuckle by the still, in fact, claimed to not know what they were. His bond was $300.

On March 7 deputy sheriffs walked in on Eva Butkovich, mother of young Matt, on Chicago Street in Sugar Creek at 6 a. m. The washtub and a coffee pot containing whiskey was brewing. George Butkovich was arrested and bond was set at $1,000. A neighbor, Joe Spallack, was also busted. He was found to have four gallons of hooch, 150 empty bottles, and 75 gallons of grape juice that had not yet fermented. That was given back to him so that it could ferment. In October the Sandbar that doomed Wayne City, now an island in the middle of the Missouri River a mile downstream from the Standard Oil refinery, was raided. A 100 and a 50 gallon still were discovered. The raid was led by Edison L. Watson, constable, four county cops and two feds. Bottles of finished stuff were found in gunny sack, tied with rope, hidden among vegetation in the river. Two pressure cookers and a 35-gallon tank; two hydrometers and several funnels were found.

On the island was a dead cow and hundreds of dead rabbits. Sugar Creek had a rat.

Fairmount Park's men's bath house was torched on May 6. The 100 ft x 45' structure, with 3,000 lockers, was badly damaged on the north end. To the rescue came the newly formed Fairmont/Mt. Washington Fire Department led by Chief C. S. Hunning. The call came in about 1:30 a. m. by C. G. McGinnis, Park Watchman. The fire was out by 3:30. Damage to the premises was set at $10,000. The area not only had Feds and rats, it had a pyro.

The park opened on Saturday, May 16. Work was progressing on the new men's bathhouse, bigger and better. With 5,000 lockers it would be ready by Memorial Day.

Dr. Carver's 18 high-diving horses and girl riders dressed in red, fresh from working the Southern circuit. Two plunges daily, 4:30 and 9:30 p. m.

Boys and girls under 16 were offered free season passes if they would register with park management opening day. They lined up between 10 in the morning until 3 in the afternoon. The kids were given numbered buttons, which gave them free access to the beach for the season, but they still had to pay a dime to get in. Was it Mr. Carlilse's idea? Probably. Suits extra.

The new attractions at Fairmount Park were a mechanical miniature city. Minona, Minnesota, a city along the Mississippi River, with scaled buildings, working street lights, and cars that moved about the town. The new ride was called the "Dodge-Ems", bumper cars. Aeroship, which Al Carlisle said was probably just one of the old rides re-painted, and a water toboggan.

Electric Park's 27th season began on Memorial Day Weekend. The feature was a staged Vaudeville review called, "Broadways of 1925." Some of the cast were, "The World's Specialist Roller Skating" "The Unusual Duo Novelty Dance," "Acrobatic Dancers," "Comedy Dancers," "Prima Donnas," "Juvenile Dancers," and a "Chorus of 18 Lovely Young Ladies." Chicken dinners and a "Colored Dixie Land Blues Band". New features included "Cave of the Winds," "China Town," and "The Kick", soon to go up in flames, and a 500-specie aquarium that couldn't burn. Also new was the admission price of twenty cents.

In May the Guinotte Dam on the Blue River, between 12th and 13th street, was dedicated, backing the water to 19th Street. The project was accomplished by the "Blue Valley Business Association", and the Kansas City Parks Board. What now is a dry slab of cement then had water, with big plans for its future. The west bank, or the Kansas City side, was pristine, with a boat house and a path running from the dam to 19th Street. The east bank was littered with junk.

On the 17th, because of inclement weather, only 500 spectators showed up for the regatta. The local Navy Reserve had parked a small steamship there, which led the parade of smaller craft down to the dam, then traversing a large body of deep water. There were more people in the show than on the shore, almost 100 watercraft. Races were held and politicians spoke of future improvements; today the area is a disaster.

Fairyland was the last park to open this season, featuring a high-wire act, working 102 feet in the air, with nothing between the acrobats and injury. They performed all kinds of crazy things, hand balancing, swinging around on a trapeze, and rings, singly, in pairs, and all four at once, followed by a high-diving act. New this year was the Crystal Cave and the Missouri Mule.

Back at Fairmount, June brought loads of company and organization picnics, like General Motors, Allied Railroad Employees, Irish-American Society, Montgomery Ward, Proctor and Gamble, Missouri Pacific Boosters, National Zinc Company, Loose-Wiles, Ford Dealers, and Commerce Trust Company. On Saturday, July 4, America celebrated 149 years of existence. There was a one-day break in the heat wave that had settled over the town. Friday was 97 degrees hot, and Sunday would be 95, so 90 degrees and a cool breeze made for perfect swimming weather. The beach at Fairmount was packed, because of the booming local economy, and the confidence that it would go on forever, how sad.

An ad in the local papers pointed out some of the reasons why, with parks going, everyone should visit Fairmount. The beach, swim, dive, big natural lake fed by springs, invigorating, cooling, new bath house, water toboggan, and floating pillows. Dancing in the Venetian Ballroom, there's a real snap to O. A. Smith's orchestra. You'll slide across the dance floor. A score of thrilling rides and concessions, never a dull moment, there's amusement at every turn, it's a big natural playground; rides a-plenty, attractions galore. Harvey Kessel sings in the ballroom every Wednesday and Sunday nights. Club dance every Monday, Wednesday, and Friday evenings. Massive shade trees, a well kept lawn, ice water, benches, ovens, it's a great place to picnic.

Dr. Carver and his two girl riders and horses spent half the summer thrilling the crowds. No one seemed to get tired of it, and everyone took a stroll down the Midway, where you might win a Teddy bear or a Kewpie Doll. Like any modern park, there was plenty of free parking for a hodge-podge of vehicles. The place to be on the Fourth of July was the racetrack at 95th street. Two steam locomotives had a head-on collision. A lone track a few hundred yards long was laid. $500 was paid to the engineer who was the last one to jump. No one died.

In the first game of a double-header at the Chrisman campus celebration, the Sugar Creek Standard Oil team beat the Knights of Pythias, 14-12. As soon as the sun went down, a fire fight developed between some white vs. black boys on Lexington street, just north of the Independence Square. The kids shot Roman candles, rockets, and threw firecrackers of all sizes at each other. Some kids left to get more ammo. It was all in good fun, and when there were no more things to throw or shoot, they met in the street to laugh and jabber. Next morning, Lexington looked like Bourbon Street Mardi Gras morning.

The crowd at Fairyland on the Fourth was the biggest ever, estimated at 30,000. By 9 a. m. the parking lot was already full of autos. At closing time there were so many people in line for the rides that the park didn't close until early the next morning.

The auto traffic to Fairmount Park was bumper to bumper most of the day.

Many people, though, prefer the open road. 40 and 50 highways were linked coast to coast, and were nearing completion. The roads in the county were getting better, thanks to future President Truman. Some families drove until they found a good spot for a picnic. Some just drove till they had to head back. Many could now easily visit friends out of town; twenty and thirty miles an hour was fast in 1925.

In Bonner Springs, the Ku Klux Klan had a Fourth of July picnic. 10,000 people showed up, including many ladies with children. A preacher spoke about the purpose of the "Man in the Klan", and Mrs. So and So spoke of the women's role in the Klan. They also swore in several hundred new Klansmen, at $10 a head. It was lucrative business, with a business model similar to Amway's.

Electric Park also had a fire. An arsonist was being paid to burn the parks. Flames could be seen from miles around. Most everything burned: The Midway; the theater was damaged, but was repaired for Broadway of 1925 and Rory Mack's Summer Show, which featured the Charleston, which was new to Kansas City. Soon every woman under 30 made it the dance of the Roaring Twenties.

Shortly after the Fourth, a young man from Kansas City jumped off the 20-ft high dive and drowned after getting stuck in the mud at the bottom of Fairmount lake. His clothes were discovered in a locker after closing time around 10:30. A search with lights soon found him lodged so tight that divers couldn't budge him. He was finally freed about 2 a. m with the help of ropes. After more than three decades silt was filling in the lake. Nature was reclaiming the land. The geological term is called "mass wasting."

On Saturday, July 18, the Allied Railway employees held their second annual picnic at Fairmount Park. Railroad men came from as far away as 800 miles, they didn't have to pay. Music was provided by three railroad company bands, the Rock Island, Missouri Pacific, and Frisco. Athletic events with prizes were held in the afternoon. Afterwards a baseball game between the Kansas City Terminal and the Rock Island Railroad people ended in the office getting beat 25 to 2. The Kansas governor was a keynote speaker, but failed to show. Representative E. C. Ellis and Manager Gordon of Kansas filled in. Electric Park's picnic were the WWI Disabled Veterans. One thing that would have been discussed would have again been the promise of a bonus; they would have to wait till 1936 when they finally got it over FDR's veto.

On August 1, J. J. Heim and some local VIP's opened a playground at the site of the old Electric Park, Montgall and Rochester avenues. More than 800 attended the ceremony. Until recently, the abandoned park was a dump. Six bathing suits were awarded to boys who had carved dead trees into something. Wednesdays will be known as "Pet Night." Prizes will be awarded to children with the largest, smallest, and the most deformed dog.

The next day, Sunday, Dr. Carver, his diving horses, and two pretty drivers, dressed in red, made their farewell performance. Harry Kessel was now a radio personality, a device that as yet couldn't be plugged into a wall socket. O. A. Smith's orchestra was still there, and there were fireworks on the lake at 9:30.

After the horses, "Zimmy the Half Man" was booked as the main attraction. Born with no legs, he held the world's record for staying under water, 4 minutes and 17 seconds. He could eat, drink, and smoke (?) under water.

While Fairmount Park on Sunday, August 16, was hosting the huge and wet Irish American picnic, with speaker/senator James A. Reed, Electric started its Corn Carnival. It was also celebrating its swan song. Electric Park was closing. Mr. Heim was selling the land. It would eventually become The Landing, a shopping center, but in its last summer the park became a long, hot party. Mardi Gras Kansas City style. Flappers and confetti fights, patrons dressed like people from every time period, and corn stalks six feet tall were everywhere, many covering the area that burned. Many, many companies and organizations held picnics at the doomed icon. There was an industrial exposition, showing some of the technological miracles of the early Twentieth Century.

At 10 p. m. September 1, Electric Park ended with a huge fireworks display which rivaled the fire which was the park's demise. Fairlyland didn't have a fire, and both fires were set, surmises the conspiracy theorist. On Thursday, September 3, a hot day, with temperatures near 100, the Mt. Washington, Fairmount and Sugar Creek boosters held the second annual Home Community Parade and Picnic. At 2 p. m. the 150 decorated automobiles, a steam calliope and the Standard Oil Band left at the Independence road and Arlington Avenue for Downtown Kansas City. Once in the city limits of Kansas City the parade got a military escort from the Kansas City Missouri Police Department. Once downtown the autos were judged, but not told the winners until the parade had wound its way back to Fairmount Park.

Prizes were donated by merchants from Kansas City, Independence, Mt. Washington, Fairmount, and Sugar Creek, to be given out as prizes for the zany contests: Boys and girls' races, Married Women's dash, Fat Women's dash, Wheelbarrow race, women's Ball Catching event, Boys' Obstacle Race, Roping contests, Monkey Race, Kangaroo Race. The oldest man and woman present received a prize, along with the oldest resident, person coming longest distance, couple married longest, largest family; a tug-of-war between the married men and the single men, and a rock-the-boat contest, etc. etc. A basket dinner was served at 6:30, followed by three comedy films at sunset.

By Labor Day the temperature was in the 80s. The annual parade downtown by the local labor unions was held, followed by a trip out to Fairmount Park. Things for now were pretty mellow between labor and management. The two main speakers were George Berry, president of the Printing Pressman's Union, and Mrs. Harriet Hyland, president of the Railroad Carmen's Union. Kansas City, Missouri Police Band furnished the music, and the park closed its gates for another long cold spell.

Things at the Standard Oil Refinery were going well. If you were a good employee and well liked, and always came to work, a person could come and go pretty much as he pleased. One young man like that was John "Pee Wee" Pavola. He had a chance to go to Madison Square Garden in New York to indulge in the sport of boxing, where he "held his own." After he returned to work at the oil plant, he traveled around Missouri and Kansas, beating up guys in small towns for money. His mode of transportation could have been his lifelong friend, my dad, Honest John, who had just bought a 1925 Ford touring car. They were $350. Dad was also a good pinochle player, being on the refinery team that won the championship, beating the smart ones in the office.

In Sugar Creek, the trolley line into the town was discontinued by January. Most everyone working at the refinery could now afford an automobile, since there were no saloons.

Blair Jones and Charles Wesner, the town radio hams, filed and received a broadcasting license. Sugar Creek had a 5-watt radio station, "AWT". Morse Code was heard from New Zealand, and voice signals were received in several East Coast states, like Massachusetts, Maryland, New Jersey, Pennsylvania, and many southern states.

In May, a new newspaper, "The Jackson Herald," published by John S. Dickey and N. R. Smith, was started. The object of the paper was to report on small communities like Fairyland Heights, Harrison's Meadow, Harrison's Park, Maywood Park, Mt. Washington, Fairmount, Fairmount Heights, Sugar Creek, Maywood, Englewood, South Englewood, Lawn Heights, Cement City and Courtney. By now this area had 20,000 people, more than Independence, and Independence would take note.

Mr. Dickey has lived in Sugar Creek since 1910 and is the postmaster. Mr. Smith is an old hand at the newspaper business, and once owned a paper in Higginsville, Missouri.

August brought in a $16,000 bond issue to Sugar Creek. Six for a cement road on Fairmount Avenue and Kentucky, and 10K for a new city hall. Both passed, 150 to 50. Work was started on the building in November and was to be completed by Spring.

"There is only one Sugar Creek." remarked Judge R. L. Bennet, who owned a furniture store in the Creek, and was also the town counselor. Right after Thanksgiving, 400 letters were mailed to the residents of the town, stating that Uncle Sam was pissed. These people had not filed an income tax returned for the year 1921. Sam wanted $5 each in penalties, even though most didn't make enough to pay taxes. They were assessed $5 anyway. The few who didn't show to pay their fine were notified to appear in downtown Kansas City Federal Court. Uncle Sam was really pissed at them.

A ball was held New Years Eve at the Slyman Hall. $150 was raised to equip six firemen with boots, hats, raincoats, etc. So much for the year that nothing happened.

Chapter 33: 1926

Former Judge Truman didn't waste any time preparing for a trip to historical immortality. On January 15 he succeeded Allan Hoyt, the District Deputy Grand Master of the 59th Masonic Lodge. A dinner was held at the Christian Church. The whole affair was broadcast on KLDS, the local radio station.

In March a dinner for the 150 Masons of the 59th district was held at the Mt. Washington Lodge No. 641. Harry was toastmaster for the evening and proved that he was getting more comfortable talking to large groups of people. He set the tone for the evening. Dinner was prepared by the ladies of the Mount Washington Order of the Eastern Star. By June, now Colonel Truman and Major Robert W. Barr had filed for ballot space in the August election for judge. Barr was going to be the Western District judge, and Truman filed for Presiding Judge. In July Mr. Truman was elected by the "National Old Trails Association," at a dinner held at the Muehlebach Hotel in Downtown Kansas City, replacing Judge Joseph Lowe, the founder. Their goal was to pave the old trail west of Kansas City to Los Angeles. The road from Washington, D. C. to Kansas City was already in fine shape. It would soon be known as Federal Highway No. 24.

The county election in November was a sweep by local Democrats. Judge Truman would be the Presiding Judge. The seven circuit judgeships were all won by Democrats. It didn't help the Republican core when they ran out of money. Unfortunately, Judge Truman had just won a job that was a political dead-end, according the pundits of the day.

Meanwhile, in Germany, a part of Herr Hitler's probation was "no inflammatory speeches." Not being the sharpest knife in the drawer, he did just that. Justice was swift, no speeches for 18 months or it was back to Spandau. Besides, who could take someone seriously who had such a striking resemblance to Charlie Chaplin, the comic silent movie star?

Nationally, the first sniffles of the coming pneumonia were heard when the Florida real estate bubble burst. Locally, the Bank of Englewood, Missouri, just east of the city limits of Independence, tapped out. Fortunately, Judge Truman and his buddies had gotten their money out of the institution a few months before this happened.

Kansas City's two remaining outdoor amusement parks opened in unison, at 6 p. m. Saturday, May 15. Prosperity was spreading even to Germany, thanks to loans from his wealthy Uncle Sam.

Sam Benjamin was in his fourth season as the manager of Fairyland Park. Several thousand enjoyed the fair weather. Fairyland boasted twelve new attractions this season. The Hey-Day, reverse engineered from England, combined The Whip with the up-and-down movement of The Caterpillar. It was described as a sensation of "skidding out of control down a mountain in a motor car." By far the most popular new attraction was the "Monkey Autodrome." A sort of miniature automobile demolition derby, with monkeys as the drivers, many laughs. An off-duty Kansas City traffic officer observed that his job would be a lot easier if "motorists exhibited as much dexterity as the monkeys." From six until midnight, the rails around the Monkey Autodrome were elbow to elbow.

Both parks joined the Orpheum circuit, meaning all acts were controlled by people from out of town. With Electric gone, the two parks were obviously in cahoots.

The Orpheum started along with vaudeville in 1880's Boston. Arthur Wortheim owned a theater that catered to small, quick acts. The first theater called Orpheum was in San Francisco in 1887. Soon they controlled a large portion of the acts. By the 1920s there were the "Vaudeville Wars," as corporations tried to control the live acts of the nation.

Fairyland Park's first act came from Chicago. Roy Max and his "Palm Beach Frolics". Roy himself attended the opening night and thought the crowd "adequate." The two stars of the musical, Victor Caplin and Gladys Kern would stay on for the entire season. While the shows and supporting acts changed every two weeks it must have made for some interesting rehearsals. In the dance pavilion was Haley's twelve piece orchestra.

By now, Fairmount Park had acquired almost 100 novelties, concessions, and rides. A new concession was the "Jolly Jungle," dark tunnels and passageways with stuffed animals in different scenes and even a ghost, then to the "White River", rolling like the waves, then deposited on a rotating disk and mercifully put back on your feet. Another new attraction was the "Jumping Jack." A new miniature city was built, this time it was St. Paul, Minnesota. On the stage were the Dixon Riggs Group, gymnasts. Skeeball machines were introduced, a game of skill.

The lake now had 100 aluminum boats. Every year they were newly painted in silver and numbered. The beach was newly sanded, more locker space and new suits were raring to go. The mild weather allowed for the beach to be opened to swimmers a week early. On May 22 the lake opened at 6 a. m. and closed at ten. Harry Smith's band played in the Venetian Ballroom. While Fairyland covered their picnic area, Fairmount covered its midway. Rain and sun no longer drove patrons under the trees. Now they would be close to the darts, balloons, and kewpie dolls. Improvements were also made to the picnic grounds.

The following week brought a real thriller for the kids, Ezra's "Barnyard Circus." The act consisted of about thirty animals, goats, pigs, chickens and dogs trained to act like lions, elephants, etc., etc. The star of the show was Mickey, "The World's Only High Diving Pig". Shows at 3:45 and 9:45.

The first large picnic at the "Home of Picnics" was held by the Missouri Conclave of the De-Molay. The Order of De-Molay was started in 1919 here in Kansas City. Sponsored by the Masons, membership was limited to boys 12 to 21, open to all, as long as they were white. Today there are about 18,000 members nationwide. The highlight of the picnic was a baseball game between a team from St. Louis and Kansas City.

Memorial Day came and went, and so did the weekly changes of vaudeville at Fairmount. June brought many picnics as the economy grew. Leisure and fun became a passion in America. Hem lines were going up faster than the stock market. Young adults danced and many of the pre-World War I generation wondered what would become of them. Today we know the answer: They were going to save the world, again. First they would have to survive the coming Depression, Fairmount Park wouldn't.

In June, the park's third week brought Merrill's Circus, ten acts meant for amusement, aerial rings, tumbling, and a mule, which was followed by "Betty's Pets," trained dogs, and "Marvelous Darro," a contortionist. "Butterfly Girls," the three Kinswell sisters, who flew about using aerial rings and a "Spanish trapeze," described as the "Dianas of the Air." June's vaudeville ended with "Stewart's Scotch Review," opening on the 20th. Six pretty Irish lassies dressed in kilts. Accompanied by bagpipes, they danced and sang songs of their native land. The "Four Sensational Jacks," comic acrobats, closed out June.

Fairmount Park was still the "Home of Picnics." Among some of the hundreds in 1926 were the Southern Kansas City Business District, Proctor & Gamble, The Syrian Club, Blue Valley Manufacturers and Business Men's Association, Missouri Pacific Railroad, Order of the Eastern Star, Spanish-American War Vets of Independence, Grand Convention of the Edwards Estate Heirs, Mt. Washington Chapter of the Eastern Star, Kansas City P. T. A. and all elementary schools, Loose-Wiles Biscuit Company, and United Country Clubs of Missouri filled the park until the Fourth of July.

A visit to Fairmount Park would have gone something like this: The first concession you would have found was a mysterious sensation, where balls roll up hill, then you would float over the darkened canals, there was an Egyptian fun house full of mirrors, the merry-go-round had tigers, a giraffe, and ponies; the model city, there were three coaster rides, the Mountain Speedway, the Jumping Jack and the Giant Dipper. They had aerial ships, the Caterpillar gave you a creepy, crawling sensation and sudden blasts from big air fans. There was the Dodge-Em (bumper cars), and a ride on the Whip. For the kids there were miniature automobiles, the Motor Speedway, and for babies there was the Umbrella Ride. Dancing in the ballroom and swimming in the lake.

Henry Whitesell came up with a money-maker for people who wanted a picnic without the hassle. He opened his Picnic Restaurant, and he catered from small to large picnics. His motto was "Coffee from One Cup to Fifty Gallons."

On the Fourth of July, just west of the Independence Square, a memorial to the fallen in the Great War was dedicated, arranged by the Tory J. Ford Post of the American Legion. Among the speakers were Col. Lewis J. Vanschaick of Ft. Leavenworth, who made the main address. Other speakers were Col. E. M. Slayton of the 110th Engineers, and Independence Mayor Sermon. The Colonel's comments on the war were direct and to the point. He said without U. S. involvement the Germans would have won the war in 1918. Divisions like the 35th stopped the Germans at the Battle of the Muse/Argonne on September 22, 1918, when 2,600 cannon, including 155mm, 105mm, and Captain Truman's 75s. 2,000 were in attendance. Colonel Truman was no doubt there. Ironically, that building would later be named after him.

Both Fairyland and Fairmount Parks celebrated the Fourth on Monday, the Fifth, making it a four-day weekend for the gate. Besides fireworks on the evening of Monday the Fifth, Fairmount Park featured a very unusual act: Captain Blake, internationally known as Skyrocket the Human Comet. Mr. Skyrocket had two assistants, a clown and a very lovely lady whose job it was to ignite him, after which he jumped into the deep part of the lake from a 100 foot tower, after which his two assistants dove and clowned around. A huge fireworks display Monday at dusk was followed by a late-night plunge by Captain Blake.

Fairyland Park's Third, Fourth, and Fifth of July started at 6 a. m. and ended at midnight, the end of a perfect day. The 27 rides and fun houses were busy all day. At 6 p. m., the amphitheater presented Roy Mack's Palm Beach Follies, still the main feature and continues non-stop until fireworks time. Dancing, which began at 7 p. m., was halted during the fireworks display of both aerial and set pieces. The crowds milled around until after midnight, lessening the usual traffic jam.

After the Fourth the parks went back to picnics and fun in the sun.

By now Kansas City had another swimming hole, Winnwood Beach. Located a mile or so north of the Missouri River, it offered swimming and dancing. A $35,000 fire convinced them that they had better not make it into an amusement park, but Winnwood Beach would last about as long as Fairyland Park.

Now that the two parks had their way with the pleasure seekers in most of Kansas City and surrounding communities, the beat went on. At Fairmount the weekly vaudeville act continued until the end of the season. First came the five Glencoe Sisters, singers, dancers, and musicians, appearing twice a day, and on Sundays they would follow the fireworks. July 18 brought the Seven Flying Melzers, who "hurled themselves through space on the flying trapeze, and while doing so execute a series of double and triple somersaults." They also performed several comedy acts.

Fairlyland sponsored a baseball game between the "Dries" and the "Wets." The Wets took the field with a flask in most back pockets. The Wets got drunk and lost 7-0, but had a much better time, owing to not taking the game so seriously by the third inning; the game was called on account of errors.

July at Fairmount ended with the Flying Bodies of the Airplane Girls, Allison and Martha Douglas, who showed their stuff on the "whirling trapeze bars." "Back by Popular Demand" meant that they worked cheap. This was followed by movies, a new one every night in the Amphitheatre, which was even cheaper. The last act of the season was a live one, the "Aerial Rutts."

Labor Day weekend was the last weekend for mirth at the parks. Kansas City Labor met at Fairmount, although this year there was no parade. It was not a good time for Labor. The Republican Administration was very pro-business. Someone gave a speech on the Joys of Labor. He, of course, didn't work, being in the business of making speeches.

In the town of Sugar Creek, much activity was afoot. For openers, the town finally moved into its new City Hall, April 16. It was a two-story red brick job, described as "plain" and "handsome." It had a garage for the city fire truck in back. The move from the Slyman Building was postponed because of a hassle over floors with the contractor. The basement was a dungeon for any prisoners. The first floor is where the city offices were located: an office for the Mayor, City Collector, Water Department Superintendent, and the Council Chamber. The second floor had five rooms, four of which were occupied by the Health Unit. The fifth was a bunk room for the fire department. On the 22nd of April a check for $5,000 was cut to Bert Elmer, contractor. It was the final payment on the $10,000 building. The council immediately took bids for sod. The residents benefitted by a reduction in home insurance. Other improvements were to build a natural gas pipeline to the city. A six-inch line was run to Kentucky Road and Fairmount Avenue, where a two-inch low pressure line spider-webbed its way through town.

Fifty street and stop signs were purchased, the names of many streets having been changed. House numbers were also introduced, making it possible for mail delivery in the future. The speed limit on Fairmount Avenue was ten miles per hour during school hours. Chief Mackey was ready with stop signs and two deputies. Stop signs were placed at strategic locations around the school, leading to the refinery. 45 people were arrested for not stopping and paid a $1 fine, netting the city $45. Since the city had no sirens the deputies blew whistles. The Chief acted as the judge and jury. Everyone was found guilty. It was mostly in fun, but Chief Mackey informed everyone that there would be an increase in the fine.

On Monday, August 2, four Italian gentlemen in a big Buick ran John Housaman, treasurer of Fairmount Park, his family, and a vice-president of Commerce Bank and over $5,000 in cash off the road. No one was shot, and the bandits got away. A taxi driver wrote down the license plate number, and it came back stolen off of a Ford. The same people had just robbed the Fairyland Park treasurer going to the bank a couple of weeks earlier. Again, no one was hurt, or caught.

On August 25, things turned ugly. Morris Rosenberg, owner of the Missouri Supply Company of Cement City, had just left the Sugar Creek Bank. On the new Cement City Road, that runs along the Missouri River, he and his security guard were accosted by four men in a Buick. This time, the hoods opened up with a sawed-off twelve gage shotgun, using double-ott buck. The shots disintegrated the windshield and struck Evestiro Hernandes, a laborer riding shotgun. He didn't have a chance. Later the car flew through Cement City at 70 miles an hour. Another Buick from the police department tried to follow the dust trail but gave up.

On October 5, an article in a local newspaper mentioned that twice a month an armored car from a Kansas City bank was filled with money to cash payroll checks for the Standard employees. Two weeks later, the Standard State Bank in Sugar Creek was visited by five men carrying .45 automatic pistols. Shortly after the armored car left, leaving behind $50,000 in cash, a nervous young man walked into the bank, produced a twenty dollar bill, and asked for change, a ten and ten ones. While Mr. Buckley, the bookkeeper, was doing his job, two more men walked into the bank, and then another. Dropping his pistol into a trash can, he figured there were too many people in the bank to start shooting. Soon, weapons were drawn. Marshal Mackey, who stood security just inside the door, was disarmed. A fifth man stood guard outside the bank. Soon one of them fired a round into the wall, and as they drove away Mr. Buckley fired six shots from his revolver into the Buick. While exiting south on Fairmount Avenue, they opened up, shattering windows, penetrating autos, but no one was hit. They left town with ten grand, leaving $40,000 in the vault. Tony Pappos and James T. Martin were charged with the crime. Pappos left an umbrella wrapper from his business in the bank, and Martin had just escaped from the penitentiary for bank robbery the day before. At the hearing Pappos didn't show and Martin was returned to prison with a 99-year sentence. A bloody coat with two bullet holes was found in the getaway car. No money was ever recovered. Insurance covered the loss.

After the annual Sugar Creek refinery picnic in August, my dad resigned from the inspection department. He and Nick Roper left for Detroit.

Chapter 34: 1927

New Year's Eve, 1926-1927 was loud. Because of the imprecise time pieces, New Year's Eve came at different times to different areas. In Independence the noise began on the southwest side ten minutes before midnight and rolled across town. Silence finally came twenty minutes later. The loudest were the many shotguns, followed by large firecrackers, church bells, automobile horns, banging, yelling, and finally dinner bells. Since New Year's Eve was on a Friday night, many stayed up all night. There were few arrests for drunkenness, even though the curbs were lined with automobiles and many residence's electric lights burned until late in the morning. By now prohibition of alcohol was becoming a joke, from sea to shining sea.

At 10 a. m., Saturday, January 1, Judge Truman took his seat on the County Court as presiding judge. All three judges were now Democrats. With Bess at his side and his mother in the large audience, the judge gave his first speech that would separate him from your average politician, and I quote:

"It is not the custom of the county court to make speeches, but there are so many here that I think that briefly we should announce our policy. We intend to operate the county government for the benefit of the taxpayer. While we were elected as Democrats we were also elected as public servants. We will appoint all Democrats to jobs appointable. But we are going to see that every man does a full day's work for his pay. In other words, we are going to conduct the county affairs as efficiently and economically as possible."

County Engineer Koelher, a member of the political opposition, expressed his regrets saying, "It's too bad we aren't all Republicans." Truman replied, "We are neither Democrats nor Republicans, but civil servants." That's the kind of talk that would make him a U. S. senator.

In May, the Independence school PTA was having a get-together. The idea of a picnic for the children of the district was discussed. Before the meeting was over it was decided to invite all the PTAs of the various school districts outside of Kansas City. A great financial bonanza for Fairmount Park's opening day, May 14. On May 9, Mayor Sermon of Independence, with a bunch of "these and those" proclaimed Saturday, May 14 "The Independence Day Picnic." He urged all families in Independence and the surrounding school districts to meet at Fairmount Park for a "good, old-fashioned country picnic." The local PTA was to get 50% of the gate, which opened at 11 a. m.

Mrs. George Randall was in charge of the athletic events held in the afternoon. Seventy-five Boy Scouts in uniform with all their badges, ribbons, etc., were to be stationed around the park, with one Boy Scout and two members of the various PTAs at every ride or concession to aid the children, who had to be accompanied by an adult, who also had to pay admission. A large tent with coffee and cake (for a nominal fee) acted as GHQ (general headquarters).

Tickets could be purchased in advance at all seven Independence schools, plus Sturgus Jewelry and Brown Drug Store. A 10-cent ticket included two rides before 6 p. m. Some of the events were a baseball game between the fathers and sons, peanut dash, potato race, 200-yard dash, Fat Man and Woman's Race.

Large delegations came from Buckner, Lee's Summit, Leeds along with the Bristol, Manchester, and Benjamin Harrison schools. The kids from Sugar Creek never paid.

On that day a 14-year-old young man began his first day of work in the boathouse. Al Carlisle, youngest son of Carl, the owner of the lake, began a career that would last until the demise of the park. He was a very lucky boy. He was paid 40 cents an hour to be the go-fer for his older brother Charlie, who, at 17, was the boss. Their father, no dummy, inquired as to who were the local toughs, then he'd hire them. John Dumsky was a life guard; he would end up wearing a bunch of Marine Corps stripes by the end of World War II, in the Pacific theater. Young Mattie Butkovich was another one. His job was to help people in and out of the boats, after which he boxed for a while before he entered the Army, bound for the Battle of the Bulge. Captured twice, escaped twice, once shooting up the place with .45 automatic. Those poor Nazis. He told me that whenever a German soldier was captured he was treated okay, but if the bastard was the Gestapo or the S. S., they were immediately executed. George Spradley, also a toughie, helped John as the life guard. Working at the Spring, doling out water for 5 cents if you had a cup, 10 cents if you used the park's cup, was the future chief of police in Kansas City and future FBI head, Clarence Kelly.

One of Al's jobs was to blink the lights at 9 p. m., alerting the lovers on the lake. Prices for boats were 25 cents for 1/2 day, 40 cents all day. The 100th boat fleet, plus swimming, made Mr. Carlisle a lot of money, which he optimistically put into the stock market and other capital ventures.

Ladies never wandered about the park alone. That was a hangover from the Victorian age. There weren't any black faces, ever. Water skiing and baptisms were popular. The skiers had to wear inner-tubes for life jackets. A 48-horsepower motor boat pulled either a skier or a surf board, attached by a rope, around the lake. Fifty-cents for four laps; if the skier couldn't get up they got half their money back.

Lately Henry Ford had been getting a lot of flack from his children. Chevy was outselling the Model T. By now there were 22,000,000 autos on America's few highways. Half were Model Ts. Ten million, or 2/3 of the Model Ts ever made, were still running. It was announced by Ford Motor Company that the 1928 Model A would be a doozy. Suddenly no one wanted the old Model T. So the local Ford dealers, along with park management, worked out a deal whereby the dealers wouldn't lose much money on the Model Ts that would be given away for publicity at the park.

The first of these automobiles was to be raffled off on Surprise Night, Wednesday, June 29. For a quarter, that had Lady Liberty on the face of the coin, a person could purchase a chance to win a piece of the end of an era. My dad won. Since he had to work, he entrusted the ticket to his sister, Mary, but made it in time for the raffle, and probably drove the car right off the stage, straight to Sugar Creek for some celebrating, I'm sure. After over a decade of service, the 25-cent auto was sold for $25 in 1941, still running.

Fairmount and Fairyland's 1927 season was like playing "New Park, Old Park". Fairyland outspent Fairmount in not just advertising, but also in entertainment. While Fairmount Park relied on its old standby, the corporate picnic, swimming, boating on a huge lake stocked every year with fish. But the rides would stay the same until the park's demise. And there was no reason to spend any money on the park, except for repairs and paint. Some of the structures by now were over 30 years old.

Fairyland flourished. The void in outdoor amusement left by Electric was filled. On Sundays there was a matinee. Dancing from 3 to 6, gents 25 cents, ladies a dime. And if you were really good looking, you might even get your dime back. After that, Daredevil Dixon landed by parachute on the athletic field. He had a knack for brushes with death, for which he was paid $100, more if he broke something. A free aerial act and a picture show, and park had a Comedy Quartette, from 9 until 10:30 the Glen Lloyd's Dance Orchestra played live while being broadcast on a local radio station, which played until midnight. Admission to the park this year was a dime for adults, kiddies free.

Fairmount Park's summer was more subdued. The big opening attraction was a chintzy swimming contest for men and women. Admission to the only fresh-water beach in the city was 35 cents for adults and 25 for youngsters and older kids that could lie about their age. There was a high-dive, a medium board, and one at the bottom, only three feet from the water. The higher boards were longer.

The park's smaller newspaper ads appealed to the nostalgia of fun, saying, Do you like merry? Laughing? Crowds? Music? Dancing? Groves of wonderful old trees? Good eats? Fast, thrilling rides? Dozens of special attractions? Oceans of fun for the kiddies? Surprises? Screams and a rollicking good time? Attractions like the Giant dipper, Puzzle Town, the Whip, Canals of Venice, Miniature Railway, Mountain Speedway, Merry-go-Round, dancing, the Caterpillar, Over-the-Top, Pony Track, and a spring-fed 18-acre lake, full of people boats and fish.

Nationally, the Fourth of July was a disaster, over 200 people were killed and hundreds more injured. Independence, Missouri was fairly quiet since a strict ordinance against selling or using big bangs was a misdemeanor. Only one person was arrested for "dealing" and was fined $5 and his stash was taken away. The worst accident of the day was when a young man was injured after being thrown from his motorcycle.

The parks had a good day. The weather was cloudy, with a high in the mid-80s. To quote a young patron, "It is the celebrationist of all the holidays." After the holiday, Fairmount Park went back to being a laid-back picnic grove. "Zimmy", the only legless diver and swimmer in the whole, wide world; he was at Fairmount training for the Wrigley Marathon in Toronto, Canada.

Fireworks returned for every Sunday night in July, at 9 p. m. Scrapping the Navy was the first theme. A bunch of miniature dreadnaughts were blown to smithereens on the lake. This reflected the mentality of most people in America. The militarism of ten years ago was soon fading. Replacing it was "screw the rest of the world and its problems, let the good times roll."

The next Sunday Col. Lindberg's Spirit of St. Louis crossed the lake, all this being reflected on a huge, dark lake. Because of a lack of light pollution, the stars would have been brighter, and one could have seen the Milky Way. The noise of the rides and the screams of joy would have made for a perfect evening.

August brought shorter days but more picnics to Fairmount Park. Zimmy was replaced by Cliff Curran. He balanced and swayed on a 90-foot pole over terra firma, billed as a "swinging phenomenon, one moment between life and death."

The first of the big August picnics was the 20th annual "Woodmen of the World" picnic. Organized in 1890, it acted like a life insurance policy while the person was still alive. At one time their tombstones resembled tree stumps. Woodmen from their respective posts included Kansas City, Missouri and Kansas, Richmond, Missouri, and Independence. Every city had a drill team. Thanks to their service during the Great War and years of practice, they were all very good. There were also games, races, and other athletic events. Not only was there a nut on a pole, Dr. Nicholas Jaime's 50-piece Mexican Band, with lots of brass. 5,000 Woodmen and friends roamed the park, swam and danced to Earl Coleman's Orchestra, which started at 8:15.

Some of the picnics "hooked" for August included the Gallileo Galilie Society, amateur astronomers, Richard and Conover Company, KC Power and Light, Cake Eater and Kiddie's Day, Rothschild's Boys' Club, Fraternal Order of Eagles nos. 47 and 87, Kansas City, Kansas Retail Grocers' Association, Loose-Wiles Biscuit Company, John Hancock Mutual Life Insurance, Gateway Railway Clerks, City Ice Company, Mt. Washington and Fairmount Association Picnic, Standard Oil Refinery of Sugar Creek, National Bellahess Company, for which my 17-year-old yet-to-be mother worked making gloves at that time.

The United States Post Office employees' picnic was held on Sunday, August 14. Postal Employees from Greater Kansas City, St. Joseph, Leavenworth, Topeka, and Lawrence, Kansas, were also in attendance. The main feature of the picnic was a horseshoe tournament between Kansas City and St. Joe. Besides a fireworks display a free six-reel movie starring Clara Bow, the "It Girl", named "Free to Love", which about sums up her off-screen sex life.

While the world mourned the premature death of Rudolph Valentino, "The Sheik", Labor held its annual picnic at Fairmount Park. It wasn't a good year for Labor, or for the farmers. There were four main speakers, and many VIPs, but Judge Truman was not among them.

1927 was Independence, Missouri's Centennial. Sunday, October 2, through Friday, the 7th became a mostly sober block party, using the Square as the block. Governor of Missouri Sam A. Baker arrived on a special train from Jefferson City to give a kick-off speech in the Memorial Hall building, with seating for 1600 people, and 200 standing. Many were turned away into a cloudburst, the result of which pushed both Blue Rivers and their creeks over the banks. The governor spoke of the kind of people that settled Independence, noting that there were never any assholes in Independence, ever. The Sunday evening gathering was sponsored by the churches of Independence, of which there were a lot. Monday was the homecoming day, starting with a sight-seeing tour of Independence at 9 a. m., a parade at 3:30, and finally a talking picture exhibit by the people at Bell Labs, starting at 8:00 Monday evening. Every day of the week had a parade. Monday's theme was "Transportation: From Mule Haul Carts of 1827 to Autos, Airplanes, and Everything In Between." The airplane was built by the students of William Chrisman. Also featured was a complete railroad locomotive and coal car from the Missouri Pacific Booster Club, Hoisington, Kansas.

The first parade proved to be a huge success. In addition to the week of parades, 500 locals volunteered to assume the role of character actors. Daniel Boone and many other characters were portrayed. Every bit actor took his part very seriously. Yanks and Rebels in costume reenacted some of the Civil War skirmishes. All went according to script.

Tuesday was "Old Settlers' Day". Every day of the week was sponsored by different organizations or clubs. The Women's Temperance Christian Union, the gals that kept Independence dry, or the Pythian Sisters, dozens of groups such as these were in town. Also a person could theoretically belong to all of them, if he or she had the time. Judge Truman was an active member of at least six such organizations. Tuesday's parade was in sharp contrast to yesterdays. The civic and fraternal order marched, led by a band. Next came students from William Chrisman, dressed in costume of the different societies and academics at the school. Tail End Charlie at the end of the parade was a brass marching band. Compared to Monday's parade, Tuesday's was a bore.

Wednesday was the day of the biggest parade and was labeled "Historical Day". It formed at Maple and Union at 3:30, went east to Main and south to Lexington, then West to Liberty, north to West Oak, ending up at Lexington and Pleasant Street. Fifty floats and dozens of decorated autos took part. As many as 30,000 people lined the streets. Many floats were sponsored by local businesses, employees donating their free time, so as not to get fired. First prize of $25 cash went to Ott funeral home. It was Daniel Boone meeting with the Indians at the spring, overlooking the fact that Daniel never got within 200 miles of Independence. First prize of $15 for the prettiest auto went to a local woman, who spent $30 on the flowers to cover her car. Many bands, including the Standard Oil Refinery Band, passed through on flat-bed trucks.

Thursday's theme, "Patriots' Day", soldiers and sailors of three wars were honored. The long procession of veterans began at 3:30 and was billed as a parade for the soldiers of all wars. Although all gone, the veterans of the Revolutionary War were represented by a drum and fife corps, leading the parade. Following were forty or so Civil War veterans from both sides, many donned their blues or grays. Their ages were from 77 to 90, and they rode in autos. Next came the guys from the Spanish-American War, they marched in unison. Last but not least, then called the veterans of the Great War, in field gray, with a sprinkling of Navy blue, or the white of the Red Cross. The disabled veterans brought many a tear as they passed by, still in the care of the Kansas City Veterans Hospital. While this was going on, the Kansas City Police Band played at the City Hall. Judge Truman was busy helping to dedicate a tree given by the Daughters of the American Revolution, planted on the courthouse lawn. He gave a very short speech and hurried off.

Friday had two parades, one for the students of the Independence School district, sponsored by the P. T. A. All of the K through 8 grade students were in attendance, but the Chrisman High Schoolers were a different story. 250 didn't show; few had excuses.

A daily feature at the Memorial Building was "Talking Moving Pictures". Paid for by Southwestern Bell Labs, every afternoon at 3:30 sharp, the one hour demonstration impressed. One electric motor ran both machines, the first being the video (film), the audio coming from the photograph needle. Very crude, but effective.

A dance at Memorial Hall Friday night ended the festivities.

Independence was proud of 365 businesses (one for every day of the year) worth $15.2 million. There were six banks, 24 real estate/insurance companies, 9 printing companies, 4 lumber yards, 12 hardware stores, 52 grocery/meat markets, 16 dry goods stores, 12 restaurants/cafes, 28 garages, 18 filling stations, 14 coal companies, 16 barber shops, and 4 radio stores. There were zero saloons, zero pool halls, and zero brothels, but it was only six miles to Kansas City, Missouri, where there was plenty of everything.

In Sugar Creek, "Daddy Thatch" was elected police judge in April. He had a few cases which he quickly disposed of. But by July, when there had been no crime, only a few public drunks, Judge Thatch was quoted as saying, "Guess I've worked myself out of a job."

Cement City had its annual murder on September 26. It was a strange case, even for Cement City. Mr. and Mrs. Robert Johnson were fighting over the family .45 automatic. Somehow Mrs. Johnson procured the weapon and capped Mr. Johnson, twice, once in the lung, the other in the abdomen. She then returned it to Mr. Johnson and fled. At 1:30 in the afternoon the cops were called, but since Mr. Johnson was black, he wasn't allowed to be taken anywhere but the hospital for Negros at 19th and Forest in Kansas City. By the time he got there he was dead. Had he been a Mexican and maybe not even a citizen, he would have been allowed in the Independence hospital ten minutes away.

Chapter 35: 1928

As mentioned in '27, there were no saloons, brothels, or pool halls in Independence, but there was one gambling casino. Located on the south side of the Independence Square, on the second floor above what is now a restaurant called the Courthouse Exchange. Today, like a lot of things on the Square, it is vacant. The Hare Gambling House had been raided the following April and justice was served. By New Years Eve they were back in business, not more than a stone's throw from Judge Truman's office, the New Year's Eve crowd being more than the cops could ignore. A dozen men, six from the Jackson County's Sheriff's department and six from the prosecutor's office, showed up on the first Saturday night of the New Year, unannounced. They rushed past the doorman, whose job it was to keep out the riff raff. The raiders found four pistols, one large knife, several bottles of whiskey, fifty dice, a half a bushel of poker chips, black jack, stud poker, and dice games in progress, with $70 in cash still on the table. 32 men were arrested and taken to jail. After posting a total of $17,000 in bonds the men were released, the bonds covering the fines.

The following Friday at 6 pm the Hare establishment was again visited on a tip. The brothers were in the process of opening up again. New gaming equipment was coming to light. The stash included a new pistol and a roulette wheel. The brothers were taken to the county jail in Kansas City, their game finally up.

Fairmount Park opened its gates officially on Saturday, May 12. The previous weekend the gates were opened free to the public. There was even dancing in the newly redecorated and enlarged ballroom, Earl Coleman's new band providing the music. Many improvements were made and park management wanted to show them off.

A 400-foot wooden walkway was added to the west side of the lake, linking the boat house and the bathing beach, which got a new coating of sand. Animals for kids to ride, like goats and more ponies, were procured.

The first act at Fairmount Park was a trick auto act labeled "Gregge's Auto". They passed through the air back and forth....

The Parent Teachers Association of the Independence suburbs was the first park picnic, followed by a Mother's Day celebration. A prize of $5 each was given to mothers with "the most girls," boys, boys and girls, the oldest and youngest mother.

Memorial Day was ruined by rain, hail, and lightning, sending everyone running for cover. The storm was responsible for knocking out 500 phones in the Fairmount, Mt. Washington, and Sugar Creek area.

This year Fairmount Park was getting a lot of competition for KC's entertainment dollars. First there was Fairyland Park, which went all out to lure the public and picnics. Two of the premier picnics were the P. T. A. of First Kansas City, Missouri, followed by the P. T. A. of Kansas City, Kas., both in May. The picnics weren't just one day affairs, each lasting three days. 600 prizes were given, number one was a Shetland pony, awarded to the child that sold the most tickets to the event. Radios and lots of athletic equipment, from baseballs to tennis racquets were given out as prizes. The main attraction was a double-parachute leap from a balloon. Second, Winnwood Beach, north of the river, opened as a $1 million amusement park. Frank Winnwood, the son a former prominent Clay County jurist, and his wife, ran the park with a hands-on style. Advertised as "The Atlantic City of the West," their niche was pretty girls (beauty contests). The park featured a Ferris wheel, dancing, swimming, boating, and various rides and concessions. There were weekly beauty contests as soon as the weather allowed the girls to take off their clothes. There was also a roller coaster, and a dance floor was built over the lake. There was a Santa Claus ride which was pulled by reindeer, and took a person through Santa Claus Land. A circle swing, a fun house, and riding academy for horse lovers. They also bought a lot of park insurance. The official opening was Sunday, May 27. Admission to the park would be free, but once inside...

The new Winnwood's first attraction was aeroplanes. The "Beals Flying Circus" (featuring mono-planes, one-wing, the latest thing) with "Daredevil Pilots", put on an air show. After the figure eight, loops, barrel rolls, flying in formation, and buzzing the crowd the five planes each dropped 1,000 long-stemmed red roses over the crowd. Every hour on the hour a bus left Seventh and Grand for the park, via the ASB Bridge.

Also competing for the entertainment dollar were movie houses, thanks to air conditioning, allowing them to stay open all year. Talkies were becoming common. The last silent movie was only a year away. A popular movie at the Liberty Theater was a serious look at the younger generation. The title was "The Road to Ruin," insinuating that the generation that will soon save the world was a bunch of crazed partiers breaking all the mores of decency, and some Commandments.

The second week in June brought the Republican National Convention to Kansas City. There wasn't a lot of debate, Secretary of Commerce, poor old

Herbert Hoover, was nominated to fill the vacuum in the White House left by Calvin Coolidge, a very lucky politician.

Monday night, June 11, the city of Kansas City and its suburbs put on one of the city's largest parades in a town once renowned for its parades. Starting at 9th Street and Grand Avenue at 8:30 p.m., the torch lit parade snaked it's mile-long, 10,000 strong, down Grand Avenue, ending at the World War One memorial. An estimated 200,000 - 250,000 lined the streets. Leading the parade was a pair of elephants. The caboose was two camels. In between were thousands carrying torches being tossed in the air, not all being caught. There were 21 marching bands; the one representing Independence was the 54-piece "Independence Co-operative Band". As the parade passed, many people crowding the sidewalks sang the National Anthem. Forty floats, some of them adorned with characters to look like deceased Republican presidents from Lincoln to Teddy Roosevelt. The Independence Missouri float was manned by the great-great nephew of John Grinter, the only man in rural Jackson County, to vote for Lincoln in 1860. Cowboys on horses, Indians, stage coaches, old railroad engines and cars. Columns of marchers carrying signs and banners for the potential nominees, mainly Hoover, Lowden, and Curtis. Sprinkled in were hundreds of automobiles decorated in red, white, and blue.

The parks profited because the convention was over before it started. President Coolidge stayed out by not endorsing anyone. Secretary of Commerce Hoover won the nomination before the first ballot. Silent Cal said of Hoover, "He gave me a lot of unsolicited advice, most of it wrong."

Fairmount Park's beach opened Memorial Day weekend. A slide and waterwheel were added to the fun. The first act of the new season was "Diving Ponies." All the way from Hollywood, the horses had been in many silent cowboy movies. Their job was stunts, like jumping and swimming in rivers. Miss Helen Manning, a Hollywood stunt lady, along with her horse, dived 50 feet from a tower into the lake. The act was free with a paid admission, and would last two weeks, every day at 4:30 and 9:30. Besides the 54 amusements and concessions, a free silent picture show was shown in the vacant bandstand, darkness permitting, no vaudeville. Coleman's Fairmount Park Orchestra played dance music every Saturday, Sunday, Tuesday and Thursdays. Plenty of free parking, with street car service to the front gate.

On Sunday, June 24, Fairmount Park, not to be outdone by Winnwood Beach's beauty contest, staged a reproduction of the Miss Missouri contest previously held in St. Louis. Miss Missouri, her attendants, and twenty-four young ladies from various cities representing their community as the prettiest girl in town. The girls modeled the latest in bathing suit attire, meaning less suit than last year. The largest picnic of June was the 20,000 employees, friends, and hangers-on of the "Allied Railroad Employees."

Winnwood Beach had a contest to name the newest ride added early in the season. A $50 prize was split between three people who submitted "The Whirlwinn." A new concession was added, the Gas House. A bathing beauty contest of sorts was held starting on June 24. Girls received a ticket every time she paid to swim. After five tickets, she was entitled to a free bathing beauty photo. Every week the prettiest girl won a season pass to Winnwood.

Fairyland Park's season opened with a Battle of the Bands. A 14-piece orchestra from the University of Missouri challenged the same from the University of Kansas. The winner in each of the numbers was judged by the response of the crowd. The Missouri Tigers beat the Jayhawks and therefore won a gig at the park, playing dance music in the dance pavilion where admission was 75 cents a couple, no singles allowed. Vaudeville was presented with two acts doing two shows a day. A movie was shown as soon as the sun set, no Daylight Savings. The Fourth of July was the hottest in ten years. Humidity plus 96-degree temperatures were responsible for two deaths in the city, but it was good for business at the swimming holes.

The diving ponies were still at Fairmount Park. A huge fireworks display again reflected off the lake, starting promptly at 9:30, according to someone's time piece. But not all, atomic clocks were in the future. Radio Station WHB every day from 11:57 to noon broadcast a time check, Monday through Friday, making it possible for people to synchronize their lives to time, the fourth dimension. There was dancing in the pavilion from 8:30 to 11:30 and a movie was shown.

Back at Fairyland, the eight Flying Le Mars, acrobats, flew around. Professor Lee Planet did a double-parachute leap twice a day. The University of Missouri orchestra had whittled down to ten musicians, thanks to summer vacation. The KC Juvenile Star Troup performed, featuring Monty Brancato, tap dancer, and Hugo, tight, rope walker. Again, a movie preceded a huge, free fireworks display.

Fairmount Park had 40,000 people on the Fourth of July, and by now 30,000 had already rode the giant dipper this season. The week of the 15th was celebrated as the park's 35th anniversary. The main attraction was Millie Florence. She climbed a 70-foot pole, swaying to and fro. Upon reaching the top she commenced to do death defying stunts. When asked if she ever got scared, she said, "Only when I look down and see movement on the ground."

Mayor Sermon of Independence held his third annual picnic for Independence children at Fairmount Park. This picnic was followed by the American Can Company, Kansas City Clearing House, Cudahy Packing Company, and the Kansas City Public Service Brotherhood. Nightly fireworks were also a part of the park's anniversary.

Some of the picnics to close out July were the Atlantic and Pacific Grocery Stores (the A & P), Public Service Employees from Ninth & Brighton, Cook Paint and Varnish, H. D. Lee Mercantile Company, and Blue Valley Business Men's Club.

If not for a small workforce, the "Park in the Woods" would look like a forest, sun and rain being job security. Push mowers kept the grass like a green, soft carpet in the many acres of picnic area shaded by huge trees. Flowers were grown in the park's greenhouse on the east side of the lake, beautifully arranged in the earth along the walkways, where they could get the most sunlight. Working out of the boathouse, Al Carlisle and crew were responsible for the weeds that grew along the bank of the lake. Working with a small scythe, it wasn't too bad a way to spend the summer vacation.

August through the Labor Day weekend brought many picnics to all three parks, Fairmount led the way. First came the annual Buckner/Blue Springs, Missouri picnic. There were races on both the athletic field and lake, in which men, women, and children participated. The Bucker Lions played the Blue Springs Tigers for the Suburban League Championship. Other picnics for the first week in August were the National Bella Hess Company, Metropolitan Insurance Company, and United Garment Workers, all scheduled on different days.

Fairyland was more than holding its own that first week in August. The park featured Captain Jack Payne, the World's Greatest Daredevil Diver, and he must have been nuts. He was the Evel Knievel of the 1920s. Before coming to Kansas City he had gained fame by diving 140 feet into Niagara Falls, a 130-foot dive off the Pittsburgh Bridge, and a 120-foot back somersault in Wheeling, West Virginia. At Fairyland, every evening at 10:00 and twice on Sunday, he dove 80 feet into a tank of water which was on fire, because gasoline burns, while doing a back flip.

The remainder of Fairmount's 1928 season was picnic time. A typical week would go something like this: Monday, the South Side Merchants' Association; Tuesday, Clearing House of Greater Kansas City; Wednesday, Knights of Columbus, Daughters of Isabel, and the Booth Hatcheries of Lee's Summit; Gettard Groceries on Thursday. On Friday it was the Grotto Chapters of Topeka, Leavenworth, Kansas City, Kansas, and Sedalia, Missouri. The park was booked.

Sunday, August 12, brought a One-Step (Fox Trot) Dance Contest. 50 couples took part. The winning couple received one Loving Cup (?). Tuesday was candy night. The prize, chocolate. On Thursday evening there was a barnyard dance. The ballroom was decorated like a barn yard and Earl Coleman's Orchestra dosee-doed. Among the contests were a rooster crowing contest, potato race, wheel-barrow race, and a hay-pitching contest. Prizes representing a farm were given. Special prizes were given to people dressed as rubes.

Winnwood had a big problem when someone spread the rumor that the lake water was contaminated. After a test, the lake was okayed for swimming, but it sure didn't help business. Winnwood was not pulling in many picnics, but dancing on the pavilion built over the lake in the evening was pretty cool.

Fairyland Park had a dance marathon. Starting at 9 o'clock Friday night 'till the last of 75 young couples couldn't stand up. The rules were simple: You danced 21 hours a day. Every hour you got a 15-minute break for a head call, drink, food, rest. Then it was up and at-em till 2 a. m., when a 3 hour sleep was allowed. Before the sun was up it was dance time. They danced outside in the Collegiate Dance Garden to an old Victrola record player. First prize was one Chevrolet Coup. Seems a little unfair. Second prize was two diamond rings, third prize was $100, down to $10 for the twelfth couple to drop. This would later evolve into the Walkathon.

Among the larger picnics at Fairmount was the Armour Packing Company's annual picnic on August 19th. Tickets admitting employees, families, and friends were liberally distributed. Games, races, swimming, and a Fox Trot contest in the evening, with the winning couple receiving one silver Loving Cup. The picnic basket was replaced by the hot dogs of the retail grocers. People, upon entering the park, were advised to save their numbered tickets, as hundreds of grocery type prizes were to be given away, the grand prize being a new Chevy Coup. Saturday brought the Kansas City Southern Railway Co. Great food and a baseball game, as well as the park's many amenities kept everyone late into the evening.

The last week in August was reserved for the annual Mt. Washington/Fairmount Area picnic. Old-time residents who had moved were encouraged to return. The park was shared by Rothschild & Sons Clothing Store, followed by picnics for the Walker Tabernacle, and the Ford Dealers of Greater Kansas City were the last major picnic of the season. No Model A's were given away this year, although it was game to make fun of the old Fliver. Prizes were given for the oldest Model T, the most comically decorated, and best decorated. The many Model A's were there to be worshipped as the savior of the Ford Motor Company.

Labor Day brought Senator James A. Reed, a power in the Democratic Party. His claim to fame was casting the deciding vote ushering in the Federal Reserve Act. In 1913, as a member of the Banking Committee, he changed his vote from "Nay" to "Yea" and the state of Missouri received two Federal Reserve Banks, one in St. Louis and one in Kansas City, out of the deal. Whatever he said was irrelevant, because he was retiring from politics, after much racial demagoguery.

The end of the season brought Carnival Week. There were clowns, and flags were flown throughout the park. The scene this year is "A Night in Atlantic City," racing being the subject, from wheelchairs to row-boats, and crab races. Much confetti and a dancing contest ended the season.

Two major projects got underway which would change the area landscape. First was Highway 24, a cement ribbon that would follow the Independence and Kansas City Road out to Lexington. A viaduct would have to be built over the railroad tracks and the Blue River on Kansas City's east side. Heading east, first through Mt. Washington, then through the Fairmount's business district, and by Fairmount Park's front entrance. East to where two farms with homes had to be condemned and bought between Liberty Street and Noland Road, where the old Lexington Road finished the journey out of Jackson County, finally hooking up with the highway coming east from St. Louis. Second was the new bridge crossing the Missouri River, connecting Jackson and Clay Counties at the old Liberty Landing. Costing $970,000, the payback was to be by toll.

In April the J. G. White Company of the Big Apple wired Judge Truman and the Independence Chamber of Commerce, who had both lobbied for the bridge, that they could announce the projects' approval. In September a contract was signed with the Union Bridge Company of Kansas City, Missouri, to start moving in equipment and build the necessary structures, including a railroad switch by the Wabash Railroad for hauling in the tons and tons of stuff. The bridge is to be 2,194 feet from South to North, most of it in Clay County. All-weather roads were promised by both counties. Obtaining the right of way on the Clay County side presented a couple of problems. First, Mr. Robert Elliott, previous owner of 20 acres purchased for $500, hadn't received his check yet. He would not allow equipment to be unloaded in his cornfield until he was paid. A check for $500 borrowed from the Independence Chamber of Commerce soon arrived. Unloading could begin. Not one to miss an opportunity, Mr. S. P. Boggess wanted $9,000 for a slice of land 1/5 of an acre. He knew that a pillar had to go there and he never budged. The dispute was still pending as the year came to an end.

Sugar Creek continued to prosper. The city taxes were actually lowered from a 95-cent per $100 valuation, to 80-per cent per, a savings of 17%. The town, including Standard Oil, was assessed at $3,754,950. Of the $30,000 paid in 1928 taxes, Standard Oil paid 81%, or $23,957. Sugar Creek's water came from Kansas City. The annual consumption was about 200,000 cubic feet per month, and there were 264 hookups. For 75 cents per month a customer was allowed 2,000 gallons. The next 13,000 were billed at 23 cents per thousand. The next 15,000 cost 22 cents. In June the city council was losing patience with water users. Some were over 90 days overdue. David Evinger, Water Superintendent, was giving warnings before taking out their water meters.

It was the first year for the "Sugar Creek Flashers, a baseball team in the Kansas City Journal Post League. By the Fourth of July they were in second place. A problem for the team had been getting to the games. The boys took an old Model-T that had been parked in front of a telephone pole for months. The auto had been abandoned and stripped down to its skivvies. Only the frame and parts of the motor were left to rot in the sun. Soon it was on the road. The only problem was money for gas. The rule was whoever bought the gas, drove. For some reason the old car would only start by raising the rear wheels on two boxes before cranking.

On September 26 the inspiration and promoter of the Air Line died in New York City. Arthur Stilwell, born October 21, 1859, used the name "Air Line," because he claimed it was built only on hot air, mainly his. He was a spiritualist entrepreneur, meaning his inspirational endeavors came to him thanks to spirits he called Brownies. Called by many "The Great Promoter," Stilwell and his Brownies would bring the world the Kansas City Southern Railway, the Kansas City Mexico & Orient Railroad, and numerous towns and cities along those roads, many named after himself. He and the Brownies also gave the world Kansas City's Fairmount Park.

Chapter 36: 1929

Things were tough at Fairmount Park in January. The Goetz Brewing Company of St. Joe, who had been leasing the park for $10,000 a year from the Cusenbary family, sublet the lake, the rides, and concessions, the money being split by the three remaining members of the Cusenbary family. All kinds of rumors about the future of the park were tossed about, since the land was valued at $5,000 an acre, as a sub-division. The merchants of the Fairmount business district were much concerned. If the park closed, many businesses would not have had a chance to be ruined by the coming Depression. The people who had the biggest stake in the park came to its rescue.

The park was making money, lots of money. The people making that money wanted to continue. So entrepreneurs like Mr. Carlisle leased the lake, pooled their financial resources, that problem solved. There were forces at work who wanted to destroy Fairmount Park for greed. On February 27, Mr. H. R. Ennis, a Kansas City realtor, spoke at the East Suburban Kiwanis Club. His main topic of discussion was what to do with the very valuable land now occupied by a summer oasis. He started his attack of the park by claiming liquor was being sold illegally on the park's premises. William Morrison, representing the park, pointed out that the park, last season, had hired a detective to investigate the charges. He found no one selling alcohol on park property. He did, however, find a very open and thriving liquor business directly across the street from the park's entrance. The business of cleaning up the illegal auto trunk sales were really the responsibility of the Fairmount community and maybe the police. Mr. Ennis, though, believed that the acreage would be better utilized as an industrial park, so that he could make a lot of money.

The same day, Cement City was raided again, resulting in the arrest of the same man that had been arrested last year. This time a five-gallon jug of corn whisky and several empty five-gallon jugs were found, along with corn whisky in half-pint bottles, along with an arsenal of rifles and pistols. The arsenal was returned by the judge, but justice would be served.

The parks were all opened by mid-May. Purchased a few years earlier by William C. Glover of Kansas City, Wildwood Beach, just outside Raytown, had plans to amuse the people of that area and beyond. Like the other lakes, land around Wildwood's three lakes was on the market. As the park grew in importance management didn't want the public to take the name "Wildwood" to mean any shenanigans were allowed. No bums allowed. The Missouri Ramblers made music for the 60' x 90' dance floor. Plans were made to turn Wildwood Beach into Wildwood Park, with all the rides, etc.

An early Spring plus great management allowed the parks to all open by mid-May. The grasses were green, the paint was dry, the beach at Fairmount Park had a new coating of sand and new fish.

Fairmount Park's first large picnic of the young season was the now-annual Independence Schools PTA Picnic. First scheduled for Saturday, May, 11, rains postponed the event two weeks.

Food would be gathered by the ladies. Most grocery shopping would have been done around the Independence Square, where a one-hour parking limit was sometimes enforced. The most popular items for a picnic, hot dogs, were 25 cents a pound, and were linked together like machine gun bullets. Sandwiches were next, mayonnaise 25 cents a quart, meat loaf 50 cents a pound, ham 40 cents, lunch meat 30 cents. Potato chips came in three sizes, 5, 10, and 30 cents a pack; sweet pickles, 20 cents a dozen, dills, 3 for a dime; oranges were 25 cents a dozen, bananas, 10 cents a pound; new potatoes were 3 lbs for 25 cents, local potatoes were 25 cents a peck; cabbage, 6 cents a pound. Prices varied from week to week. Chickens were a special order, came whole and were not cheap.

When the PTA picnic was finally held, all went well. The ladies not only took care of the food, they manned some of the concessions. The Boy Scouts were in uniform, and again took the children whose parents couldn't make it under their wing. As in the past, every ticket of admission entitled the holder to two free rides, except for the roller coasters. The park gave a percentage of the day's profits to the P. T. A. In the afternoon games and races were held on the athletic field. Prizes from local Independence merchants were awarded the winners. All were encouraged to come early and stay late, and they did.

A month later, the mayor of Independence, Roger Sermon, held his annual picnic at Fairmount Park. Mayor Sermon, like Judge Truman, was a Captain and Battery Artillery Commander in WWI. First elected as mayor in 1924 at 32 years old, he's best remembered for saving the Independence Electric Power Plant from unscrupulous forces. He updated the Water Works and the gas system. On Thursday, June 27, the third annual Mayor's Picnic began early. Free tickets were available at several locations. The gates opened at 10 o'clock. By noon all of the tables in the pavilion were taken. For one hour, all rides in the park were free. The lines were long. 2,000 kids ran amuck throughout the day and into the late evening.

Between the two picnics were picnics, hundreds, some large, some small, all fun. The free attraction from Memorial Day until the Fourth of July was "Fearless Gregg's Autos". Like last season, the jalopies were put through their paces.

The bathing beach had some new attractions, like new diving boards, slides, and a device called a "rolling top". This year's aquatic fun would be a "Water Sports Carnival". Every Sunday, fun in and on the lake brought prizes for the participants. Races, water polo, diving contests and canoe tilting were well supervised by Harry I. Strandhagen, physical instructor on KMBC radio.

In the ballroom Earl Coleman's Band played peppy music seven days a week. Every night had a different theme, starting with "Candy Night". The dance contest winners received boxes of Vassar chocolates. Then came "Carnival Night," where prizes were given for the best costume. Rattles and whistles were some of the prizes. Applause by the crowd selected the winners.

The Fourth of July fireworks at Fairmount Park were a little different. The Ralph Rhodes Fireworks Company used the bathing beach area instead of the east side of the lake for Ground Zero. A new Ford was given away. Every Sunday night for the remainder of the season ended with a fireworks display. This year Wildwood Beach had a daylight Japanese fireworks display. For the patriots, Swope Park would have been their forte. Six local organizations participated, including the Veterans of Foreign Wars, American Legion, Boy Scouts, and Daughters of the American Revolution. The celebration started at 11 a. m. Playing and singing of patriotic songs like God Bless America was followed by the reading of the Declaration of Independence and the Constitution, ending with a Benediction, after which blankets and picnic baskets were spread out around the bandstand. Starting at 7 p. m. and ending at 10, Ben Kendricks band played popular music. Other amusements were baseball games and a lot of golf tournaments. Throughout the day the temperature was mild, in the mid-80s. Many people walked to the air-conditioned movie house.

Following the Fourth of July the Kansas City Journal Post held a much publicized picnic for the children of Kansas City at Fairmount Park. Thursday, July 11, was cool, with skies threatening rain. Special cars were added by the Kansas City Public Service Company. On the front of the cars signs designated the cars' destination as Fairmount Park and "Kansas City Journal Post's Kiddie's Day." All a kid 12 or under had to do was to pay a one-way fare to the park. The trip back to the big city was free. Entrance to the park was free to everyone. Five concessions were free for the kids. Long lines formed for the Merry-Go-Round, The Whip, Aerial Swing, Mountain Speedway, and the Fun House. Early rain chased many picnickers into the dance pavilion, changing the affair into a huge, family-like gathering. By 2:00 the sun was burning off the clouds, leaving the afternoon a mild 80 degrees.

There was so much going on the kiddies seemed confused. They just couldn't keep up. Hiram and His Mule performed. The laughter and screams of joy could be heard all over the park. One of Earl Coleman's three bands played kids' stuff, with Earl on the drums, Hilda Olson doing the vocals. A pie-eating contest was held in the open-air theater, followed by games and contests of skill at the Athletic Field. Every child upon entering the park received an all-day sucker, and popcorn and drinks were given away first come, first served.

The Prettiest Boy and Girl contest was held, breaking the hearts of many parents. Two 2-year-old girls tied for first place, applause from the crowd picking the winner. After six tries to thunderous applause, two loving cups were given. L. L. Warren, the Kansas City Supervisor of Playgrounds, was in charge of the games, which attracted a large crowd.

The contests consisted of Boys' Lock-Leg Race, Girls' Egg Race, Boys' Shoe Scramble (throw 'em in a big pile, find 'em and win), Boys' and Girls' 25-Yard Dash, ages 8-10. A nurse set up shop in the Ladies' restroom, but was not needed for any of the 5,000 youngsters in attendance.

It was back to large picnics every day, starting with the Post Office and the American Legion. Basket dinners were followed by dancing in the Pavilion. The Liberty Garment Company followed on Tuesday, Aines Farm Dairy on Wednesday, Bemmis Bag Company, which was followed by churches, unions, and corporations for the rest of the summer.

Every week starting Sunday, July 14, brought a new act of some sort. First came a bunch of people on a trapeze. That week the Kansas City Grocers came to the park to give things away. Thousands of grocery items were handed out. The largest prize that day was a new Chevrolet. A fireworks display by the Ralph Rhodes Fireworks Company put an end to the evening, and then the long drive back to Kansas City, Kas., without power steering. Hot weather set in, and all of Kansas City's parks, lakes, and pools were packed. Starting the first week of August through the end of the season, every week brought new themes to Fairmount Park. First was Circus Week, with vaudeville. Jack Wade and Company did circus stuff. Bozo and Elmer, clowns, Tusker's Trained Goats, featuring "Little Cutlet", the world's only globe-walking goat. The main attraction, however, was Uncle Charles's Trained Animals, ponies, monkeys, and dogs doing tricks for treats. This was also the week of the Old Settlers' Get Together. The old pioneers were starting to thin out. Prizes were given to the oldest person, oldest couple, and oldest twins. Fiddles were brought out and music of the Sixties filled the air, the 1860s.

Next came Hawaiian Night, with Ralph Rhodes and his Hawaiian Review, starring the Palis Hawaiian Serenaders, featuring Mrs. Bobby and Virginia Lea. The mule was back, there were lots of pretty girls doing the Hula and giving out leis. A huge volcano was built next to the beach, which acted as Waikiki. Every evening, promptly at 10 p. m., the volcano would roar to life. Fireworks also erupted with a roar. Earl Coleman's Band was still belting out the hits in the ballroom. The lighting in the dancing pavilion was impressive. A mirrored ball reflected light, the effect seemed amazing.

Hundreds of picnics ended the season. Due to the warm weather, the lake and bathing beach stayed open after Labor Day. Management complimented the local constables for running off the riff-raff peddling booze in the parking lot.

For the first time in four years, Labor had a parade Downtown. Starting on Journal Post Hill, 10,000 people and horses started to assemble by 8 o'clock that morning. Labor was pissed. It felt that technology was killing their membership; so everyone walked. The ten floats were pulled by horses. Bands were pulled, except for the pianos, their operators ordered to walk. Every trade in town was represented. Most of the brewery workers were gone. There were a few, however, who made soda pop. After their long walk, they got into their automobiles and headed for Winnwood Beach. At Winnwood, the unions called for a 40-hour work week. A zero-hour work week would be in their future.

The big news locally was the Independence/Liberty Bridge across the Missouri River. As the time for the ribbon-cutting grew closer, excitement grew. The new bridge, going from South of the river to Liberty, would knock an hour and a half off the trip by auto. President Hoover was invited but the bridge had to settle for Henry S. Caulfield, Governor of Missouri.

As early as March, news trickled through the community. Many braved the rotten roads to view the site. As completion drew near, the traffic through Sugar Creek was sometimes bumper to bumper.

On March 6, the bridge claimed its first life. A KC man, working for the KC Bridge Company, was felled by an iron derrick on the Jackson County side. A few weeks later a stiff was discovered hanging from the bridge as the sun rose in the East.

A seven-mile ribbon of concrete, starting at the northern edge of the Independence city limit, was laid north to Courtney, Missouri, then on to the bridge. The entire project was planned to be completed by September 1, but there was no way.

In late May the Independence Chamber of Commerce met to decide what kind of celebration to throw. Some wanted a three-day affair, but a one day celebration won out. Floats, tours up and down the river, and motorboat racing were planned. The Independence Bridge Road started just south of the entrance to the bridge, then two miles to Courtney.

In late July the last pier was positioned in the river. Traffic in Sugar Creek was getting worse. Besides the regular employees entering the Standard Oil plant, bridge construction employees had no choice but to come through Sugar Creek, six 5-ton trucks coming through town 24 hours a day, six days a week. 55 tank trucks hauled oil for the county roads, and 75 batch trucks hauled cement and various types of gravel en route to various locations, along with the regular business traffic in the bustling little town.

As the formal opening of the toll bridge drew nearer, plans for the celebration intensified. Twenty communities from both sides of the river planned to have floats in the parade, which would be held in Independence on the Square. The bridge was opened for business on Saturday, September 28, but the official opening was Saturday, October 5.

The charges for crossing the bridge were as follows: Automobile & driver, 25 cents, five cents for each additional passenger; a truck under one ton, 25 cents; a truck one to three tons, 40 cents; for people using the bridge on a regular basis a book of 50 tickets could be purchased.

Signs announcing the shortcut over the Missouri River were scattered everywhere within 100 miles:

GOING NORTH AND EAST, CROSS THE MISSOURI RIVER BY INDEPENDENCE LIBERTY BRIDGE GOOD ROAD, DIRECT ROUTE

The signs were placed as far north as Bethany, Missouri, south to Clinton, Missouri, and Joplin, east to Columbia, Mo.

Three toll takers were hired, working twelve hours on, twenty-four hours off. The toll booth was at the north end of the bridge. A Buckner girl, 19-year-old La Verna Foley, would reign as "Queen of the Bridge," along with her eight attendants. The barricades came down at 05:55. The two-mile cement strip, between the bridge south to Courtney, was okay for auto traffic only. The road to Lexington Street was not yet complete, so traffic was re-routed to River Boulevard. The first car to cross the bridge was 15 minutes after the barricades came down. By ten o'clock that morning only twenty cars had crossed. They only had to make another $874,995 to break even. On the big day, Friday, October 11, a day of much to celebrate, it rained. The governor claimed it to be "tears of joy." Things started late at the bridge because of the weather. The governor's entourage and the Independence county delegation could not use the new road because some of it had washed away. The only way to the bridge was through Sugar Creek/Cement City.

At the bridge American flags with 48 stars flew every 60 feet. Red, white, and blue bunting hung the length. Around noon, five aeroplanes from the North Liberty airport dropped flowers, did loops and stunts until one quit working and had to make a dead stick landing in a potato field. After the speeches the Queen untied a ribbon in the center of the structure, officially linking Jackson and Clay Counties. Cement City and Sugar Creek once again became a parade of sorts as hundreds of autos and limos had to backtrack to the Independence Square. Starting at 2:30, an hour late, the parade slowly traveled from Noland and State Highway 24 around the business district. The parade route was lined with people, some six deep. For the first and last time ever, Kansas City cops directed traffic, as they were better than the local police. The Kansas City Police Band led the procession, followed by everybody else. There were half a dozen marching bands, including Standard Oil's. Floats were soggy, but neat. Orrick's was a huge, wet potato. The Square was decorated to the nines. The parade ended at the Chrisman Campus, where speeches were followed by a football game between William Chrisman and Lexington, Mo., the locals winning 6 - 0.

In January of 1929, my Grandpa Novak died of pneumonia. He left my grandma with seven kids and my Uncle Jerry a fetus. After Grandpa Novak was laid to rest, my bachelor father quit his job as a messenger Downtown, and went back to work at the refinery. On Saturday, October 19, he married my mother. After the ceremony at St. Cyril's Catholic Church the wedding party had breakfast at my widowed grandmother's house. Following this ritual and a little small talk, most went home to rest. Later in the day the good times would begin. The ladies would prepare the food, the men would bring cigars and booze. The reception would have been held in Slyman's Hall. The crowd would have been large, bearing gifts of mostly cash, and there would have been live music and dancing. As the refinery ran 24/7, men in work clothes would drop in. Kids would have been everywhere, maybe even tending bar. There would have been no closing time. The next day being the Sabbath, anything left over would be consumed and the evidence destroyed. After a honeymoon at the Lake of the Ozarks, they bought the house they would live and die in.

1929 was an election year in Sugar Creek. Mayor H. R. Boehner had done his job. Sugar Creek was probably the best Fourth-Class city in the state. There were few fires, because almost everyone owned his own American Dream. Much of the building material was liberated from the refinery, being of good quality. In April, rallies were held for both the Republicans and Democrats. The Democrats had Judge Truman as their principal speaker. The Democrats swept. John Kelley beat out I. D. Sutton for mayor.

Work at the oil refinery was dangerous. Walter Ray Griffith, 21 years of age, lived with his aunt and uncle in Independence. He was fatally burned. At breakfast he told his aunt he'd had a dream that he would be hurt at work that day, and he was.

In April, a very wealthy man asked psychic Edgar Casey if he should sell his stocks, or keep them. He told the man to sell; he didn't. He ended up broke, like the world would soon be. The total financial meltdown would put an end to Fairmount Park.

My Mom and Dad, Engaged at Fairmount Park, 1929.

Chapter 37: 1930

Since the park had closed in September, a few things had changed. First, the stock market had crashed. Second, by Spring, 1930, things were not getting better; the market kept jerking (down). Unemployment started to surge. But at the Kansas City parks, there was only optimism. By Spring President Hoover was declaring the Depression over. But in reality it had 11 more years to go, followed by four years of war.

Fairmount Park's last year as an amusement park began on Friday, May 9. In their optimism (or desperation) the owners made improvements and changes. First, Sam Benjamin was re-hired to manage the park. Second, over $100,000 was spent on lighting. Colored light bulbs hung from the branches of the big trees, giving the illusion of a jeweled canopy. The lake was also circumvented with lighting. Sam had traveled back east to Coney Island, which had had a bad year. He brought back a new ride and several concessions. A zoo was built by the spring. Admission to the park for the first time was free. Ingersoll rehired Sam, who had opened and had been managing a new park in Minnesota for three years. Sam, being a bachelor, lived in the second-floor office/bedroom. In the winter he managed the Orpheum theater downtown, now air conditioned, along with most talkie theaters. Sam brought with him 30 years in the amusement/theater business.

His career started in the 1890's with the Heim Electric Park, located in the East Bottoms of Kansas City, Missouri. There he racked up nine years. The new Electric Park, seven years; Fairmount Park, seven years; Fairyland Park four years; Minnesota, three years.

In an interview he was quoted as saying that his, "management will be such that Fairmount Park is to be the amusement center of the suburban district, Independence and the Eastern part of the county. It is to be run in a clean and orderly manner, and the support and interest of the community will be invited." Optimism in the face of disaster.

Friday, May 9, Fairmount Park opened for the season. The local Kiwanis Club held their annual dance at the newly-enlarged pavilion, now big enough for 500 couples.

Most of the amenities were ready for the anticipated crowds, the park sporting a new coat of lead-based paint. They included a Ferris wheel, Tilt-a-Whirl, miniature golf, miniature railroad, Heyday, Lindy Loop, Mountain Speedway or the Monkey, or the three roller coasters. On the lake were the Swooper Water

Wheel and the Serpent through the Everglades. There was the Midway, a cafe, dozens of ice cream, soda pop, popcorn, etc., etc., concessions, and a lot of noise. A speaker was hooked up to a radio, positioned in the center of the park, so people wouldn't need to be by their radios from 7 to 7:15 p.m., seven days a week, until 1943, to listen to the antics of Amos and Andy.

Fairyland Park spent money, also. Twenty area businessmen now owned the park. A new ride called the Waltzer, a miniature golf course, and several new concessions were added. Opening week at Fairyland featured two vaudeville acts, Prince Hoshi and his Fight for Life, as well as the Aerial Holts, presented twice daily.

Picnics were going to be a main feature at Fairyland this year. Some of the biggest were booked months in advance. The Retail Grocer's picnic was the largest in the city. Other huge gatherings were the Kansas City PTA picnics, lasting nine days, starting with Kindergarten Day to Day Nine, for all the grades. The Shriners followed this, then the Gas Company, the railroads, and the Loose-Wiles Biscuit Company. The dance floor was also enlarged, making it the biggest in Kansas City.

Management promised to bring big names to Fairyland, like Rudy Vallee and the Paul Whitman band. Neither would play an amusement park. They were the Rolling Stones and Elvis of an earlier generation. The patrons would have to settle for Benny Moton and his Victor Recording Orchestra.

On Sunday, May 25, a motorcycle rodeo came to Fairyland, a four-state affair, sponsored by dealers and six-thousand fans of the "murdercycle." The rodeo was something like a much more innocent version of Sturgis. At 1 p. m., they rode into Fairyland through the main gate, then to the athletic field, where they would destroy the grass.

The first event was a motorcycle broad jump, assisted by a four-foot high runway, a real nut-buster. Next came a pursuit race, followed by a motorcycle polo game. Cash prizes were given for: the guy that walked funny because he rode his bike the farthest, the oldest machine, and the prettiest. Although there were minor injuries, no one was killed.

Winnwood Beach became the town's Northern oasis. Mr. Winn had sunk a lot of money in his dream this year. Winnwood's third season promised to be its best. He recruited a 12-piece orchestra, who'd just spent two years booked in the Bear Club at Lake Placid, New York. The Tores Brothers played 30 different instruments, and each musician took turns playing solo.

A new roller skating rink, said to be the largest west of Chicago, featured a hard, maple floor. Another free attraction was the Monkey Jungle. The primates lived in a natural habitat, except for the rock houses. Another new attraction was a funhouse, called "The Devil's Cave." A new miniature golf course was under construction, the lake had new rowboats, and a motor boat with a capacity of 30.

On May 11, at 1:30, the newly sanded beach at Winnwood opened. Many plunged into the cold water without a wetsuit, people being tougher in 1930 than they are now. Admission to Winnwood was still free. Winnwood also had skee-ball, a game of skill, the Japanese Bazaar, the Whirlwind, and the Windy Chutes.

Early June brought warmer, but wetter weather. Not good for the park business. The free admission to Fairmount brought in many more family picnics, but as the economy sank, so did the park's cash flow. Many businesses suffered the same problem, causing a decline in company and large and mid-sized events. Thanks to the free admission, Memorial Day, 1930, brought a huge crowd to Fairmount Park. There were still large picnics. The local PTA, sponsored by Independence Mayor Roger T. Sermon, drew 10,000, mostly kids. The three biggest prizes given away were a Shetland pony, and a boys' and girls' bike. The cities Catholics held a picnic, then Sheffield Steel, Montgomery Wards, and Carpenters' Union #61 followed immediately.

The free zoo, with 24 separate cages, featured both predators and prey. From 10 a.m. until close, there was much curiosity by our species of mostly children and dogs. The dogs liked to bark and arouse the anger of the captive big cats and bears. Thus, management asked that if you are going to visit the zoo, please leave pets at home. Life was much different for dogs 80 years ago. If an animal screwed up, there was no dog-catcher. It were just shot.

By the 8th of June the parks were packed. The wet spring would give way to a hot, dry summer. Grain Valley, Missouri's wheat crop dried up to a dead brown. Hard times were coming.

Fairyland Park's dance floor was drawing so many hoofers that people were being turned away. One of the city's largest picnics was held this week, the Ford Dealers' Association, drawing 40,000 visitors, eager to see Henry Ford's latest improvements. Three new Model As were given away. The new Fords came in a half-dozen colors besides black.

Winnwood Beach had motor boat races. A field of many was narrowed to a few. The fastest boat in town won $100 cash. The miniature golf course was nearing completion, and the Monkey Island was no disappointment. An interesting hype was the Al Jolson photoplay scam. Girls were encouraged to do their best solo dance in hopes of getting a part in a big-time Al Jolson movie. It would run for two months, giving every girl in Kansas City a fatuitous hope for a life of glamour, breaking hearts, bringing tears and disappointment, and sometimes rage. But, it was all in fun.

Things were going fine at the Home of Picnics, at least in the second week of June. Company picnics like Western Union, City Ice, Forum Cafeteria, Chevrolet Motors Employees, Munger & Root Dry Goods, and the Missouri Garment Company all had picnics there that week.

Haley's Dance Orchestra kept the dance floor jumping. Requests were their forte. They had a huge repertoire. The zoo was a popular place. Every week one or more species would be switched. Animals were constantly being rotated from one cell to another.

The swimming beach at Fairmount Park was starting to come to life. The hours were from six to midnight, still only 25 cents for all day. This included a suit, not necessarily dry, the same for the towel and locker. A newly sanded beach awaited, with lights, a water wheel, big top, high dive, and a boardwalk.

In the middle of June the politicians voted in the Hawley-Smoot Tariff. The bill was ready for President Hoover to sign, and he did. Nobody had any idea what it would do to the world economy. The Republicans said, "Final passage of the bill will do more towards reassuring industry and restore confidence to business." A Democratic Congressman said, "I don't know, and I don't believe anyone else knows what will be the material effect of this bill on the country." It was a disaster.

What happened was a very serious global trade war, all mad at the U S of A. The Canadians were the first to strike back, making it impossible to sell American wheat, hurting the very people (agriculture) the bill was supposed to help. Prices for commodities dropped precipitously, along with the already battered stock market. "In actuality, any tariff is a tax on the consumer," said Adam Smith in "The Wealth of Nations," c. 1776.

June 15 was the much-delayed Jackson County Democratic picnic at Fairmount Park. Twice before the event had been rained out and hundreds of pounds of barbecued ribs had to be disposed of at great loss. The third picnic no one bothered to cook, so only about 1,000 loyal Democrats showed up. Seven candidates gave short speeches. The main speaker, former Senator James A. Reed, was introduced by Independence Mayor Sermon. What was to be a short statement turned into a lament of the current administration and Prohibition. Judge Truman was there, but didn't speak.

At about noon, Friday, June 20, payday at the Portland Cement Plant, two young ladies were driving with $1,200, withdrawn from the Standard State Bank in Sugar Creek by the Missouri Supply Company at Cement City. Upon reaching the high ground between the two villes, a big Buick with three big fellows drove them off the road. Armed with an arsenal, they forced the girls on the Buick's rear floor board. They turned around and headed back through Sugar Creek. Then heading east on Kentucky Rd., the girls were dropped off a mile out of town. The men wore handkerchiefs over their faces and were all dressed in overalls, but they didn't smell of oil. Instead of heading towards Kansas City, only a few miles away, they turned back towards Sugar Creek like they were on a lunch break from the Standard Oil Company. The entire felony took about twenty minutes. The perfect crime.

By the end of June at Fairmount Park, the free zoo was the big draw, but people were going broke. Prices were dropping to pre-WWI levels. The free admission with the picnic amenities attracted crowds without money. In the zoo, the monkeys became the stars. Jigs was the Alpha-Male; Barney was at the bottom of the pecking order. There were twenty monkeys that Jigs dominated; he was old and mean. Whenever one of the other primates took a shot at Barney, all Hell broke loose. He was Jigs' buddy, to the amusement of the humans.

It's about this time that a comic icon enters by chance. Richard "Red" Skelton's early life is an enigma. Born in 1910, his birth certificate is dated 1913, the same year his clown father passed away. Red didn't like school. In the summer of 1923 he took a job with a grifter selling iodine and water as a cure-all. Red's job was to fall off the stage, make 'em laugh, then sell them poison. Later, he worked a river boat. He ended up in Kansas City in 1930 with a gig at the Gayety Theater at 12th and Wyandotte in Downtown, Kansas City. The Gayety was a high-class burlesque house. The difference between the high class and low class burlesque was the women wore pasties. Lurking not far away was Edna Stillwell. She was a sixteen-year-old usherette at the Palladium, a more moral type of entertainment venue, and it paid better. Red hung out there, hoping to get a break and go on stage. He also had an eye on Edna. A man of the world, he stood six foot three inches tall and was handsome, with dimples and wavy red hair. He had a great sense of humor and was destined to be a huge success in the entertainment world, but Edna couldn't stand him.

One day the regular emcee at the Palladium couldn't make it, so Red got his chance. He did his regular stuff. He fell off the stage, told some jokes, did a few imitations, and introduced the acts. Edna went to her boss and told him that Red should be fired because he wasn't funny. Two years later they were married.

Rumors of Fairmount Park's eventual demise started in July, and there was good reason. Even with free admittance, there just wasn't enough money being spent to keep the operation in the black. For example, while Fairyland Park had a mother lion and her two adorable cubs, Fairmount Park had a water fountain. There were no longer lines to most of the rides, as in the immediate past.

After the Fourth of July Fairmount Park's manager, Sam Benjamin, met with the local Kiwanis. The purpose of the get-together was the discussion of the fate of the park. The local businesses knew that a closed park would mean financial disaster. The Fairmount/Mt. Washington area was also fighting incorporation by Independence, Missouri. Another big problem discussed was the Fairmount/Mt. Washington Fire Department, who hadn't been paid in a month. The department didn't have the money to replace fire hoses. At the fires, the local brats would cut the hoses, so what hoses the department had been repaired repeatedly. There wasn't money to replace them. The Depression was moving slowly through the economy.

Explaining to the Kiwanis, Sam put the free admission to the park as the problem, as well as the lowering of the price of swimming at the beach, that brought in "negroes." He said that problem had been addressed by again charging a ten-cents admission at the gate, and the beach back to a quarter. In turn, the Kiwanis promised to put on a community, all-White picnic. Other groups pledged help also.

On Sunday, July 13, thousands of railroad people from Kansas, Missouri, and Texas, held their last annual picnic at Fairmount Park. They came by rail, free, from cities like St. Louis, Tulsa, Oklahoma City, Dallas/Ft. Worth, Waco, Temple, Austin, Santa Ana, Houston, and Galveston. Tons of ice were delivered prior to the ten a. m. opening of the park. The heat of summer drove many of the railroad people into the spring-fed lake. The shade of the big trees dropped the temperature ten degrees. The most popular rides were the ones that created the most breeze. A baseball game was featured in the afternoon. The zoo was still a popular attraction. This was the tenth annual picnic at Fairmount Park for the Missouri, Kansas, Texas railroad, and would be the last.

Meanwhile, Fairyland Park had become KC's most popular resort. The picnics which attracted the larger crowds now came to Fairyland. A perfect example was the Chevrolet and Ford Dealers' Association. Chevy started their annual picnics at Fairmount Park. They gave away cars through a raffle. Now the cars were gone, and so were the huge crowds. In 1930, the Ford Picnic drew 52,000 on the 20th of July; Chevy drew 50,000.

Because Fairmount Park's cash flow was no longer flowing, management decided to put on prize fights. Starting Tuesday, the Third of July, several African American boys started the show. The fifth and final match was between two heavies, Tiny Burgess knocked out Willy Johnson in the first seconds of the first round, by a one punch knockout, before Willy saw the Sunday punch coming. Management was very encouraged by the 5,000 mostly males that paid admission at the gate, so every Tuesday night from then on would be fight, drink, and gamble night at Fairmount Park.

The first day of August was the day of the promised Kiwanis picnic to bring the neighborhood together in support of Fairmount Park. Named "The Community Church School Picnic," every merchant in the Inter-City district gave a little green card to their patrons that were good for several freebies. One, free admission to the park and a free ride on the Mountain Speedway, Merry-go-Round, Giant Dipper, and the Fun House. The card was not just for the kiddies, adults were allowed the same privileges. What the hey, the park was going broke anyway. On the day of the picnic crowds started to enter the park at 11 a. m. The fun lasted all afternoon. 7,000 kids were in attendance, with another thousand green cards being used by adults. In the evening the crowd was entertained by the East Suburban Kiwanis Club Juvenile Band, boys and girls. They started in the band shell at 7:15. The seventy young musicians were directed by Wilfred Schelager.

On Sunday, August 3, three large picnics were held at Fairmount Park. Two Philco radios, thirty other prizes, and 3,000 souvenirs were given away. A large picnic for the residents and former residents of Cass County, Missouri, was held the following Sunday. The gates opened at 10 a. m., but because of the Sabbath most arrived after noon.

Starting on Saturday, August 9, the Kansas City Journal-Post held a huge picnic for employees, their families and readers of the late Col. Van Horn's newspaper. Since the gates were wide open, there was no accurate way to tell the size of the crowd. It was estimated to be between 30,000 and 40,000. It would be the last time that that many people would be in Fairmount Park. All rides were a nickel. The Mountain Speedway, Tilt-a-Whirl, Fun House, etc., all five cents, the lake amusements being packed. Long lines of now mostly dead people snaked through the park. The picnic ground was crowded like never before. Buckets of free spring-fed ice water were a relief in the 95 degree heat; the previous day it was 104 degrees. The air temperature was ten degrees cooler in the shade of the big trees, with a cool breeze blowing off the 18-acre lake. Management, anticipating the crowd, hired scores of extras to help sell hot dogs, ice cream, soda, and to pick up the trash.

Before the supper picnic, scheduled for the late afternoon, there were many contests and races on land and sea. At the athletic field there were eleven contests for boys, girls, men, and women. Starting with the Boys' Shoe Race, won by Mike Rahrye of Sugar Creek; second was the Boys' 25-yard Dash. The longer runs were cancelled because of the heat. Third was the girls' 25-yard dash, fourth was the men's' three legged race, fifth was girls' egg race, sixth was the men's' 25-yard dash, seventh was the women's 25 yard dash; eighth was the cracker eating contest, ninth was the backward race, fun to do when you'd been drinking, tenth was the women's pop drinking contest, eleventh was the Men's Beauty Contest, for the most homely-looking man. It was won by M. H. Leslie of Fairmount. His prize was a loving cup.

In the lake, the first contest was the men's 50-yard freestyle, won by George Bradley, who lived just north of the park and was also a lifeguard there. Second was the women's 25-yard freestyle, third was men's backstroke, four, women's breast stroke, fifth, the boys' 25-yard freestyle, won by Marvin Evans of Sugar Creek; sixth was the Men's Breaststroke. Most of the winners resided in Kansas City, Missouri.

The swimming contest was followed by a late afternoon picnic. The well-maintained acres of picnic grounds under the huge shade trees was saturated with blankets, picnic baskets, adults, kids, and people in motion, after which it was back to the nickel rides and the cool lake that many never left.

Business was so good for the vendors that shortages appeared. Hardest hit was the hot dogs and soda pop. Many of the ring-tosses, balloon busting, and ball throwing concessions ran short of prizes.

The next day, Sunday, August 10, thirty lodges of the Woodmen of the World and the Women's Circles held their picnic with the usual games and fun at Fairmount Park. The ladies packed picnic baskets. The festivities started early in the morning with games and races. Three prizes were given to the prettiest and healthiest boy, girl, and baby. At 5 p. m., sharp, the Woodmen of the World Drill Team marched around the park. While the men were drilling, prizes were still being given out for families. An American Austin Auto was given away after the fireworks display. Starting at 9 p. m., the dance floor was packed until midnight.

The whole third week in August at Fairmount Park was given to the "Northeast Kansas City Fair." Rain kept the crowds down on Sunday and Monday, but the rest of the week was typical summer. The Alpha Industries of the Northeast District and Blue Valley erected 25 booths set up on the picnic grass. These booths represented industries, like the Englewood Fur Farm, Norway, Gliders, World Book, Loose-Wiles Biscuit Company, and many, many more.

Thursday evening was the beauty contest. Mrs. Northeast and Mrs. Jackson County were picked. A parade of all contestants wound its way around the park. Leading the girls was Mrs. Northeast of 1905, wearing the lucky bathing suit that she wore twenty-five years ago. It weighed in at over fifteen pounds.

Friday was the day of the great Carnival. The Fairmount Business District was decorated in red, white, and blue bunting. It was professionally done by the Craig Decorating Company of Kansas City.

The last Labor Day at Fairmount Park started with a parade of 7,000 union members from Downtown, Kansas City, to Fairmount Park. The crowd swelled to around 10,000 as families joined in on the festivities. Starting at 3 in the afternoon, union leaders and politicians manned the bandstand shell for speeches. The supposed main attraction drew few spectators. The few Republicans on the program caught hell. The winner in the float contest was won by Local 61 of the Carpenters' Union. It was a scale down of a real house, with small doors and windows. It was put on display in the park and attracted much attention. But, in reality, labor had little to celebrate as the Depression was not yet the Great Depression. The economy of 1930 slowly slipped into an abyss.

Starting around the Fourth of July, every Tuesday night was Amateur Fight Night at Fairmount Park. The star of the show was a local kid by the name of Tony Manure. Earlier in our story Tony, 17, had lost to Nick Roper, 24. Now it was time for Tony to take revenge. Boxing as a light heavyweight, 160 to 179 pounds, he never lost a fight.

On July 30, 9,000, a thousand more than the week before, came from afar to see the boxing match. The fights were held in the band shell, so there was plenty of room for the crowd.

Tony was given a loud ovation upon entering the ring and an even bigger one in the third round when he KO'd Kid Roberts. Another popular fighter was Tiny Burgess, 210 pounds, a proud product of the Independence school system. Jimmy Moran, of Fairmount, barely 180 pounds, bet $50 he'd whip Tiny. He lost.

On August 19 Tony was the main feature. With a smile on his face, he pretty much beat the tar out of Jack Smith from the West Side Athletic Club. Tiny and Tony were the favorites at Fairmount Park. They had beaten most anyone tough enough to get in the ring with them. The following week two fellows from St. Joe, Missouri came down to be beat up. For Tony, the test came on September 5, the final fight at the park. Mike Uras was a hard-hitter from California. Mike hit the mat in the third round, Rough House Tony won by decision, but most of his wins were by knockout. After this, the fights would be held in Fairmount at the

Claude Brown Motor Company garage. Tony's name was changed to Manors and he later boxed professionally at New York's Madison Square Garden. Rumor has it that he had a crook for a manager.

Thanks to an arrangement early in his presidency, Hoover and many of the heads of industry, like Standard Oil, men were put to work at the refinery, temporarily boosting the local economy. But nothing could stop or predict the train wreck still to come.

> **"Believing that the fundamental conditions of the country are sound, my son and I for some days have been purchasing sound, common stock.**
> **-- Rockefeller.**

> **"Sure, who else had any money?"**
> **-- Eddie Cantor**

Chapter Last: 1931 - 1935

Both Fairmount and Fairyland Parks opened in mid-May, 1931. Fairyland Park was now the most popular place for summertime fun. From the beginning of the season Fairyland labeled itself as the only amusement park in KC. But Fairyland would eventually get theirs. Lamar Hunt's Worlds of Fun, just north of the Missouri River, easily outclassed Fairyland in the 1970s.

Fairyland Park's first year as the only amusement park in Kansas City began with dancing, followed a month later by a rodeo. The picnics that once flocked to Fairmount Park didn't. Some of the bigger picnics that had deserted over the last few years were Ford and Chevy, Kansas City Grocers, the Kansas City Journal, and to add insult to injury, even the Independence, Missouri School District.

There was also plenty of competition from other venues. Swope Park now offered a sandy beach for swimming. Adults 25 cents, kids 15 cents, which included one of 1,500 new suits, towel, and a locker. Swope Park Lagoon featured "The Red Wing," a large, outboard motorized boat, ten and fifteen cents per trip. Dickinson Lakes, one mile east of Independence on 24 Highway and north on Dickinson about a mile, offered fishing and picnics. Wildwood Lake in Raytown had swimming and dancing to McElroy's Orchestra, and good eats. Speed boat races at Lake Quivira, auto races in Smithville every Sunday, six races starting at 2 p. m.; a dollar to get in, fifty cents more for a box seat. Winnwood Beach drew large crowds. There was dancing to the music of Andy Kirk and his Twelve Clouds of Joy, "They are Plenty Hot." Parachute leaps, Monkey Island, and a little elephant named Babe. Also swimming and fishing, of course. Campbell's Lake on Merriam Lane, a mile west of Rosedale, offered swimming, boating, dancing, and fishing.

Kansas City, Missouri, had twenty-three neighborhood movie theaters, 1931 being the first year of the double-feature. Air conditioning in the hot summer to come made the Depression years profitable for the motion picture industry. The city's suburbs had almost as many movie theaters. There were golf courses and many tennis courts. A third of the households in America had radios. Autos could take people many miles from the city in an hour or two, thanks to Judge Truman's foresight for an excellent county road system. Lastly, there were plenty of saloons and whore houses.

The nails in Fairmount Park's coffin started late in 1930 when the "Fairmount Beach Co." filed for bankruptcy. Worse, to manage the park in 1931, the Cusenbary family took over the park and hired John D. Chapelle, an attorney. He didn't have a lot of money to work with. Twenty-five acres north and northwest of the park across the ravine were cleared for picnicking. City water was piped to the area. Picnic tables, ovens, and a new road and bridge were in place for the May opening. Many additional attractions were promised, but never delivered. This year entrance to the park would be free until 6 p. m., because of poor attendance. That would soon change to free admission. All the mechanical rides worked fine. All concessions opened on time. The only thing missing were the crowds and money to spend.

The beginning heat wave of 1931 was in full blast by the end of June. Not only was it hot, there was no rain in the immediate future. Back then, the weather forecast came out of Chicago, which was 94 degrees; Minneapolis, 98; Wichita, 95; Omaha, 100; Oklahoma City, 100; St. Louis, 102; Kansas City, 101. The weather people sent a message to President Hoover stating that this was the hottest June in history, and if the trend continued there could be trouble, which there was. The heat was good for Fairmount's swimming hole, and anywhere there was an air conditioner. I was told by someone who was a kid then that they slept on the cement floor in the basement to stay cool.

The "Home of Picnics" were sorely lacking in that endeavor. Few wanted to book a picnic at Fairmount Park when it might close before the date of the reservation. Sadly, attendance was poor.

On the Tuesday before the Fourth of July, Mayor Sermon of Independence threw his fifth and final picnic for local students at Fairmount Park. Every kid upon entering the park received an all-day sucker, because in the past the best free ride tickets were traded or bullied from the smaller children, the old pecking system. This year all rides were free to the young 'ens for two hours, from noon till 2 p. m. The next major picnic was not to be till July 16th, given by the Blue Valley Manufacturers and Businessmen Club, and was to be an all-day affair.

Winnwood Beach caught hell because of truth in advertising. Some of their ads in the local press claimed the lake was under the supervision of the Kansas City Health Service. Winnwood was in Clay County, across the river, and not in Kansas City, Missouri. It turned out that the lake had been tested by a dairy inspector. Calvin Cooper, Director of Health, was livid but powerless.

Fairmount Park's last Fourth of July as an amusement park drew only 5,000 people. The heat wave was temporarily put on hold for several days, but the holiday was cut short because of a cloud burst. The 4 p. m. storm cut short all outdoor activities throughout Kansas City. By the time the rain had stopped there were few people left at Fairmount Park. The fireworks display was postponed until the following Sunday evening. Social gatherings in the form of picnics were rare at Fairmount Park in 1931, while Fairlyland was stealing the summer show.

One of the biggest picnics to move from Fairmount to Fairyland was the Second Annual Journal-Post Picnic, held on July 18. The gates were opened at 10 a. m., admittance was free. The price of the crystal pool's filtered water was reduced from 50 to 25 cents for admittance. All rides were a nickel. Since the hot weather had returned, no swimming or diving contests were held, so that the masses could enjoy the cool water all day. Additional life guards were brought in to handle the expected overflow crowd. There were a number of contests, like hot dog and pie eating, nail driving and foot races, with prizes given. The following week was booked at Fairyland by the Ford Dealers of Greater Kansas City. It was the largest crowd of the season. The oldest Ford had a serial number of 312,000, where as a 1931 Ford number was 21 million. There were so many autos that an extra twenty acres were thrown open as a parking lot.

Though Charles Carlisle had lost a fortune in the market collapse, the entrepreneur still had the Fairmount Lake concession. To help the local Kiwanis and the Mt. Washington Fire Department, in early August, he donated 150 swimming tickets to those two organizations. The plan was for those organizations to sell them for fifteen cents and keep all the money. Unfortunately, some of those tickets would go unsold. Time was running out for Fairmount Park. The last Type-A picnic held at Fairmount Park was the Western District of the Missouri Pacific Railroad Booster Club, held on Sunday, August 2, 1931. Over 5,000 were in attendance. The entertainment featured a baseball game between the railroad people and Baily Manufacturing Company of Leeds was held in the afternoon, followed at 4 o'clock by boxing and wrestling matches. At 6 p. m. a bathing beauty contest was held at the beach. It would be the last activity held at Fairmount Park until the Walk-a-Thon.

On Monday morning, August 8, the gates failed to open. Fairmount Park was quiet, and the local economy had lost about $35,000 in annual wages.

1932 didn't start out any better for Fairmount Park. On Friday night, March 25, kids, vandals, or volunteer firemen, needing some quick cash, practically burned Fairmount Park to the ground. The first alarm came in by phone around 11 p. m., to the Mt. Washington/Fairmount Volunteer Fire Department. The Sugar Creek fire department also responded. The two fire companies battled the flames, cutting off the advancing inferno before it could get to the boat house. The dressing rooms were saved by keeping the roofs wet as thousands of embers from the buildings and leaves from the dying, huge oak trees threatened what little there was left of Fairmount Park.

At first there was not enough hose available, so both Kansas City and Independence fire departments were called for help. Only KC Fire responded. Independence Mayor Sermon, who had just held five picnics at Fairmount Park in five years said, "No." When the KC fire people arrived, there was now plenty of hose, but not enough fire plugs. I was told by Al Carlisle that while the men were fighting the huge blaze that could be seen for miles, the local brats were busy cutting the hoses. And this is going to be the Greatest Generation?

By the time the sun came up, Fairmount Park no longer existed. The huge 100+ year old oaks were black stumps. Among the casualties was Jackson County's second biggest elm tree.

Before the fire everything that could be carried had been stolen by the vandals. After the fire, there wasn't anything worth stealing. The fire had destroyed the café, pool hall, and contents, Fun House, most concession stands, and the buildings holding games like shooting galleries, where the people threw soft baseballs and knocked down wooden milk bottles to win a Cupie doll, or break balloons with darts, etc., etc. The east end of the mile-long Giant Dipper was gone.

Mr. Carlisle's lake buildings were saved because of the competence of the local volunteers, who had braved the intense heat. That heat had melted glass, copper wire, and transformers. Damage had been done to his roofs, ironically 1932 is also the year that the Zippo lighters were il-nvented. Sadly, most of the park was not insured. This Depression was snowballing through the economy.

The biggest losers were the Cusenbary family, who had hoped to open the park once again for the 1932 season. Things were worse in the real world. 1616 US banks would fold this year. 20,000 businesses would go bankrupt. There were 21,000 suicides. There were between 15 and 17 million unemployed. The Dow hit bottom at 41.22, down from 381.17 on September 3, 1929.

The Summer of 1932 was not a good year for Charles Carlisle. The only thing left to do was swim, fish, boat. Many couldn't afford it, so in September Mr. Carlisle and the Inter-City News made free tickets available to any kid willing to pick up a free swim pass at the newspaper office (and get your name in the paper as being poor). Only 145 partook. That closed the 1932 season.

The years 1933 and 1934 at Fairmount Park were maybe the wildest yet, a fitting end to an amusement icon. As everywhere in America, things in the Fairmount business district were critical. Only the newly-minted 3.2 beer saloons seemed to be making any money.

The local Kiwanis, along with the Frank Fraas VFW Post 1000, Independence, Missouri, had a band that played 8 concerts in May and June in downtown

Fairmount, to help bring Saturday night alive. Special sale prices were printed on page 3 of the Inter-City News.

In early May, 1933, something magical happened. M. C. Tabbett met with the local Kiwanis club with a proposition, at their weekly Wednesday luncheon. Mr. Tebbeth and his two associates, General Manager Jack Frogmann, and Floor Comedian Dick Buckler, had pulled off a successful walk-a-show at the El Torreon Ball Road on Gilham Road. In the later Thirties the El Torreon would be a roller rink. In the 1970s it was called the infamous "Cowtown Ballroom". To see a Hollywood version of a Walk-a-Thon, check out a 1969 flick named, "They Shoot Horses, Don't They?". The movie has a happy ending, though. That commie bitch Jane "Hanoi Jane" Fonda gets her head blowed off.

The Walk-a-Show of 1933 and the Walk-a-Thon of 1934 brought money, controversy, and a future comic legend to Fairmount Park. The first Walk-a-Show started on Memorial Day weekend and ended rather abruptly in July. The Dance Pavilion was enlarged to 60 feet long, and seating for 2,500. Thirty couples were rounded up. While participating, the contestants were fed and under the care of Fred W. Hink, M. D.

Radio stations WHB and KMBC both promised to broadcast the show. WHB in the morning, KMBC at 10 p. m., bulletins any time. Allen Franklin, Chief Master of Ceremonies, and Sammy Jarvis, Floor Comedian, ran things.

There were only two concessions open. The German Village (anguish to the Vets of the Great War), the beach, but others were in the works.

Things went fine until the Fourth of July. On the Monday morning following a great weekend, three men, one armed with a Thompson sub-machine gun, .45 caliber, interrupted Garnet Gilmer, making him open the safe and liberate $1,500 in Walk-a-Show money and a pistol. There were no witnesses, as there were few patrons. Mr. Gilmer was blindfolded and chloroformed, later discovered unconscious. It put a real damper, as there was no insurance.

The first of two Walk-a-Thons lasted until Friday, September 29, 1933. Russell Gerken, Fairmount, and Mildred Gore Englewood won first prize in the Walk-a-Show at Fairmount Park. They endured 2,834 hours of torment. First prize was a certified check of $500 each. Second went to Alice Barker, Winner Road and Blue Ridge Blvd, won a free trip to Chicago, Murder Capitol of the World. Her partner, Bob Parratt, Mound City, Missouri, was forced out of the contest Friday night because of a bad leg. Miss Barker had 48 hours in which to solo before being disqualified, and the show was over before that time ran out. All contestants gained weight during the show, Gerken taking on 26 pounds.

Nowhere in the press was the future great Red Skelton mentioned, probably meaning that there were a lot of talented people involved.

The big news locally this Spring wasn't about Fairmount Park. It was about how many places in Sugar Creek were selling 3.2 beer legally. The saloon was back. Soft drink establishments started selling Pendergast whisky, wine, brandy, mixed drinks, and 3.2 beer. A city liquor license cost $50 a year. By June of 1934 all cities in Missouri with a population of less than 20,000 had to vote to condone sales of liquor.

What wasn't so good was the once-solvent Standard State Bank of Sugar Creek going bankrupt. The doors to the bank just closed, leaving the locals with money in the bank, but no way to retrieve it. The huge Rockefeller fortune, via Standard Oil, bailed out the depositors, 90 cents on the dollar, or, $50,000, thus allowing assets to be liquidated in good time. Today, the bank building is empty and probably haunted.

The Standard Oil generosity would be forgotten two decades later when an unneeded 8 month strike broke their Union.

Back at the Walk-a-Show, many various comedians/emcees passed through. One was a tall, red-headed, handsome fellow by the name of Richard "Red" Skelton. He had arrived in Kansas City in about 1930, and didn't stay long. But in the meantime, in 1932, at the Aladdin Hotel, where Red resided, he married Edna Stillwell, on June 1. The next year would have been when he was in town. Because in 1934 he was making a name for himself on the East Coast.

So, he must have been at the 1933 Walk-a-Show. It's hard to believe, but such a future star was not ever mentioned in the local papers. It's as if he wasn't there. But he was. Stories abound. By now, Edna would have been part of the act. Her job was to harass her husband without anyone knowing that they didn't hate each other. He was known for his antics, and on many a later occasion was threatened with dismissal, only to be saved by loyal Edna. Some of his best stuff was very unconventional, like riding a horse, a motorcycle, or a bicycle onto the floor while the show was in progress. His method of dismissing a participant in the show was by hitting them with a roll of toilet paper. He was very agile and could, on his knees, circle the dance floor on the railing, using just his knees. It was not unusual for one of the local females to form a crush on him.

1934 was Fairmount Park's last year before simply becoming a run-of-the-mill lake slowly filling with silt.

Address _____ *Alladen Hotel* _____

Application No. A _____ *48767* _____ For License to Marry

STATE OF MISSOURI,
County of Jackson, } ss.

(AFFIDAVIT OF MALE)

I, *Richard (Red) Skelton*

of *KC* _____ County of *Jackson*

and State of *Mo* _____ party of the first part, desiring to procure a license to marry

Edna Stillwell — 382869

of *KC* _____ County of *Jackson*

and State of *Mo* _____, party of the second part, do hereby solemnly swear that we

are of the ages of *21* years and *18* years respectively and that we are both single and unmarried and

not first cousins, and may lawfully contract and be joined in MARRIAGE. *July 18-1931 Mar 5-1932*

(SIGN HERE) x *Richard (Red) Skelton*

Subscribed and sworn to before me this *1st* day of *June* _____ 193 *2*

JOSEPH W. CORDER, Recorder.

By _____ Deputy.

STATE OF MISSOURI,
County of Jackson, } ss.

(AFFIDAVIT OF FEMALE)

I, the undersigned, party of the second part, do hereby solemnly swear that I am

the person named in the above application for a marriage license and that I am the age of *18* years and

that I am single and unmarried and may lawfully contract and be joined in MARRIAGE.

(SIGN HERE) *Edna Stillwell*

Subscribed and sworn to before me this *1st* day of *June* _____ 193 *2*

JOSEPH W. CORDER, Recorder.

By _____ Deputy.

STATE OF MISSOURI,
County of Jackson, } ss.

I, the undersigned, do hereby solemnly swear that the said party of the second part

named in the foregoing application for marriage license is personally known to me, and that she is over the age of

eighteen years and may legally contract said marriage.

(SIGN HERE) _____

Address _____

Subscribed and sworn to before me this _____ day of _____ 193 ____

JOSEPH W. CORDER, Recorder.

By _____ Deputy.

(Consent of Parent or Guardian to the Marriage of a Minor.)

STATE OF MISSOURI,
County of Jackson, } ss.

I, the undersigned, do hereby solemnly swear that I am the _____

of the said party of the _____ part, named in the foregoing application for marriage license, and do

hereby give my consent to _____ marriage _____

(SIGN HERE) _____

Address _____

Subscribed and sworn to before me this _____ day of _____, 193 ____

JOSEPH W. CORDER, Recorder.

By _____ Deputy.

11

219

The local economy was making a comeback. Lots for new homes were starting to sell. Rental property was getting hard to find. Hope that the worst was over. Too bad it wasn't. 1934 was the end of the streetcar / trolley. Buses were seen as a technological step into the future. They would run the same routes as the old technology.

The last good news for Fairmount Park came in mid-July. Although the lake was still good for fishing, swimming, and boating, most of the park had been hauled off.

Last year's Walk-a-Show lasted too long, eighteen weeks to whittle the contestants down. This year would be different. A quote from the Inter-City news in July set the theme:

"The endurance contest this year will probably last only until the middle of October, with derbies and sprints for walkers being staged from the first to keep interest at the highest point and cut down on the number of contestants."
Many of the walkers in the show will be experienced and several are winners of former endurance contests, according to Mr. Burns. Master of Ceremonies will be Frank Hamilton, formerly of the Parody Club in Chicago. Ducky Narcaratto, 'Spark Plug of Comedy", and Bob Brodie, who was formerly at the Belvedire Club, also of Chicago."

All were experienced Vaudeville artists from Mafia Town, USA. Makes one think of the thugs from last year's heist. The locals were unceremoniously pushed out.

Music was furnished by Jimmy Smith and his recording orchestra, also of Chi-town.

Some of the contestants were former Vaudeville artists who had fallen on hard times, as Vaudeville was on its way out, being replaced by the Talkies in air conditioned theaters. They would entertain the crowd and get a following. Sometimes the hat would be passed around for a couple who were popular. Gambling on contestants happened. It was also a good place to get drunk. Although no alcohol was sold on the premises.

Al Carlyle remembers Frank Hamilton, the Emcee of the show, making a deal with him. Every Sunday morning whoever was left in the show swam free in the lake, in return Al had a free pass to the entire show.

Every decent Walk-a-Thon had a band. This year, Jimmy Smith and his Recording Orchestra played every evening.

The show was broadcast via AM radio at 8:30 a. m., 12:45 p. m., 5:30 and 10:30, four times a day, seven days a week, fifteen minutes per period.

The carpenters, electricians, and stagehands were back enlarging the dance floor capacity.

The contest began Friday night, July 30, at 9:30 p. m. with 30 couples. By the beginning of the second week all but 18 couples and 5 singles had been eliminated. This year the one-fall rule was in effect. If a knee touched the deck, you were out, but your partner could continue.

This year's contest was a lot more brutal and loud as the patrons were encouraged or discouraged accordingly.

The trouble started at the Men's Bible Study get-together in Mount Washington. The non-fun guys of the neighborhood led by Phil De Hart, father of Dave De Hart, one of Van Horn's finest teachers. The problem was all those patrons of the Walk-a-Thon having fun 24 hours a day, 7 days a week. On the first of August, an injunction shut the Walk-a-Thon down. Over 100 locals signed a petition that read:

"We, the undersigned citizens of the Inter-City district and contiguous territory, hereby protest the continuance of the Walk-a-Thon at Fairmount Park, Fairmount, Mo, as a nuisance and detrimental to the best interest of the said community."

The promoters of the said nuisance responded thus:

"The Walk-a-Thon has spent thousands of dollars since opening this show, most of it in the Inter-City district. Approximately 20 persons from the Inter-City district are employed at the show.

"The contestants are being fed seven times every day, have the best medical attention (Dr. Hink), are well-clothed and clean (a once a week dip in the lake, as far as clean), and in good health.

"Promoters have lost money on it to date, and the walkers have wasted their efforts if they are not allowed to continue." Two locals have dropped out. Most of the Mules and the Pros remained.

There was a wholesale arresting of the contestants, manager, nurses and employees, Wednesday morning, August 1. The whole bunch were released on $20,000 bond. The show was allowed to continue without any music or patrons. The God-citizens released the following statement:

PURPOSE
"The purpose of the Association is to promote good government and good citizenship. To aid and assist its respective communities in its problems of local regulations concerning their peace, health, and MORALS and to render such charitable service to said communities as is within our power."

A few days later Federal Judge Darius A. Brown ruled the Walk-a-Thon to continue until the defense and prosecutors worked out their briefs.

Nothing was to bother the contest further. It was important for the proprietors of the Walk-a-Thon to win in court as pressure mounted across the country at the inhumane treatment perceived by a minority of the public at large.

"They're walking again at Fairmount Park, with Father Time as their opponent." So read the Kansas City Journal-Post of August 5, 1934. The Walk-a-Thon/Speed-a-Thon field had narrowed to 14 couples and one single. So far only 360 hours were on the clock. Kiddies got in for a dime. Adults, 15 cents for the matinee, 25 cents after 7 p.m., or listen on the radio, four times a day on KMBC. Phone number, Independence 3620. By August 11 the contestants had shrank to 10 couples and 2 solos, with 528 hours of elapsed time. Added to the fun was a little Vaudeville put on by the contestants.

The show featured a bathing beauty contest, along with a comic act. The following Sunday, with over 550 hours, larger crowds were an indication that Kansas City enjoyed this sort of sadistic entertainment.

If today was Tuesday, August 14, 1934, and you followed the Walk-a-Thon on the radio, you would turn it on to 810 Kz, KMBC. At 12:45 Live From the Big Show at Fairmount Park would crackle through the atmosphere for 15 minutes. It would be followed at 1 p. m. by L. A. La Forge Berman, Musical.

1:30 p. m. – Goodwill Industries – 1:35 Waltz Time – 2:00, On the Village Green – 2:30 DAR Talk – 2:45 The Instrumentalist – 3:00 Jack Brooks, Tenor – 3:15 Between the Bookends – 3:30 Milton Charles at the Organ – 3:45 Two Pals and a Gal – 4:00 The Village Choir – 4:15 The Collegian's – 4:30 Journal-Post News Flashes – 4:40 Program Bugle – 4:45 Blipois Balalaika Orchestra – 5:00 Big Brother Club with Willie Botts – 5:15 Happy Hollow – 5:30 Big News from the Walk-a-Thon. By now many autos also had radios. Motor-ola. One thing that would have been missed would have been commercials. For the record, America in 1934 owned 40 million radios. The 5:30 p. m. 15-minute Walk-a-Thon radio slot would have updated fans and they were updated on what had happened since lunch.

Today's big news was "A March to the Altar". Couple #19, Gene Williams and Miss Lou Martin would get married at 9 p. m. tonight. They are sponsored by Heckers Market, 63rd & Prospect, Kansas City, Missouri. So far the 600 hour mark had passed. Be there!

Also, since the end of Prohibition, several "night clubs" were making their debut. There was the GROTTO, with a band and floor show. 85th STREET CLUB, dining and dancing with an outdoor garden; ZAZINO GARDENS, forty entertainers; SILVER SLIPPER, variety entertainment; SPORTSMAN'S CLUB, boring. The BEETLE CLUB's draw was 75 women/girls to dance with for a small fee, the Depression-era's version of speed dating.

The #1 club in town was the HARLEM NIGHTCLUB, conveniently located at 15th Street and the Paseo. As of yet clubs didn't have to close at 1:30. In fact, they didn't have to close at all.

For 25 cents, a person could have hours of fun. The master of ceremonies, Maceo Burch, introduced dance bands like, "Benny Moten and his Victor Recording Orchestra." There was the Harlem Review, featuring Olive and Joe; and their version of "Society Dance." Three Chocolate Drops, back by popular demand. James Rushing, singing "Little Man, You Had a Busy Day." Mr. Shorty and Mr. Jack, comedians. Three shows nightly, the first at 11 p. m., 1 a. m, and 3:30 a. m. Largest bar in the Midwest. Age was irrelevant. Color of skin was. "White People Only" (an exception was made for the entertainment) and legally, only 3.2 beer could be sold, but there were exceptions to that rule, too.

Meantime, the Walk-a-Thon cranked on. By August 19 the ten couples and two solos passed the 700 hour mark. Manager Jerry Burrows vowed that the contestants would be narrowed down with hourly sprints in prime time. The patrons loved to see people drop out, unless they had a side bet on them.

By Labor Day, the 1000 hour had passed. There were seven couples and one solo. They were Jimmie J. and Darline Ferrell, Spud Murphy/Teddie Chadwick, Jimmie and Helen Zimmerman, Mary Lewis/Marty Ford, Tommie Hart/Maxine Merritt, Sid Rufus/Irene Carter, Ray Hall/ Kay Burrs, with Lon Williams as the "only lonely."

At 10:30 p. m., September 18th, just in time for the radio show from the Walk-a-Thon, Tommie Ford, a floor judge, and Katherine K. Burns, contestant, got hitched. The Rev. Arthur Burch, doing the nuptials. The couple met for the first time July 20th as a flirtatious affair led to their Walking Wedding. Something to tell the grandkids, unless this was just another publicity stunt.

Another stunt was Charles "Dutchman" Loeb, a man who traveled from Coast to Coast and allowed himself to be buried six feet under. He will not attempt to break his previous record of 37 days. Communicating with a ten-inch by 6' pipe. He was wired to radio station KMBC, where he had his own radio show for as long as he lasted every evening, at 8:30 (?). The 7 and 1 had just passed 1,224 hours.

The contestants were slowly dropping in the heat of 1934, the year of the Dust Bowl. The local papers treated the contest as if it didn't exist; the Journal's advertisement was posted stamp-size. Someone called the Walk-a-Thon radio show the most boring radio show yet.

Early in the evening of Sunday, October 7, the next to the last person couldn't move. James Thomas "Gigolo," Zimmerman, had bested the best after 1,897 hours and 35 minutes. Not much was said in the Inter-City News.

1934 was an off-year election. President Roosevelt was still very popular, but that would soon end as his economic experimentation didn't help, the Depression ending thanks to the Japanese. Judge Harry Truman ran for the Senate. His opposition, Republican Party's Roscoe C. Patterson; Social Labor party, William W. Cox; Socialist Party, Walter Charles Meyer; Communist Party, Frank Brown. Commies had one other candidate for State Superintendent of Public Schools. The facts about the candidates were thus: Roscoe C. Patterson, incumbent, lived at the Newbern Hotel here in Kansas City. Born and educated in Springfield, he'd lived in Kansas City nine years, and he was going to lose big time. Harry S. Truman was the local favorite. His first job was wrapping newspapers, then served as timekeeper for a railroad, bank clerk, salesman, artillery officer in WWI, served two years as Eastern Judge of the Jackson County Court, and was nearing the end of an 8 year service as presiding judge of that party. Note was made of his road building and honesty, etc., etc. The Democrats were overwhelmingly picked to not lose one race. Truman, 716,258; Patterson, 459,113. It's the first time that a person from Independence, Missouri, would go to Washington, D. C., as a Senator (and there hasn't been one since).

The 1935 season of Fairmount Park was short. On Sunday night, April 13, fire consumed the men's bath house. The first fire in 1932 burned most of the Midway, as you will recall. This one put the park out of business. Without a bath house, the only alternative was military-type tents for the boys and girls to change in. It was short-lived. The last activity besides swimming at Fairmount Park Lake was motor-boat racing in 1936.

The Kansas City Star's article of July 18, 1936 read:

FAIRMOUNT FIRE DESTROYS PARK

The Examiner's front page noted:

SIX HOUSES BURN AT FAIRMOUNT

The Journal-Post simply said:

FAIRMOUNT COTTAGES BURN

The dance pavilion, where the Walk-a-Thon was held in 1933-34, had long been robbed of everything, including the dance floor. There simply was nothing left to burn except the canvas tents used for swimming. Six of the nine cottages, the last buildings standing from what was once "The Prettiest Park in the USA." Kansas City, Sugar Creek, and the Mt. Washington/Fairmount Fire Departments were called out just after midnight. 900 feet of hose had to be laid. The Greatest Generation started out as a bunch of juvenile delinquents. Once the water was turned on, some joker along the hose passed the word to shut off the water. Six families were made homeless. One of the two room cottages held a family with eight kids. Furniture saved by removing soon burned after the water was cut off. The burning dry grass and trees helped by wind, created small fires, threatening even local property.

In 1950, as the lake filled with silt, Mr. Carlisle went to the state to try and preserve the lake as a state park, but failed. Motor boat races in August of 1935 were the last attraction at Fairmount Lake until August of 1952, when a crowd anticipating the rupture of the dam. Many locals camped out as the weather was perfect. It finally caved in on the 25th at 2 in the afternoon, leaving behind mud, covered by dying fish. Dozens of hand fishermen scooped many up, the rest left to die a horrible death.

In Memory of
Alfred C. Carlisle

1915 ~ 2012

Learn more about Kansas City's history, people, and places at

VintageKansasCity.com

**Look for more Vintage Antique Classics
Books including:**

The Trial of Jesse James, Jr.

Vintage Kansas City Stories

The Merry Widow Hat

**Vintage Antique Classics
Book of Obscure Poetry**

*Visit us online at
VintageAntiqueClassics.com*

Made in the USA
Middletown, DE
04 November 2017